JOSHI'S HOLISTIC LIFE PLAN

HOW TO BE HAPPY, HEALTHY, RADIANT – FOR THE REST OF YOUR LIFE

NISH JOSHI

HODDER
MOBIUS

First published in Great Britain in 2006 by Hodder and Stoughton
A division of Hodder Headline

The right of Nish Joshi to be identified as the Author of the Work
has been asserted by him in accordance with the Copyright, Designs
and Patents Act 1988.

A Mobius Book

1

A CIP catalogue record for this title is available from the British Library

ISBN 0 340 83844 2

Set in FranklinGothic
Designed and typeset by Smith & Gilmour, London
Photography © Liberty Silver

Colour Reproduction by Dot Gradations Ltd, UK
Printed and bound by CPI Bath Press

Hodder Headline's policy is to use papers that are natural, renewable
and recyclable products and made from wood grown in sustainable
forests. The logging and manufacturing processes are expected to
conform to the environmental regulations of the country of origin.

Hodder and Stoughton Ltd
A division of Hodder Headline
338 Euston Road
London NW1 3BH

The Joshi Clinic
57 Wimpole Street
London
W1G 8YP
T: 020 7487 5456
E: info@joshiclinic.com

JOSHI'S
HOLISTIC
LIFE PLAN

HOW TO BE HAPPY, HEALTHY, RADIANT –
FOR THE REST OF YOUR LIFE

ACKNOWLEDGEMENTS

I would like to thank Jane Alexander for helping me to piece together my philosophies and to write this book. I would also like to acknowledge the patience and guidance of my agent and publishers, in particular Helen Coyle for holding my hand through the editing process. Also Josh Tuiffa, soloist at The Royal Ballet for posing for yet more photos and Ross Harrington for spending his precious time taking them.

I dedicate this book to my patients. Their belief in my abilities encourages me to continue to learn and be a better practitioner.

CONTENTS

INTRODUCTION 8

CHAPTER 1 **THE FOOD EQUATION** 12

CHAPTER 2 **EXERCISE FOR LIFE** 38

CHAPTER 3 **HEALTHY MIND = HEALTHY BODY** 78

CHAPTER 4 **PREVENTING ILLNESS AND TREATING AILMENTS WITH COMPLEMENTARY MEDICINE** 98

CHAPTER 5 **HOLISTIC BEAUTY** 118

CHAPTER 6 **THE FOUR-WEEK PROGRAMME** 140

CHAPTER 7 **HOLISTIC WELLBEING** 162

CHAPTER 8 **RECIPES** 166

CHAPTER 9 **DIRECTORY** 185

INDEX 189

INTRODUCTION

How would you like to feel? It's a question I ask all my patients and they usually say much the same things – that they would love to feel healthier, more energetic and happier in themselves. Many say they would like to feel ten years younger or to regain the joie-de-vivre that has become a distant memory. Well, I *can* make you feel better; not just better, but the best you've ever felt. This is not an idle boast, as any of my patients would tell you.

In this book, I will give you the precise tools you need for complete and total wellbeing. You will be able to follow the same strategies, tips and recipes that I give my celebrity patients – such as Sadie Frost, Cate Blanchett, Gwyneth Paltrow and Patsy Kensit – and the many other people who come to my clinic. It will require some work on your part, some shifts and changes in the way you live, but I promise I will make them as easy as possible.

You know, I don't wave a magic wand and transform people overnight – *you* are the vital part of the equation. You and only you can make the vital decision to change your life. You can choose to be overweight, unhealthy and unhappy or you can make up your mind to do a real-life 'Cinderella' rags-to-riches transformation. Truly, it's up to you. Don't think, 'I'll do it tomorrow'. Set a date. Every day promises a new beginning, a new dawn. Start your new life right now. I'll be there all the way to help you. I will tell you exactly what you need to do to have the wonderful results you deserve. You're not alone. You can join the thousands of my patients who are living the life they want in the body they always wanted.

HEALTHY FOR LIFE

Many diet and health books are focused around short 'quick fixes'. This book is different, very different. My Holistic Life Plan is about having total, vibrant good health forever. It's a plan for life. I recognise that you have busy lives and that you work hard, play hard and want to enjoy your life to the max. So do I. I promise you that I lead by example – there is nothing in this book that I do not use myself. If I can do it, so can you. I know that, like me, you enjoy going out, having fun, eating in good restaurants and entertaining your friends at home. Now you can – but without compromising your health in the process. I'm a pragmatist – I accept that you are short on time and high on commitments. I know full well that you have more to worry about than your shopping basket. Nobody can devote huge chunks of their lives to their health – it's unrealistic. This Plan teaches you the ground rules, the bedrock of pure unadulterated health. Once you have these rules in place, good health becomes a natural, everyday part of life. I will show you, week by week, how to adapt and adjust your life, a little touch here, a tiny switch there, so you barely notice you're changing. By the end of four weeks, you will have the blueprint of healthy living forever, and you will have transformed your life painlessly and effortlessly. You will have created a solid foundation of habits that will, quite literally, change your life, your body and your health.

THE FEELGOOD PLAN

This Plan is not designed to deprive your body; it's not about giving things up; it's not about iron willpower and restriction. It's not a hair-shirt regime – quite the contrary, in fact. My Holistic Life Plan shows you how best to nurture yourself by being kind to both your body and mind. It's about giving yourself the very best you can. Think about it: you go on the best holiday you can afford, you live in the nicest house you can afford, you always try to give your children 'the best' – so isn't it time you started giving yourself 'the best'? It's a tough world out there and, if you're going to survive and thrive, you need to look out for Number One. You.

My first book, *Joshi's Holistic Detox*, gave you the chance to spring-clean your body from top to toe. It's been used successfully by tens of thousands of people. This book goes a stage further, looking at how you can be not just a healthy individual but a happy one, too. I will give you the secrets I share with my patients on how to live healthily and happily forever.

THE ANCIENT WISDOM OF AYURVEDA – AND BEYOND

This book is steeped in the wisdom of Ayurveda – the ancient Indian system of mind-body medicine that has been healing people for around five thousand years. It is actually more than a form of medicine – it is a total way of living. My family is from Gujarat, in North West India, and I have grown up with Ayurveda. It has informed every part of my life. My mother will automatically use particular spices or certain combinations of foods and, when I ask her why, will shrug and say, 'Because that's the way it's done.' She is creating balanced meals that heal both body and mind.

Nevertheless, my approach is not limited to Ayurveda but is truly global and, ultimately, *holistic*. I have travelled the world, from Italy to India, from Egypt to Eastern Europe, to train in therapies that complement my Ayurvedic training. In my clinic, I also use acupuncture, massage, herbal medicine and cupping techniques. I frequently refer my patients for hypnotherapy, psychotherapy, yoga and Pilates.

WHAT TO EXPECT FROM THE HOLISTIC LIFE PLAN

We will start, in Chapter 1, by looking at diet because it *is* the bedrock of your new healthy life. I'll show you how to use food as a means to vibrant energy, a calm focused mind, glowing skin and lustrous hair. There is so much conflicting advice given on food that it's easy to become confused. I'll make it all crystal-clear, giving you simple lists of what to eat and what to avoid. But most importantly, I'll give you the tools you need to shape your own diet and your own life.

In Chapter 2, I'll introduce you to exercise that you will actually enjoy (I promise), in a form that fits in with your life. I will explain the real reason why you have found exercise tough in the past and encourage you to try wonderful movements with deep healing powers. Too busy to exercise? No excuse in *my* book! I'll show you how even the busiest person can squeeze serious amounts of exercise into a hectic schedule.

Chapter 3 moves from your body to your mind. I'll explain how to beat stress, soothe your sleep and make you positively brim with confidence and calm. There's nothing arcane or weird about it, I assure you. I will let you in on amazing mind tricks that can literally shift the way you think, the way you behave and the way you cope with stress. We'll also take a look at your home and work environment and discover how to rethink your surroundings to get more out of life.

Nowadays, most of us are concerned about chronic illness: we all know someone suffering from heart disease, cancer, diabetes, arthritis or some other serious ailment. In Chapter 4, I'll show you how to protect yourself from such conditions, as far as you humanly can, by boosting your immune system and disease-proofing your life. I'll also arm you with a battery of home remedies for common ailments – simple medicines that you can make yourself with store-cupboard ingredients. Call it a holistic first-aid kit – it works a treat. From an early age, I watched my mother, cousins and aunts whip up and use gorgeous beauty potions that can make your body glow and your hair gleam. In Chapter 5, I'll share them with you – just as I do with my patients, many of whom have to look perfect, day in and day out, for their high-profile work. Your friends will badger you for the details of your new facialist or hairdresser. It's up to you whether you let on!

So, by the end of Chapter 5, you will have learned the simple yet deep-working ingredients for a healthy, happy, fabulous life. In Chapter 6, we put it all together in a life-changing four-week programme. You will start by making small, almost imperceptible shifts. I'll show you how to fine-tune your diet, ease yourself into exercise, train your mind and clear your environment. As the weeks progress, and you become more proficient, I'll teach you deeper techniques, coax you into more effective exercise, expand your mind and stretch your muscles. It's all so easy that I promise you will find it simple – and fun. Bodies and minds are intended to be used; yours will adore my Life Plan.

At the end of the book you'll find a selection of gorgeous recipes to get your taste buds tingling and your motivation sky-high. No soggy salads or diet meals here – just absolutely stunning food, packed with nutrients and taste, from all around the globe.

HOW TO USE THIS BOOK

Ideally, I'd advise you to read this book through, chapter by chapter, rather than launching straight into the four-week Plan. If you understand why you are eating certain foods, doing particular exercises and so on, your motivation on the Life Plan will be much higher. We are rational beings and our minds like to know *why* we are doing something. Also, by understanding the reasons behind the various elements of the Life Plan, you will be taking full responsibility for your own health, which is a vital part of the process. I am not a guru, giving you prescriptions from on high as to how to live your life. I am simply providing you with the tools you need to make your own best choices and to take charge of your own life. It's an important distinction. I may give my patients the pointers and tools they need, but it is *they* who make the changes and do the work.

Choose to take responsibility for your own self. Think about what you do to your body. It's your choice – nobody else's. Throughout the book, I'll give you examples of people who have used the Holistic Life Plan, and had wonderful results. I find them inspiring and hope you will, too.

Now it's time to stop chatting, and get to work. Welcome to the rest of the book and the rest of your life. Live every moment of it to the full.

CHAPTER 1
THE FOOD EQUATION

FOOD CAN HEAL. FOOD CAN HARM. I TALK ABOUT DIET BEFORE ALL ELSE BECAUSE, QUITE SIMPLY, THE FOOD YOU EAT CREATES THE PERSON YOU ARE. IF YOU WANT TO LOOK GREAT, FEEL WONDERFUL AND BOUND WITH ENERGY, YOU NEED TO PAY CAREFUL ATTENTION TO WHAT YOU DECIDE TO PUT INSIDE YOUR BODY. FOOD AND WATER ARE FUEL: WHAT YOU EAT AND DRINK AFFECTS EVERY ORGAN, EVERY MUSCLE, EVERY BONE AND EVERY LAST CELL OF YOUR BODY. GIVE YOURSELF POOR FUEL AND YOU CAN EXPECT A MEDIOCRE PERFORMANCE – BOTH PHYSICALLY AND MENTALLY (REMEMBER, YOUR BRAIN CHEMICALS ALSO NEED FOOD). GIVE YOURSELF THE OPTIMUM DIET AND YOU TURN YOURSELF INTO A TOP-OF-THE-RANGE TURBO – FIRING ON ALL CYLINDERS AND FEELING FANTASTIC.

THERE'S A DEEPER, PSYCHOLOGICAL FACTOR, TOO. HOW YOU EAT – WHAT YOU PUT INTO YOUR BODY – REFLECTS HOW YOU FEEL ABOUT YOURSELF AT A PROFOUND LEVEL. FOR EXAMPLE, IF YOU ALWAYS EAT ON THE GO, IT'S AS IF YOU'RE SAYING YOU DON'T HAVE TIME TO TAKE CARE OF YOURSELF. ON THE OTHER HAND, IF YOU TAKE THE TIME TO EAT GOOD, HEALTHY FOOD, YOU'RE GIVING YOUR SUBCONSCIOUS THE POWERFUL MESSAGE THAT YOU'RE WORTH IT.

THROUGHOUT THIS CHAPTER WE WILL LOOK AT THE FACTORS THAT MAKE UP YOUR OPTIMUM DIET FOR HEALTH AND HAPPINESS. WE WILL BUILD ON THE INFORMATION GIVEN IN MY FIRST BOOK, JOSHI'S HOLISTIC DETOX, TO COMPLETE THE PICTURE, SO YOU CAN MAKE THE VERY BEST POSSIBLE CHOICES. THE DIET I WILL ASK YOU TO FOLLOW IS BASED ON THE REBALANCING REGIME I INTRODUCED IN MY FIRST BOOK, BUT IT GOES MUCH DEEPER. I'LL ALSO BE INTRODUCING YOU TO NEW INFORMATION AND SHARING WITH YOU THE VERY LATEST CUTTING-EDGE RESEARCH IN NUTRITION.

YOU AND FOOD

Even before you begin the Holistic Life Plan, I would like you to start becoming more aware of your relationship with food. What kind of foods are you drawn to – and why? Are you looking for comfort, or staving off boredom, or worried about feeling empty (in all senses)? Try to find the connection between food and your emotional life – you may be surprised.

Please don't panic about this. Food is such an intrinsic part of our lives that it can stir strong emotions. My Life Plan is not about deprivation. You won't go hungry, I promise you. You're probably thinking you have bad habits – that secret chocolate fix or a serious caffeine habit. Well, who doesn't have some guilty secrets? Don't worry; you don't have to give them up all at once. Instead of having, say, five mugs of coffee a day, make it four, then three, two, one . . . and then shift to herbal tea or try a coffee substitute. Gradually substitute more healthy options. Start doing this right now and then you won't suffer the side effects of withdrawal when you begin the Life Plan.

YOUR FOOD DIARY

One of the most effective tools for examining your relationship with food is to keep a food diary. This can give you surprising insights into how everything you eat and drink affects both your body and your mind. Right now, even before you begin the Life Plan, I'd like you to start on your diary. It will help to shift your awareness and can also show you how often you kid yourself (we frequently eat far more than we care to believe, or else we conveniently 'forget' about the odd snack or treat!).

Here's how your food diary might look:

DAY: MONDAY
Time: 7am
Where you are/what you are doing: at home, having breakfast, listening to radio
Food eaten: muesli, milk, banana, 2 cups coffee
Physical symptoms: energy good, slight backache
Mental symptoms: anxious about meeting

Time: 9.45am – at work – headache

Time: 10.15am
Where you are/what you are doing: at desk, working on report
Food eaten: chocolate muffin, coffee
Physical symptoms: heart racing a bit
Mental symptoms: irritable; concentration poor

It's important to note down how you feel, both physically and mentally, throughout the day. Do this every time you eat, but also note down any feelings or symptoms that crop up independently of food. At the end of the day, you can look back and see if any symptoms came about as a result of your food choices. You can also gauge whether you are eating at the best times for your body. We are all different: some of us thrive on three solid meals a day; others work much better on several smaller meals so that the blood sugar does not drop too far. A food diary will help you see that the sugary snack you craved only provided you with a short-lived energy spurt before plunging you further into lethargy. It teaches you to listen to your body. Once you have regained this knowledge, your food choices will become second nature and it will become almost impossible to eat the wrong foods.

DETOX FIRST

Before you start on my 28-Day Life Plan, you really do need to detox first. In our modern world, nobody is immune from toxicity and you will never be able to live a full, healthy, happy life if you are laden down with toxins. In my first book, *Joshi's Holistic Detox*, I gave a full 21-Day Detox Programme. If you have already read, and followed, the Detox, then you're already there. If not, I would strongly advise you complete that Detox before starting on this plan.

The Detox is designed to last for 21 days. Please don't be tempted to skimp on this and do a shorter detox. Although it may sound arduous, most people find it quite easy to adjust their diet, not least because, after a few days, they are already brimming with energy – and losing weight. Having very limited choices is actually easier than trying to eat healthily on a varied diet.

Why detox? Several reasons. Firstly, you cannot truly expect miracles from a body loaded with toxins. If you don't detox first, the Life Plan won't work so spectacularly. Secondly, and this is very important, there is a psychological reason for starting with the Detox. Habits take at least six weeks to form. By taking the Detox (three weeks) and then following it with the Life Plan (four weeks) you are giving yourself a rock-solid habit of health – for life. After seven weeks of healthy eating, your body and mind will have fallen in love with the feeling of being energised, enthusiastic and free of aches and pains. You won't want to go back to your old way of feeling – not even for the sake of a slice of double-chocolate fudge cake! Thirdly, the Detox acts as the starting point for discovering any intolerances or allergies, as we'll discuss next.

THE FOOD CHALLENGE

Once you have completed the Holistic Detox, you can start to reintroduce foods (those we eliminated for the 21 days of the Programme) slowly back into your diet. Because your body has not had to deal with these foods for 21 days, you should notice a swift reaction if your body is intolerant of any particular food.

This reintroduction process needs to be precise and disciplined. You must test only one food at a time, and that needs to be in its purest form. So, for example, on day one you could try tomatoes – a few raw tomatoes, not tomato sauce that will contain other ingredients. If you notice any old symptoms (refer to your list) recurring, then it's highly likely you are intolerant of tomatoes. If so, wait a day before trying your next food. Note – it's worth testing all types of a food. For example, it's quite possible to develop an intolerance to raw tomatoes while having no reaction to cooked tomatoes.

This is a slow process but it is a sure-fire (and free) way of testing for intolerances. If you are not so patient, there is a shortcut. I often refer my patients to allergy therapists who use NAET (the Nambudripad allergy elimination technique); this employs kinesiology to test for intolerances and then treats them using a method based on Chinese acupressure (see the Directory). The whole process is gentle, painless, non-invasive and extremely effective.

NOTE: you will not be testing wheat or cow's-milk products at the end of the Detox, as you will not be eating them on the Life Plan. You can test them at the very end of the whole programme.

EATING FOR LIFE

Now you are ready to embark on my Holistic Life Plan. The eating plan will actually be very easy because you will already have shed a host of toxins and accustomed your body to eating good, healthy food. You will also have adjusted the pH balance of your body towards its optimum, slightly alkaline state (see page 19). The aim of the Holistic Life Plan diet is to expand your options and tweak your diet for total health and vitality. Over the next few pages, I'm going to give you all the information you will need to review your shopping, cooking and eating habits for the Holistic Life Plan. Most people find that this new way of eating is too good to limit to a month; they go on to use it as the blueprint for a lifetime of healthy eating. This is not surprising. If you're feeling full of energy, optimism and bounding with good health, you're not going to wish to go back to feeling tired and dispirited, are you? Once you have experienced for yourself just how good the optimum diet can make you feel, you won't want to accept anything less. I'd like to stress, again, that this isn't about deprivation. If you really crave a pizza, or an ice cream or a large glass of red wine, I won't stop you – but you may well find that your body will! Once you have detoxed your body, it becomes far more sensitive and quite intolerant of less than wonderful food.

THE pH FACTOR

A vital part of the Life Plan is shifting your body to its ideal, slightly alkaline state – your body's pH neutral. Unfortunately, most of us are generally far too acidic because of all the acid-forming foods we eat – in particular, chocolate, alcohol, sugar and red meat. Even some healthy foods – such as tomatoes and potatoes – can increase acidity. When your body is slightly alkaline, it finds it easier to eliminate toxins and to break down the acidic deposits that lead to sluggish digestion, fat and arthritis.

Many people find this concept hard to grasp because the foods that *seem* acidic (lemons, for example) don't have an acidifying effect on the body, while those that seem *unlikely* to be acidic (meat, sugar) *do* acidify the body. Forget about how a food seems to be in its natural state; instead, you have to learn what it does inside your body. The food we eat interacts with oxygen in our cells to create energy – this is our digestive process. A by-product of digestion is a kind of 'ash' that can be acidic, alkaline or neutral in action. Your body naturally sweeps up the alkaline or neutral ash without any problems (we are designed to be slightly alkaline, remember). It can also handle a little acidic ash (so you don't need to shun tomatoes completely!); but, when you overload your system with acidic residues, it simply cannot cope. The acidic ash builds up and your body becomes imbalanced and toxic.

The results of over-acidity include many of the scourges of modern life: osteoporosis, arthritis, fatigue, weight gain and poor skin tone. However, as I am always telling my patients, nearly everything is reversible. Start eating an alkalising diet and you will lose weight, you will find your energy levels soaring and you will notice your skin and hair starting to look great. You can even reduce or eliminate the symptoms of arthritis and stave off osteoporosis.

ALKALI-FORMING AND ACID-FORMING FOODS

FOODS IN RED ARE:

Acid-forming in the human body
Make blood, lymph and saliva more acid and
Cause acidosis – too much acid in the body
(lower pH number)

FOODS IN BLUE ARE:

Alkali-forming in the human body
Make blood, lymph and saliva more alkaline
and Cause alkalosis – an excess of alkali
in the body (high pH number)

Remember, this chart shows foods that are acid or alkali *forming* when digested. So, just because the lemon might taste acidic, this does not mean it is so after it has been combined with the digestive juices. It does, in fact become alkaline – hence its appearance, here, in blue.

PROTEINS AND FRUITS

Beef	Apples
Buttermilk	Apricots
Chicken	Avocados
Clams	Berries (all)
Cottage Cheese	Cantaloupes
Crab	Cranberries
Dairy Products	Currants
(except goat's milk)	Dates
Duck	Figs
Eggs	Grapes
Fish	Grapefruit
Goose	Honey (pure)
Jelly	Lemons
Lamb	Limes
Lobster	Oranges
Mutton	Peaches
Nuts	Pears
Oyster	Persimmons
Pork	Pineapple
Rabbit	Plums
Seeds (cooked)	Prunes
Sugar (raw)	Raisins
Tomatoes	Rhubarb
(processed)	Tomatoes (raw)
Turkey	
Veal	

NON-STARCH FOOD (VEGETABLES)

Alfalfa	Kelp
Artichokes	Kohlrabi
Asparagus	Leek
Aubergines	Lettuce
Beans (string)	Mushrooms
Beans (wax)	Okra
Beets (whole)	Olives (ripe)
Beet Leaves	Onions
Broccoli	Parsley
Cabbage (white)	Parsnips
Cabbage (red)	Peas (fresh)
Carrots	Peppers (sweet)
Carrot Tops	Radishes
Cauliflower	Rutabagas
Celery	Savory
Chicory	Seeds (sprouted)
Coconut	Sea Lettuce
Corn	Sorrel
Cucumbers	Soybean
Dandelions	(products)
Endives	Spinach
Garlic	Sprouts
Greens (leafy)	Summer Squash
Horseradish	Swiss Chard
Kale	Turnips
	Watercress

STARCHY FOODS

Bananas	Peas (Dried)
Barley	Potatoes (Sweet)
Beans (lima)	Potatoes (White)
Beans (white)	Pumpkin
Beans (kidney)	Quinoa
Breads (all)	Rice (Brown)
Buckwheat	Rice (White)
Cakes (all)	Rye Flour
Cereals	Sauerkraut
Chestnuts	Squash
Chick peas	Tapioca
Cookies (all)	Wheat Flour
Corn (processed)	(all, including
Corn Meal	Spelt, Semolina
Corn Starch	and Couscous)
Crackers	
Grapenuts	
Gluten Flour	
Lentils	
Macaroni (any)	
Millet Rye	
Oatmeal	
Pasta (any)	
Peanuts	
Peanut Butter	

HOW TO SHOP

We've lost the art of good shopping. Most of us buy our food from supermarkets. In fact, many of us don't even get as far as the supermarket but make our choices at the click of a mouse. We have jettisoned our relationship with the food we eat and with the people who produce our food. Is it any wonder that our children don't know where food comes from? Is it any wonder that we're tired, overweight, irritable and low? The Ayurvedic way is to be mindful about every single aspect of food – from choosing it, through preparing and cooking it, to eating it. Try not to race through your shopping. Take a leaf out of the books of other cultures where food shopping is both art and science. Develop a relationship with the people who sell you your food – that's impossible in a supermarket, so choose small, specialist shops. In France, nobody would buy a melon without feeling it and sniffing it; and nobody would *dream* of buying a chicken without knowing which farm it came from and what it ate.

You wouldn't buy a nasty, tacky pair of shoes – would you? – or a horrid, cheap jumper? You wouldn't opt for plastic when you could have leather, or put up with acrylic when you could have silk. So why, when it comes to buying food, are so many people willing to accept bargain-basement, jumble-sale-quality food?

TOP TEN GUIDELINES FOR GOOD SHOPPING

1. Buy the best-quality food you can afford – not necessarily the most expensive, but food that is as fresh and chemical-free as possible.
2. Shop as frequently as you can to ensure your food is fresh and nutritious, instead of doing huge, bulk supermarket shops. It's less wasteful, too.
3. Opt for organic produce wherever it's available; it uses less chemicals and produces less toxins.
4. If you can, find biodynamic food, this is the very best you can get.
5. Support farmers' markets and organic-box schemes.
6. If you have the choice, pick small, individual shops – they will know where their produce comes from and how it is produced. Don't be afraid to ask for information – it will boost the demand for accountable food.
7. Eat food that is seasonal and local. Try to avoid racking up huge 'air miles' for fresh produce – long-distance food is not so good for your health or the environment.
8. Shun genetically modified food – we just don't know what it does to our bodies.
9. Avoid ready-made meals and fast food. Instead, choose simple, wholesome ingredients and make your own meals. The one exception to prepared food is frozen vegetables. These, ironically, can be more nutritious than fresh (but old) veg.
10. Read labels carefully to weed out undesirable additives and chemicals. Use foods before their sell-by date to ensure that optimum nutrients remain.

HOW TO COOK

Cooking healthily for life is not difficult. In fact, the best ways of cooking are actually the quickest and easiest – you don't need to be a Michelin-starred chef. I promise.

Preparation is important. All vegetables and fruit (even organic) should be washed, and preferably soaked, before using. Discard outer leaves and any damaged parts. Prepare your food when you are ready to cook – don't be tempted to peel and chop vegetables in advance because you will lose vital nutrients.

A salad is, of course, the ultimate no-cook food. Simply break, chop or slice, then pile into a huge bowl and off you go. You can add a little cold-pressed olive oil and lemon juice for dressing. Chopped garlic and herbs give it a lift. Sprouted seeds and pulses pack a huge nutrient punch and give added bite. Ring the changes by adding chickpeas, cooked beans, grilled chicken, steamed fish or stir-fried tofu. Can't live without croutons? Use gluten-free bread lightly fried in olive oil if you really must (but be aware of the calorific load!).

I'm a huge advocate of fresh vegetable juices – they're tasty, filling and packed with goodness. If you like something warming, whiz them up into a soup and pile in herbs or spices to give added flavour. There is no limit to the combinations (see page 32 for some ideas).

I personally advocate steaming or grilling fish, chicken and vegetables. You do need a little oil for grilling so make sure you only use the best-quality extra-virgin olive oil; it contains fewer chemicals than a lot of the cheaper processed varieties.

For stir-fries (another healthy option), I recommend sesame or sunflower oil. There's really no end of choice: kebab chicken, fish and vegetables, North African tagines, Thai curries. Throw together Mediterranean fish stews, Greek salads or Asian-fusion vegetables and noodles. I've given some of my favourite recipes in Chapter 8 to get you started.

THE MINDFUL COOK

Prepare your food with awareness. In many yogic traditions, the cook would chant and meditate while preparing the food so that it absorbed as much positive energy (known as *prana*) as possible. I'm not asking you to sing to your supper (unless the idea appeals), but it's worth using the preparation and cooking of food as a form of mindfulness – a simple type of meditation that is deeply relaxing and beneficial to your body and mind (and, according to some researchers, your food as well). Add a healthy pinch of love when you prepare each meal. We'll look at this in greater detail in Chapter 3.

For now, simply be aware of what you're doing at each stage of your cooking. Think about where your food came from, who grew it and how it came to your kitchen. Be grateful for having good food: say a word of thanks or some form of grace. Prepare only as much as you need – waste not, want not.

Always think about your food as fuel for your body and affirm that your aim is to give it the best possible food you can. In Ayurveda, fast food, leftover food, red meat and fried food is considered to be low in vital energy – poor, low-grade nourishment that will lead to lack of energy, weight gain and low mood. Good enough reasons to shun the fast-food counter, surely?

HOW TO EAT

Start shifting the way you eat your food, too. *How* you eat is almost as important as *what* you eat. In the Ayurvedic tradition, it would be anathema to eat at your desk or while walking down the street or when hunched over a tray while watching television. Food should always be eaten slowly, with awareness and while sitting down at a table so you can digest it fully and properly.

⇢ Try to sit upright while eating at a table, and, preferably, make the table attractive, with flowers or a candle.

⇢ Don't be tempted to watch television or read a magazine while you're eating – give your food your total attention. It's fine, though, to hold a conversation while you eat – as long as it's not a heated argument!

⇢ Don't pile up your plate with food. Make the plate look attractive; arrange your food with care.

⇢ Before eating, look at your food. Smell it. Observe it.

⇢ Breathe deeply and slowly – this helps your body become more alkaline and also helps to focus attention on your meal.

⇢ Now, bring the food to your mouth. Feel it in your mouth, notice the texture, the taste, the temperature.

⇢ Chew thoroughly to release the enzymes that start the digestive process. Aim to chew each mouthful 8–12 times.

⇢ If your digestion is slow, try drinking a cup of ginger tea before you eat. In Ayurveda, cold water is avoided at mealtimes as it slows down *agni*, the digestive 'fire'. But you should sip warm or room-temperature water, or warming herbal teas (such as ginger, cardamom, fennel or aniseed).

⇢ Pause between each mouthful and put your knife and fork down.

⇢ Notice how the food makes you feel. When you start to feel full, stop eating. You don't have to eat everything on your plate.

THE HOLISTIC LIFE PLAN'S GOOD-FOOD GUIDE

Providing you do not have intolerances, you can – and should – eat as wide a diet as you possibly can. There is some evidence that eating a very limited diet encourages intolerances to develop. So, once you have completed the Holistic Detox and ascertained any problem areas, you have a wide choice stretching out in front of you. However (there had to be a 'however', didn't there?) some foods should remain out of bounds for the duration of the Life Plan. Please steer completely clear of:

⇢ All convenience food – fast food, ready meals, junk food, packaged and processed food

⇢ All deep-fried food, including crisps

⇢ Caffeinated and decaffeinated drinks and products (tea/coffee/hot chocolate)

⇢ Artificial sweeteners

⇢ Sugar

⇢ Refined (white) carbohydrates

⇢ Cakes, biscuits, cookies

⇢ Red meat

⇢ Seafood – prawns, shrimp, mussels etc, lobster, crab

⇢ Dairy produce (cow's milk, butter, cheese)

⇢ Alcohol

⇢ Fizzy drinks

⇢ Wheat and gluten products

This leaves you with a wide choice of foods. Choose from:

⇢ Brown rice, millet, quinoa, spelt
⇢ Gluten-free cereals, breads, pasta, rice noodles
⇢ Oats (if not intolerant)
⇢ Sheep and goat's cheese and milk (if not intolerant)
⇢ Rice and almond milk
⇢ Soya products (if not intolerant), including tofu and tempeh
⇢ Live yoghurt (if not intolerant)
⇢ Dark-green vegetables (avocados in moderation as acidic and high in cholesterol)
⇢ All other vegetables and salads
⇢ Fish (except tuna and shellfish as can be high in heavy metals)
⇢ White meat – chicken, turkey, pheasant, partridge, guinea fowl
⇢ Pulses/lentils/peas/beans
⇢ Honey and maple syrup
⇢ Cold-pressed olive oil
⇢ Herbal teas

BAD BASKET, GOOD BASKET

How can you make the switch to really good nutritious food?
Let's see how you could begin to change your shopping choices:

BAD BASKET	GOOD BASKET
White bread	Gluten-free bread
Red meat, sausages, bacon	Chicken, turkey, tofu, pulses, lentils
Ready meals	Fresh ingredients
Tinned vegetables	Fresh vegetables and salads
Cereal	Gluten-free muesli, porridge oats
Pasta, white rice	Brown rice, brown-rice pasta, gluten-free grains
Seafood, lobster, crab	Deep-water oily fish
Butter	Olive-oil or pumpkin spread
Cow's milk	Rice, almond or soya milk
Table salt	Rock salt or sea salt
Ice-cream, jelly	Bio-yoghurt, soya yoghurt, fresh fruit
Crisps	Seeds, unsalted nuts, dry-roasted pulses
Muffins, cakes, biscuits	Rice cakes, oatcakes, hummus
Tea, coffee, decaffeinated tea and coffee	Green tea, herbal teas, coffee substitutes such as No-Caff
Sugar	Honey/maple syrup
Chocolate	Bananas
Wine, beer, whisky	Organic vodka with pure cranberry or pomegranate juice (if you really must!)

WATER

We are water creatures – up to seventy-five per cent of our bodies is made up of water. Drinking plenty (at least 2 litres a day) of fresh, clean water is one of the most important steps you can take towards a healthy body and a sharp, focused mind. Water helps your skin and kidneys eliminate toxins; it also stimulates and flushes out the liver. Water softens your faeces and helps waste pass more quickly through the gut. Sadly few of us have the luxury of clean, pure water. Here's how to improve the quality of the water you drink and use.

- If you can, fit a combined reverse-osmosis and activated-carbon unit to filter your water supply.
- Cheaper, but still effective, are activated-carbon filters that are placed in a water-filter jug. However, these filters cannot remove nitrates or dissolved metals such as iron, lead and copper.
- Bottled water is another option, but not infallible. Some brands have been shown to contain 10,000 bacteria per millilitre. If you do choose bottled water, go for glass bottles rather than plastic ones that leach chemicals into the water.

SPICES FOR HEALTH

Ayurveda uses spices for far more than mere flavouring; each spice has specific properties that can help boost your health in particular ways.

- **Black pepper:** can ward off colds and throat infections. A digestive stimulant, antiseptic and anti-bacterial. Warming and toxin-releasing.
- **Cardamom:** helps prevent the formation of kidney stones; a digestive stimulant and antispasmodic, can prevent cramps and bloating. Can also prevent coughs.
- **Cinnamon:** helpful in fighting diabetes and food poisoning, boosts circulation and lowers blood pressure. Anti-bacterial, antifungal and antispasmodic, so useful in digestive problems and in preventing colds. **CAUTION:** avoid during pregnancy.
- **Cloves:** antiseptic; controls gum and tooth infections; anti-nausea, combats colds, strengthens nerves and improves the circulation.
- **Coriander:** eases indigestion. The seeds can help reduce cholesterol.
- **Cumin:** a good digestive aid, can settle the stomach after a heavy meal and reduces bloating. Also reputed to combat insomnia.
- **Garlic:** helps lower cholesterol, inhibits rheumatism, and has anti-cancer, anti-flatulent and anti-bacterial/parasitic properties.
- **Ginger:** improves digestion, helps lower cholesterol, controls blood pressure, inhibits cancer, prevents coughs and colds, and has anti-nausea and anti-clotting properties. **CAUTION:** do not take in therapeutic doses if you are taking aspirin as a blood-thinner.
- **Nutmeg:** said to relieve stress; commonly used in China for nausea, indigestion, chronic diarrhoea and gastric upsets. It's also an anti-rheumatic. **CAUTION:** large doses (over 7.5g) produce convulsions and palpitations. Do not use during pregnancy.
- **Red chilli:** useful in that it stops you eating too much. It does, however, encourage the stomach to produce more acid, so use sparingly.
- **Saffron:** an excellent heart and nerve tonic, it has anti-ageing properties and is said to cure anaemia. It can ease period pains, relieve indigestion and soothe urinary disorders. **CAUTION:** do not use large doses during pregnancy.
- **Turmeric:** a potent blood purifier, it also improves liver function, prevents coughs/colds, improves skin tone and is antiseptic.

HEALTHY HERBS

Herbs are to the West what spices are to the East – powerhouses of healing. Think about using these in your cooking, or adding to salads, juices and soups. Many also make wonderful tisanes (herbal teas).

- **Basil:** antidepressant and cheering, basil is an uplifting tonic for depression and nervous exhaustion. It's antiseptic, anti-nausea and soothes coughs. Shred leaves in salads, add to pasta sauces and pizzas; rub the leaves on insect bites.
- **Celery:** mild digestive stimulant, anti-rheumatic, diuretic and antitoxin. Reduces blood pressure. Helpful in joint and urinary-tract problems (rheumatoid arthritis, cystitis, urethritis). Eat as a vegetable, juice, or add to salads. A tea made from the seeds can help rheumatoid arthritis and gout.
- **Chamomile:** anti-inflammatory, soothing to the mind, prevents nausea. Can help IBS, indigestion, insomnia, anxiety and stress. Best as a tea. **CAUTION:** do not use during pregnancy. Can cause contact dermatitis in sensitive individuals.
- **Dandelion:** power-herb for the liver and digestive system, a wonderful tonic; diuretic, anti-rheumatic, antitoxin. The young leaves are great in juices, salads and soups. Or drink as tea. Don't pick leaves growing by the side of the road – they will be laden with toxins.
- **Fennel:** a great breath freshener, appetite suppressant, sore-throat soother and cough beater. It calms the gut, relieving indigestion, wind and hiccoughs. Great as a vegetable, in soups or as tea. **CAUTION:** avoid high doses during pregnancy.
- **Lemon balm:** antidepressant, relaxing, antispasmodic, relaxes the peripheral blood vessels and stimulates digestion. Anti-bacterial and antiviral, so great at warding off colds and infections. Make a tea out of fresh leaves or add to salads.
- **Mint:** wards off nausea, travel sickness, indigestion, wind, fevers and can soothe migraines. All types of mint can be used as a tea or added to vegetables, sauces and marinades. **CAUTION:** peppermint can reduce milk flow so avoid during breastfeeding. Mint can irritate the mucus membranes – use cautiously with children.
- **Rosemary:** improves circulation, stimulates digestion, soothes headaches, boosts energy and battles depression. Good for 'cold' complaints, such as rheumatism and chills. Add to stews; drink as a warming tea. A pad soaked in hot rosemary tea can ease sprains.
- **Sage:** memory-enhancing, a tonic and a liver stimulant. Improves digestion and circulation. Reduces night sweats in menopause. Antiseptic and makes a great mouthwash. Add to cooking, or use as a tea. **CAUTION:** avoid large amounts when pregnant. People with epilepsy should avoid sage as it contains thujone, which can trigger seizures.
- **Thyme:** antiseptic and expectorant, so useful for chest infections. Improves digestion, soothes diarrhoea, stomach chills and IBS. Gargle to help a sore throat. Add to cooking or use as a tea. **CAUTION:** avoid large amounts when pregnant.

SUPERFOODS

Some foods really do have 'superhero' stamped all over them. Scientists are discovering more and more the hidden properties of everyday foods, and sometimes the most humble foodstuffs really do pack a huge healthy punch.

Once you have your basic alkalising diet in place, I'm going to be urging you to add in some of these superstars on a regular basis.

Let's start with a huge favourite – sprouts – no, not Brussels sprouts (although they're pretty fabulous, too), but sprouted seeds and grains.

SPROUTING

There's a huge range of sprouted seeds, grains and pulses now available: alfalfa, radish, mustard, aduki, mung, quinoa, red clover, fenugreek, chickpeas, lentils, broccoli and so on. They really are superfoods, packed solid with vitamins, minerals and phytonutrients. All along, I've been asking you to choose really fresh food – well, there is absolutely nothing fresher and more packed with essential enzymes than newly sprouted seeds. Sprouts have extraordinarily high levels of antioxidants (which neutralise the free radicals responsible for much of the ageing process and many degenerative diseases).

Research into sprouting broccoli seeds at John Hopkins University Medical School in Baltimore found that broccoli is rich in sulforaphane glucosinolate (SGS™), a precursor to sulforaphane (an extremely powerful antioxidant that can even help to detoxify cancer-causing chemicals). The research team found that SGS is twenty times more concentrated in young, three-day-old broccoli sprouts than it is in more mature broccoli plants.

Throw a handful of sprouts into salads to give some extra 'crunch' – or nibble them as a nutritious snack. You can buy sprouts from most good health stores or even order them on the web. However, I'd suggest you try growing and harvesting your own so that they will be super-fresh. Truly, it's a very simple process.

HOW TO SPROUT

→ Choose organic seeds and buy in small quantities to ensure complete freshness. You will also need a few large glass jars, some fine mesh and a few rubber bands.

→ Put a couple of tablespoons of dry seeds in each jar. Cover the jars with mesh so water can be drained out and air can circulate.

→ Soak your seeds, pulses or grains for several hours to start the process. Different sprouts need different soaking times: alfalfa, radish, mustard, fenugreek, red clover and quinoa need 5–7 hours; lentils, aduki, mung beans and broccoli seeds need 8–12 hours; chickpeas require about 15 hours.

→ Then, drain the seeds by keeping the jars tilted downwards at a 45-degree angle so that the water can run out and air can circulate. Prop them against a dish rack, for example.

→ Make sure your sprouts have warmth but are protected from direct light and heat while germinating (keep them off window sills, avoid radiators).

→ Rinse them twice a day (three times a day if the temperature is high) as this will make them grow faster.

→ As they sprout, pick and eat immediately. Always handle sprouts gently and be careful not to damage the growing shoots and leaves.

CAUTION: the vast majority of people will thrive on sprouts but it's worth mentioning that a few people are allergic to sprouted grains and seeds.

WHEATGRASS

Wheatgrass is another superfood. I love it for its detoxifying, colon-cleansing, blood-purifying and cancer-fighting properties. Wheatgrass is high in a vast range of vitamins and minerals, in particular beta-carotene, vitamin K, vitamin B6 (pyridoxine) and calcium. Wheatgrass is also, you may be surprised to hear, a superb source of protein – it contains all the essential amino acids in the right amounts needed by the body.

It is such a strong detoxifier that – if you have not already detoxed – you may find it causes a little nausea because it starts up an immediate reaction with the toxins and mucus in the stomach. For this reason, I suggest you begin with 1 oz (25g) of juiced wheatgrass a day in a small amount of water. Once you can tolerate this diluted version well, leave out the extra water and work up to 6 oz (150g) of wheatgrass juice a day. Ideally, mix the wheatgrass juice with your saliva before swallowing, and drink it very slowly, one hour before your meals. You can mix it with other juices such as ginger if you do not like the taste.

Growing wheatgrass is very straightforward and – unless you have an organic store or juice bar on your doorstep – the best way to ensure your supply.

HOW TO GROW WHEATGRASS

You can obtain wheetgrass seeds from organic stores or health-food stores. One tray will last one person about a week (giving you one shot per day).

⇢ Fill a seed tray with 1 inch (2.5 cm) of general compost.

⇢ Add the seeds and water daily. Keep the tray away from direct light and excessive heat. It does, however, need to be kept warm and so must be grown inside.

⇢ After about 6 days, your wheatgrass should be ready to be cut and juiced. You will need to keep planting fresh seed to ensure a steady supply.

TEN SUPERFOOD SUPERSTARS

These are the other heavyweight superfoods that really deserve to make up a regular part of your optimum diet.

⇢ **Beans/pulses/peas.** Packed with vitamins particularly thiamine, riboflavin, niacin and folate (all B vitamins), plus the minerals calcium, iron, magnesium and potassium, beans are also a superb form of low-fat protein. They promote a healthy heart, they balance both blood pressure and cholesterol and reduce the risk of diabetes. Beans help balance blood-sugar levels, thus keeping energy high and weight down.

⇢ **Berries/pomegranates/fruit.** Blueberries have been labelled 'youth berries' because they are loaded with antioxidants – lowering your risk of a huge range of chronic disease and maintaining healthy, age-defiant skin. They are high in vitamins C and E; the B vitamins riboflavin, folate and niacin; carotenoids, polyphenals and phytoestrogens; minerals iron, manganese, magnesium and potassium. While blueberries really are superstars, pretty well all fruit packs a hefty health punch. I particularly love pomegranates. The pomtini (a pomegranate martini) was the official cocktail of the Oscars because Hollywood stars couldn't get enough of this 'death defying' juice. Personally, I'd go easy on the alcohol, but down the juice for all it's worth. Why? Because it has more antioxidants, vitamins and minerals than pretty well anything and can even help prevent your arteries hardening.

⇢ **Broccoli/all green leafy vegetables.** Possibly the most powerful anti-cancer weapons at your disposal. Broccoli, spinach and other green vegetables not only help prevent cancer, they also boost the immune system and the cardio-vascular system and protect bones and eyes. Broccoli, itself, is one of the most nutrient-rich foods known, packed with vitamin C, beta-carotene, calcium, folate and vitamin K. As I mentioned under Sprouting, broccoli has superstar anti-cancer nutrients and, further-more, broccoli sprouts are even more powerful than mature broccoli.

⇢ **Fish.** Few of us eat enough of the omega-3 fatty acids that are so essential for preventing heart disease and cancer. Oily fish is full of it. Omega-3 increases 'good' cholesterol, reduces blood pressure and stabilises your heartbeat. It can alleviate arthritic conditions and improve eye health. It is also, surprisingly, a 'good mood' nutrient – highly effective in reducing depression, ADHD (Attention Deficit Hyperactivity Disorder), bipolar disorder and dementia. Sadly, much of our fish is highly polluted with heavy metals such as mercury. Wild salmon, trout and sardines (fresh or tinned), however, are good choices. Tinned tuna should be eaten no more than once a week because of its mercury content. Swordfish, shark and mackerel are, sadly, highly contaminated.

⇢ **Green tea.** All types of tea contain literally thousands of chemical compounds. Some of the most important are the flavonoids – powerful antioxidants that can reduce the risk of cancer, heart disease and stroke. Drinking tea can reduce gum disease and dental caries. It also seems to help prevent kidney stones. Some of the flavonoids in tea have phytoestrogenic activity so may improve bone density. Evidence shows that tea can help with atopic dermatitis, and it is also touted as an aid to metabolism and, hence, weight loss. Green tea is recommended because it is less processed and higher in flavonoids. It does contain caffeine so, if you are caffeine-sensitive, don't leave the teabag in for too long (it also gets very bitter if you steep for over three minutes).

⇢ **Nuts/seeds.** The healthiest snack going. Nuts reduce the risk of heart disease, diabetes, cancer and many other chronic diseases. Top nuts are walnuts and almonds; top seeds are pumpkin and sunflower seeds. Walnuts, for example, are rich in omega-3 fatty acids, plant sterols (important in lowering serum cholesterol), fibre, protein, vitamins, essential amino acids and minerals. They are wonderful antioxidants, too. Nuts and seeds *are* fattening if you eat buckets of them but, given that a handful is no more calorific than a cookie, they make a great snack. Try to avoid peanuts and pistachios. They harbour mould and are potentially hugely toxic to the liver.

⇢ **Oats/other wholegrains.** A diet high in oats can reduce your risk of coronary heart disease and your serum cholesterol levels. Oats are high in protein and fibre, Vitamin E, thiamine and pantothenic acid, and the minerals copper, magnesium, manganese, potassium, selenium and zinc. They also have a beneficial effect on blood-sugar levels and can reduce the likelihood of diabetes. All the other wholegrains (brown rice, barley, quinoa etc) are excellent too.

⇢ **Soya/tofu/tempeh/miso.** Providing you're not intolerant of soya, it is an excellent superfood – a prime protein packed with vitamins, minerals, phytoestrogens and omega-3 fatty acids. It's been shown to play a part in easing menopausal symptoms and in preventing cancer, cardiovascular disease and osteoporosis. It is also very useful if you are lactose-intolerant as it makes a great alternative to dairy produce. It can be a little mucus-forming, though, so go easy if you suffer from congestion.

--> **Squashes (pumpkin/butternut etc)/carrots /sweet potatoes.** These foods are sky-high in carotenoids – potent antioxidants that balance our immune system, boost cell communication, fend off cancer and heart disease, and protect our eyes (lessening the risk of cataracts and macular degeneration). They are also packed with vitamins C and E, pantothenic acid, and the minerals magnesium and potassium. Plus they're full of fibre. They all taste great roasted or grilled and make fabulous soups – and try pumpkin risotto!

--> **Yoghurt – plain, 'live', natural yoghurt.** If you are lactose intolerant, keep it to a minimum or try goats' milk yoghurt. Teeming with beneficial bacteria, live yoghurt helps heal the digestive tract and balances your bowels. It can help lower cholesterol levels, enhance the immune system, clear skin and protect against osteoporosis and rheumatoid arthritis. Yoghurt is high in vitamins B2 and B12, and minerals calcium, magnesium, potassium and zinc. It can ward off candida and gastric ulcers. It can even help lower your blood pressure. **NOTE:** ensure the yoghurt you buy is rich in live, active cultures – the more active cultures the better. Plain yoghurt is the best as the fruit versions are usually very high in sugars or contain artificial sweeteners. You can always add your own 'extras' such as fruit, grains, honey or maple syrup.

GLYCONUTRIENTS FOR SUPER-HEALTH

Trust me, you'll be hearing a lot about glyconutrients in the future. They're the latest buzzword in nutrition – and for a very good reason. Glyconutrient is the common name for a food that provides various types of vital sugars to the body. Sugars? Yes indeed. Just as we know that there are good fats as well as bad fats, science is now discovering that there are good sugars, too. Not just good, even, but *essential*. We used to think sugar was merely a fuel needed for energy but that is just the tip of the iceberg. The sugars in glyconutrients have an enormous range of functions – scientists are unravelling more and more possibilities as they research these clever nutrients. Already we know that they directly affect the immune system: helping the body recover and heal more quickly, improving resistance to disease, accelerating wound healing and reducing infections. They have phenomenal antiviral, anti-bacterial, antiparasitic and anti-tumour effects and help the immune system to recognise and deal promptly with invaders. They have a direct effect on the brain, improving memory and sleep while lessening anxiety and depression.

In our bones and muscles, they have an essential role in lessening wear and tear, replacing tissues and cells (you may be aware of one of their derivatives – glucosamine – which many people find invaluable in easing joint pain). They also affect our cholesterol levels, lowering triglycerides and LDL – bad cholesterol – while raising HDL – good cholesterol. They may even play a role in slowing down the ageing process.

While research is still continuing, and many studies have not yet been duplicated on humans, it seems possible that these sugars could help in a huge variety of conditions, including, to name but a few:

--→ Allergies

--→ Anxiety

--→ Arthritis

--→ Burns

--→ Cancer

--→ Chronic fatigue

--→ Depression

--→ Diabetes

--→ Ear infections

--→ Gingivitis

--→ Herpes

--→ Hepatitis

--→ HIV

--→ Insomnia

--→ Lupus

--→ Influenza

--→ Kidney disease

--→ Osteoarthritis

--→ Poison ivy

--→ Psoriasis

--→ Ulcers

THE EIGHT ESSENTIAL SUGARS

There are more than two hundred types of sugar, and these exist in many different forms. At present, it is surmised that eight are essential for the body.

SUGAR FOUND IN THE BODY

As you can see from the chart opposite, there are plenty of crossovers with the foods I'm already advising you to eat plentifully, so don't panic about the shark cartilage! For instance, all those leafy green vegetables, ripe fruits and berries. Many, we've already seen, are superfoods, and now you can understand that their glyconutrient status is part of their power. However, do make sure you eat naturally sun-ripened fruit and veg as far as possible; the levels of glyconutrients are much higher when the food has been allowed to ripen naturally.

It's also worth mentioning two foods that we haven't already covered which are extremely high in glyconutrients:

Aloe vera – contains over two hundred active compounds including 20 of the 22 vital amino acids, 12 vitamins and glyconutrients. Aloe-vera juice is now readily available from health shops and can be mixed with vegetable or fruit juices as part of your daily diet.

'Medicinal' mushrooms – high in glyconutrients and other active micronutrients. Types to look out for (and eat) include coriolus, cordyceps, maitake, reishi and shiitake. Button mushrooms are *not* high in glyconutrients and should not be eaten raw in salads. All the medicinal mushrooms can be, variously, grilled, baked, added to stir-fries and salads or taken as a tea. Health shops, once again, are your best source.

JUICING

If you read my earlier book, you will know I'm a huge fan of fresh (and, by fresh, I mean just-that-minute-made) juices. To recap, juicing is the quickest, most effective way of providing the body with all the nutrients it needs for good health and super-abundant vitality. Juices act so fast it's like having a blood transfusion! I mean that literally because, by removing the fibre from the vegetable or fruit, you are left with the vitamin and mineral-rich pulp that can then be absorbed directly into the bloodstream. In the first book, we used juices to help detoxify your body. Now you can follow on from that, fine-tuning juices to give you any number of health benefits.

TOP TEN TIPS FOR JUICING

1. Start out with an inexpensive juicer – no point in spending a fortune if you discover you don't like juices, or juicing!

2. Start slowly – your body will need to get used to such a concentrated form of nutrients.

3. Drink juice on an empty stomach – this allows it to pass into your intestines more quickly.

4. Buy the best-quality vegetables and fruit you can – organic if possible.

THE EIGHT ESSENTIAL SUGARS

SUGAR	FOUND IN THE BODY	PROPERTIES	FOOD SOURCES
⇢ Fucose	Kidneys, testes, skin, nerve-junctions	Cell communication, brain development, immune modulator, anti-inflammatory, anti-cancer	Mushrooms/kelp and other seaweeds/beer yeast
⇢ Glucose	Widely, especially liver, fat/muscle tissues, brain	Enhances memory, stimulates calcium absorption, cell communication, brain function	Primarily sugar. However healthy sources include honey, grapes, bananas, cherries, strawberries, mangoes, garlic, licorice root
⇢ Galactose	Widely, especially brain, kidneys, intestines, testes	Enhances memory, anti-cancer, anti-rheumatic, wound-healing, anti-inflammatory, inhibits cholesterol absorption, maintains bacterial flora	Dairy, fruit: especially cranberries, oranges, prunes, rhubarb, pineapple, dates, nectarines, peaches. Fenugreek. Chestnuts. Vegetables: especially broccoli, Brussels sprouts, asparagus, mushrooms, beetroot, onions, pumpkin, spinach
⇢ Mannose	All cell membranes, brain and nerves	Anti-inflammatory, tissue regeneration, anti-infection (particularly of the urinary tract); anti-bacterial, antiviral, antifungal, antiparasitic, anti-tumour	Aloe vera gel, fenugreek, green beans, blackcurrants, peppers, aubergine, tomatoes, turnips, shiitake mushrooms, kelp, gooseberries, black/redcurrants
⇢ N-acetylglucosamine	Small intestine, blood vessels,endocrine/seba-ceous glands, thyroid, eyes, brain	Immune modulator, anti-cancer, repairs cartilage, hormone balancing, gut-soothing, insulin and cholesterol decreasing	Shiitake mushrooms, bovine/shark cartilage
⇢ N-acetylgalactosamine	Widely. Especially brain, nerves, eyes, skin, testes, hair	Cell communication, anti-tumour, immune enhancer, possibly nerve and joint protection	Bovine/shark cartilage
⇢ N-acetylneuraminic acid (sialic acid)	Widely. Especially saliva, urine, cerebrospinal fluid, amniotic fluid, brain, adrenals, heart, kidneys	Immune modulator, anti-bacterial, antiviral, memory and performance enhancing, antihistamine	Eggs (chicken), whey protein
⇢ Xylose	Particularly digestive tract, kidneys	Anti-bacterial, antifungal, anti-cancer, promotes probiotics	Aloe vera gel, aubergines, beans, cabbage, corn, broccoli, spinach, okra, peas, guava, pears, berries, kelp, psyllium

5. Soak fruit and veg before juicing.

6. Drink juice immediately after you make it – it's highly perishable and swiftly loses its active ingredients.

7. Don't mix fruit and vegetable juices; they will ferment in the gut and cause bloating.

8. Start by trying the vegetables and fruits you like non-juiced.

9. Once you've got a taste for single juices, experiment by adding additional vegetables or herbs.

10. Remember, don't eat all your fruit and vegetables this way. Juices do not contain fibre and so should not totally replace whole fruits and vegetables in your diet.

THE ONE-DAY JUICE FAST

If you really love juice, you might like to consider an occasional one-day juice 'fast' in which you only drink freshly juiced vegetables or fruits. It gives your digestive and detox systems a lovely break,

and can have astonishing effects on your skin, eyes and hair. Many people like it so much they do it on a regular basis – even once a week. If you like this idea, make sure it's a day when you don't have heavy commitments, and don't juice fast for more than one day a week – your body needs other nutrients.

THE GOOD-MOOD JUICE GUIDE

You can use juice to lift your mood as well as tone your body. Here are a few suggestions to try:

- Anti-anxiety: banana/yoghurt/honey/nutmeg
- Aphrodisiac: broccoli/red pepper/ tomatoes/ginger
- Calm and cool: carrot/celery/mangetout
- Concentration: carrot/spinach/celery/ watercress/basil
- Depression beater: carrot/beetroot/ sprouts/ ginger
- Energy: strawberry/blueberry/apricot/ yoghurt/maple syrup
- Get up and go: pineapple/mango/banana/ coconut milk
- Stress-basher: lettuce/celery/avocado/ peppermint
- Super sleep: sheep's milk/banana/cumin

TOP TEN HEALTHY SNACKS

1. Rice cakes – load them with dips or use instead of bread for 'sandwiches'. If you find them too thick, try those designed for babies – thinner and more dainty.

2. Gluten-free oatcakes – nutty and delicious topped with sheep's cheese or grilled vegetables.

3. Hummus – great for dipping, home-made is best.

4. Guacamole – another fabulous dip or topping. Again, home-made is streets ahead of the shop-bought stuff.

5. Chopped carrots, celery, cauliflower and mangetout to dip or crunch alone.

6. Nuts – walnuts, pecans, almonds, Brazils.

7. Seeds – sunflower, linseeds, pumpkin.

8. Ripe fresh fruit – bananas, blueberries, apples etc. Ensure they are really ripe and, ideally, naturally ripened.

9. Organic dried fruits – raisins, sultanas, prunes, currants, apricots, mango, pineapple etc.

10. Falafel – delicious Middle-Eastern chickpea patties (see Chapter 8 for the recipe).

SUPPLEMENTS

If your eating is following the guidelines for my Plan, you will be getting the nutrients you need from your food. I would not be happy about you self-prescribing supplements as, without wanting to alarm you, you can do more harm than good – even to the point of giving yourself chronic conditions. For example, excess intake of calcium can cause a rise of calcium in the blood, and this can lead to cramp, lethargy, confusion and, in extreme cases, coma. Large doses of iron are fatal in children; in adults, they can bring on constipation, vomiting, nausea, stomach pain and an increase in blood pressure. Taking more than 1.5g of vitamin A per day over many years can make your bones more vulnerable in later life. And excess beta-carotene and Vitamin E supplementation has been linked to an increase in the risk of lung cancer developing in smokers. The problem with self-treating is that many supplements contain the same micronutrients so it is quite easy – unwittingly – to be taking several doses of the same nutrient, thus hiking your overall levels too high. Also, nutrition is highly individual – the micronutrients you need at 20 years of age are different from those you need in your thirties, forties, fifties and so on. As your lifestyle and the seasons change, so, too, do your micronutrient levels: if you lose weight, if you gain muscle mass, if you start or stop exercising – all these will affect your needs.

Having said all this, I often give my patients carefully chosen supplements – on an individual basis – and I do feel they can be very useful. However, I only do so after a personal consultation, taking into account all the factors in their life and condition. I would urge you to consult a well-qualified nutritional therapist or naturopath (see Directory) who will look at all aspects of your health, lifestyle, and any medication you may be taking, and prescribe accordingly. If you do want to take supplements, periodically give your body a break to rebalance itself.

AYURVEDIC METABOLIC TYPE CHART

CHARACTERISTIC	VATA	KAPHA	PITTA	YOUR METABOLIC TYPE (V, K OR P)
Body weight	Low	Overweight	Average	
Body Size	Slim	Large	Average	
Skin Type	Thin, dry, rough, dark, cold	Thick, oily, cool, white, pale,	Smooth, oily, warm, rosy	
Nails	Dry, rough, brittle, thin	Thick, oily, smooth, polished	Sharp, flexible, luminescent, pink	
Eyes	Small, sunken, animated	Big, calm, soft	Sharp, bright, sensitive to light	
Hair	Dry, brown/black, brittle, thin	Thick, wavy/curly, oily, lustrous	Straight, oily, blonde/grey/red, bald	
Lips	Dry, cracked, black/brown, tinged	Smooth, oily, pale, white	Red, inflamed	
Chin	Thin, angular	Rounded, double	Tapering	
Cheeks	Wrinkled, sunken	Rounded, plump	Smooth, flat	
Neck	Thin, taut, long	Big, folded	Smooth, flat	
Chest	Flat, sunken	Rounded, pendulous	Average	
Belly	Flat, sunken	Rounded, extended	Average	
Hips	Slender, thin	Heavy, rounded	Average	
Joints	Cold, crack a lot	Large, move freely	Average	
Digestion	Irregular, gassy	Slow, forming soft stools	Quick, burning sensation, acidic	
Appetite	Irregular, scant	Slow, steady	Strong, always hungry, eating often	
Cravings	Sweet, sour, salty	Bitter, pungent, astringent	Sweet, bitter, astringent	
Thirst	Changeable	Sparse	Surplus	
Elimination	Constipated	Thick/sluggish	Loose	
Physical activity	Hyper	Sedentary	Moderate	
Mental activity	Hyper	Slow thinking	Moderate	
Emotions	Anxious, fearful, nervy	Calm, needy	Extreme swings	
Intellect	Quick, spontaneous	Slow, exact	Precise	
Memory	Short term good, long term poor	Slow and sustained	Distinct, clear	
Dreams	Quick, active, prone to nightmares	Romantic, pleasant, calm	Fiery and violent	
Sleep	Insomniac, broken	Deep, long, uninterrupted	Little but sound	
Speech	Rapid, unclear	Slow, monotone	Sharp, distinct	

Vata total:

Kapha total:

Pitta total:

Dominant *dosha* :

YOUR AYURVEDIC METABOLIC TYPE

In my first book, I introduced the Ayurvedic concept of *doshas*. To recap, Ayurveda teaches that the world is made up of five building blocks – earth, water, fire, air and ether. These elements combine to create three distinct *doshas*, or metabolic types:

1. Air and ether combine to form *Vata dosha*
2. Water and earth combine to form *Kapha dosha*
3. Fire and water combine to form *Pitta dosha*

All three *doshas* are present in our bodies, but one or two usually dominate. We all have our unique combination of the three *doshas* but this itself may need rebalancing depending on lifestyle, age, and numerous other factors. In an ideal world, our *doshas* would all be balanced. However, as you can imagine, our rushed, hurried world, our dodgy diet – and any number of other irritants – can put us out of balance. Spend a little time filling in the chart opposite to determine your own Ayurvedic metabolic type (AMT). Throughout the book, we will be using that information to tailor various elements of the Life Plan so that it is uniquely yours. If you find it hard to answer some of the questions, ask a friend or your partner.

Most people will find one *dosha* is prominent, a few will have two *doshas* approximately equal – and even fewer will have all three *doshas* in equal proportion. If you are in doubt, go by your basic build and personality to gauge your 'fundamental' *dosha*:

Vatas are usually fine-boned, slight people who have quick, restless, imaginative minds. Think of a Siamese cat, sinewy and graceful.

Kaphas are usually heavy-boned, solid, steady people who are peaceful, tolerant and forgiving in nature. Think of a big, cuddly brown bear.
Pittas are usually of medium-build but recognisable by their keen intellect, competitiveness and quick tempers! Think of a pugnacious Jack Russell terrier, running round in circles, barking its head off.

YOUR DOSHA AND YOUR DIET

Towards the end of the Life Plan, I will be suggesting you refine your diet in order to help balance your *doshas*. Certain foods can aggravate or ease each *dosha* and so – with a little careful planning – you can tailor-make a diet that really supports your *doshas*. This is particularly useful if you suffer from health conditions associated with a particular *dosha*. For instance, *Vata* conditions include anxiety, tension, depression, migraine, IBS (irritable bowel syndrome) and nervous disorders. *Kaphas* are susceptible to such ailments as diabetes, asthma, weight gain, eczema, and gall-bladder problems. *Pittas* may be prone to such problems as ulcers, digestive problems, skin conditions, headaches and liver problems. At this stage, just look through the chart that follows and notice which foods are contraindicated for your predominant *dosha*. Ten to one, they are foods you love! It's a sad truth that our bodies can become addicted to the very foods that are so bad for us. Think about adjusting your diet to work with, rather than against, your *dosha*.

SIX TASTES CHART

SOUR

Foods: Yoghurt, vinegar, cheese, sour cream, green grapes, lemon (and other citrus fruits), tamarind, pickles, and herbs such as coriander, and cloves.

Effect: Reduces Vata, increases Pitta, increases Kapha. Stimulates appetite and sharpens the mind. Although foods are acidic they will slow the metabolism.

SALTY

Foods: Table salt, sea salt, rock salt, crisps, marine fish, vegetables; remember, there is also a lot of salt in tinned and processed foods, which should always be avoided where possible.

Effect: Reduces Vata, increases Pitta, increases Kapha. Helps digestion; acts as a laxative.

SWEET

Foods: Fruits, sugar, cakes, honey, syrup, molasses, certain vegetables such as carrots and beets, dairy produce, rice, bread. I recommend that you continue to avoid highly processed sweets such as chocolate bars and sugar.

Effect: Reduces Vata, reduces Pitta, increases Kapha. Excessive amounts of sugar will make you put on weight. The problem with eating sugary foods such as chocolate and cakes is that they also contain additives, food colourants and preservatives, which will have an adverse affect on your fat levels. Fizzy drinks can also raise your Vata.

ASTRINGENT

Foods: Vinegar, pickles, unripe banana, cranberries, pomegranate.

Effect: Increases Vata, reduces Pitta, reduces Kapha. Astringent foods can promote healing as they have a sedative action but they also produce a lot of gas and acid.

PUNGENT

Foods: Onion, pickles, spices, aromatic foods, chilli, ginger, garlic, mustard.

Effect: Increases Vata, increases Pitta, reduces Kapha. Spices stimulate digestive juices and increase production of acid, which will raise your Pitta. Also helps with Kapha problem of obesity, slow digestion.

BITTER

Foods: Coffee, wine, alcohols, greens such as Romaine lettuce, spinach, and chard.

Effect: Increases Vata, reduces Pitta, reduces Kapha. Most bitter foods are stimulants and promote digestion and cleanse the blood.

LUISA'S STORY

I went to Joshi in the first instance for help with a back problem. I knew from a friend that he had an excellent reputation as an osteopath and since I don't like taking lots of medicines for things, the fact that Joshi was also a general holistic practitioner appealed to me.

At my first consultation we had a very honest and open chat about my health. He asked me what I thought had caused my back problems and I explained that there was no single event that had triggered them but that I suspected that my weight gain had caused them. Having been a slim person all my life, after a stressful divorce I put on 30 kilos in three years. The strain placed on my back was just too much. Joshi told me he intended to work on my back first and then address my weight problems. After visiting him three times in one week for back cracks, acupuncture and infra-red treatments, my back was improved so much

that I was able to fly to an important business meeting. It felt like a turning point and gave me a huge incentive to start on the Detox Programme. I followed it religiously and found it pretty straightforward. It all made sense to me and in fact, it didn't even feel like a diet, because there were no longer any food cravings and I didn't have to waste time counting calories.

That was all six months ago and I am still on the Life Plan. I went from a size 18 to a size 10 in seven months and I have so much more energy and feel so much better. I didn't have a single cold over the winter so my immune system is obviously in better shape, and my back problems have not returned. I genuinely feel that I have regained control over my body. I recognise myself again.

LUISA PEREIRA, 40, IS A HEAD HUNTER AND WORKS IN LONDON AND THE STATES.

CHAPTER TWO
EXERCISE FOR LIFE

EXERCISE IS THE NEXT ESSENTIAL PART OF MY HOLISTIC LIFE PLAN. AFTER DIET, IT'S THE SIMPLEST YET MOST POWERFUL KICK YOU CAN GIVE TO YOUR HEALTH AND HAPPINESS. GOING TO THE GYM IS LIKE AN ADDICTION FOR ME NOW. I'M JUST SO IMPRESSED WITH MYSELF FOR HAVING THE WILLPOWER TO PUSH MYSELF AFTER AN EXHAUSTING DAY. IT'S A CHALLENGE, BUT I COME OUT TOTALLY INVIGORATED AND ENERGISED – IT'S MENTAL THERAPY AS MUCH AS PHYSICAL THERAPY. EXERCISE HAS BECOME SOMETHING I LOOK FORWARD TO AND I REALLY ENJOY IT. YOU CAN, TOO.

STILL SURGICALLY ATTACHED TO THE COUCH? LET ME CONVINCE YOU. REGULAR EXERCISE KEEPS YOUR HEART AND LUNGS WORKING AT OPTIMUM LEVELS AND HELPS WARD OFF HEART DISEASE. EXERCISE KICKS STRESS BACK INTO ITS BOX AND IS A NATURAL, SIMPLE, WILDLY EFFECTIVE MOOD ELEVATOR. MAKE EXERCISE A REGULAR HABIT AND YOU WILL PERK UP YOUR LIBIDO AND HELP TO GIVE YOURSELF A GOOD NIGHT'S SLEEP. IT CAN HELP KEEP YOUR BLOOD PRESSURE NORMAL AND BOOST YOUR IMMUNE SYSTEM SO YOU BECOME IMPERVIOUS TO COLDS AND FLU.

IF WEIGHT IS AN ISSUE (AND WHEN ISN'T IT?), EXERCISE IS THE VERY BEST MOVE YOU CAN MAKE. THE POUNDS AUTOMATICALLY DISAPPEAR WHEN YOU START TO WORK OUT; YOU BECOME MORE FLEXIBLE AND MORE TONED. THE MORE MUSCLE YOU HAVE, THE MORE FAT YOU NEED TO BURN: YOU CAN'T HELP BUT GET SLIMMER AND TRIMMER. STUDIES SHOW THAT PEOPLE WHO EXERCISE EVEN LIVE LONGER THAN THE REST OF US. LET'S BE HONEST, WHAT DOESN'T EXERCISE DO?

WHY WE DON'T EXERCISE

Despite the fact that exercise is indisputably wonderful, many of us choose to find a million and one reasons why we can't slide off our backsides and move a bit. My role as a practitioner is to guide you, encourage you, but I can't drag you up the hill. You know the story: 'I'm too busy . . . I'm the wrong shape . . . I've got dodgy joints . . . I'm so unfit, it would be dangerous.' Well, now is the time to change all that. When you decide to do it, you can do it. But we tend to procrastinate: we say we'll do it tomorrow, next week, next month, next year. There are two reasons, real reasons, why we don't exercise. Firstly, time *is* an issue for most of us. Secondly, most of us simply haven't found an exercise that really suits us. I'm going to show you how – now – to overcome both reasons. We'll start with finding the right kind of exercise.

NOTE: If you haven't exercised for a long time, or you have chronic health conditions, you should see your doctor and get the all-clear before any kind of exercising. You may need to work out under supervision or to choose particular types of exercise. Talk to your GP or ask for information from your surgery. Check out local education authorities and sports centres as these often run programmes for specific groups of people. There are, for example, plenty of gyms that run cardio-clubs for people with heart conditions, and many clubs have fitness classes aimed specifically at people who are older or overweight. Aqua aerobics may be suitable if you have weak joints. Don't use your health as an excuse; exercising will *improve* your health, no question – just do it sensibly and with guidance.

YOUR AYURVEDIC METABOLIC EXERCISE TYPE

In the last chapter, I talked about the three major metabolic types of Ayurveda – *Vata* (air/ether), *Kapha* (water/earth) and *Pitta* (fire/water). Interestingly, this knowledge can be very useful when it comes to finding the kind of exercise which will suit you and which will motivate you to keep going. So many of us were put off 'sport' when we were young simply because we just weren't good at the sports we were pushed into. Let's face it, some of us, with the best will in the world, are never going to cut it as gymnasts – we simply don't have the physical make-up for it. Equally, others won't ever have the strength and stamina for long-distance running or shot putting. We are all different, and not liking one form of exercise doesn't mean that you are not a 'fitness' person. You simply haven't yet found the form of exercise that is tailor-made to suit your Ayurvedic metabolic type. If you haven't already taken the test, do it now and discover which *dosha*, or type, is predominant. If you fall between two types (many people do), you will need (as far as exercise goes) to look primarily at your physical characteristics. To sum up:

Vata: slim, slight people who are often underweight. You have a small delicate frame with long fine bones. Generally, you are flat-chested and have prominent joints (that often crack or click). Your features are fine and pointed; your eyes animated but often deep-set; your skin dry, rough and cold. *Vata* people are quick in their movements and in their minds, highly imaginative and somewhat nervy.

Kapha: heavy-boned people with a solid, broad frame. You put on weight easily and can be plump or overweight. You are often heavy-breasted and broad-hipped. You tend to have thick, cold skin that can be oily. Your eyes are big, soft and beautiful. *Kapha* people are slow in speech and movement but have great stamina and are calm and focused in nature.

Pitta: people of average build who are often well toned. You can put on weight but lose it again quite easily. Your skin is smooth, oily and warm – *Pittas* are generally very warm-blooded and easily overheat. Your eyes are sharp and sensitive to light. *Pitta* people are smart, precise and highly competitive. They can be quite fiery in nature and swing from one mood to another.

YOUR IDEAL EXERCISE

Ten to one, if you have tried and failed at exercise in the past, it's because you were doing the wrong kind of exercise. Most people never even think about the kind of exercise that would ideally suit – you simply trot along obediently to the gym and sign up for weight-lifting or aerobics. You read about Madonna doing ashtanga yoga or Gyrotonics and think you should be doing the same, or else your best friend is passionate about netball/salsa/kickboxing and you get hauled along. No wonder you don't keep it up. Unless you are very lucky, you are most probably doing a form of exercise that runs directly counter to your natural inclinations. Stop! Put on hold all your expectations about what exercise you *should* be doing and think about what you actually *like* doing. The best way to do this is to think back to when you were young. Were there sports you enjoyed at school? What did you play with your friends? What would you have liked to have played? Were you in love with ballet or happier tossing a ball around? Did you go doe-eyed over ponies or live in your swimming costume? What's to stop you rediscovering those childhood passions?

How did you like to play sport? Did the loneliness of the long-distance runner or solo swimmer strike you with an enjoyable frisson or a horrified shudder? Did you get a kick out of battling against an opponent – going head-to-head in tennis, badminton, squash or judo – or did you relish being part of a team? Take these preferences into consideration when planning your born-again exercise habit.

Ayurveda, of course, also has the answer. Certain sports dovetail with each *dosha*. If you're new to exercise, it's a good idea to play to your strengths, to try a sport in which you have a good chance of success. This will really boost your motivation in those vital early weeks. For instance, a *Vata* type would excel on the race track but simply not have the stamina for long-distance swimming. These are the forms of exercise that work best for each predominant *dosha*:

VATA: You are a natural sprinter or runner. You may be good at gymnastics. Pretty well any kind of field sport (running, jumping, hurdling) will suit you – with the exception of the shot put! Pick sports or exercises which capitalise on your speed and agility and which won't call for a lot of endurance (your weak point). If you play team sports, such as football or netball, put yourself in a position where the emphasis is on speed. You have innate grace, too, so consider dancing, ice-skating or trampolining.

KAPHA: *Kaphas* are built for endurance, strength and power, so pick out sports needing these qualities. Any shot-putter is bound to be a *kapha*, as are wrestlers and heavyweight boxers. You will flourish with team sports because you thrive under the motivation of others – you're a generous and good-natured team player. Anything involving distance also works well – whether long-distance swimming, cross-country running or mountain biking – because you have great stamina. You thrive at weight-training at the gym and do well at circuit-training, too.

PITTA: You have good coordination and can be very (and I mean *very*) competitive. *Pittas* thrive under healthy stress, so don't bore yourself rigid by taking up synchronised swimming or long-distance running. Join a team or get involved with a league – *Pitta* can work well in most positions. If that isn't possible, then try to exercise with someone – competitive *Pitta* will even get a kick out of meditating better than someone else! Aerobic classes are great for you, and so is horse-riding or cycling – you like to feel the wind in your hair.

FINDING TIME – THINKING OUTSIDE THE BOX

'I don't have time to exercise' is the second most common excuse (after 'I don't like exercising'). It's tough, I know that. I used to go for weeks without seeing the inside of my gym, but now I have learned that, if I want to stay calm, focused and energised, I must find time for my sessions. I commit to three times a week, after work, without fail, and feel fabulous.

If I can do it, so can you. Often, it's just a case of reframing. Here are my top ten suggestions:

1. Be an early bird. Many people find they set themselves up for the day by setting the alarm an hour earlier and working out before breakfast. Drop in on the gym on your way to work; take an early morning run; literally salute the sun with a home yoga class (see page 52).

2. Do a business 'breakfast' on the hop: in America, it's a given – you go on the treadmill and do business, or else thrash out deals over a pre-work game of squash.

3. Use your lunch hour. Hit the gym, not the merlot. Many fitness centres have lunch-hour aerobics, or circuit workouts, or yoga/Pilates classes.

4. Become ladies who stretch, rather than ladies who lunch. Get together a group and commit to regular classes, or club together to get a personal trainer (cheaper and more motivating). Many of my patients do this – and love it.

5. Get your colleagues on track – pull together teams at work for five-a-side football, netball, volleyball, whatever takes your fancy. Have a league for tennis/squash/badminton/table tennis. Schedule matches for after work – and make after-work drinks a post-match wheatgrass juice.

6. Turn your gym/riding stables/tennis court/yoga studio into your social club. Persuade your friends to commit to getting fit – together. Just remember you're there to work out, not chat!

7. Families who play sport together, stay together. All of you go swimming or hiking at the weekend. Start children doing yoga from an early age with you – they'll develop a great habit for life.

8. Multi-task – it's not ideal, but, if you're really strapped for time, take your work reports and read them on the bike while you're doing your spinning class, or jump on a rebounder (mini-trampoline) while you're watching the news.

9. Go for court-ship – getting hot and sweaty with your partner is a great way to bond and makes for a healthier date than a heavy restaurant meal. Remember, too, that exercise (temporarily) increases adrenalin and that, for us humans, elevated stress hormones equate with increased desire!

10. A little and often. You don't have to do mega sessions of exercise to reap the benefits – squeezing in ten minutes of stair-walking between meetings counts. So does five minutes of stretching or yoga (see Office Yoga on page 60).

MOTIVATE YOURSELF

There's really no excuse for not exercising and yet still we seem to find plenty. It can be tough to get started; however, if you commit to a regular exercise programme, you will start to notice changes quite swiftly. At first you might be out of breath after just two minutes of jogging or cycling, but, rest assured, after a few sessions you will be up to a good six minutes and within six weeks should be able to breeze through thirty. Follow these tips to help you boost your motivation levels:

THE THREE STEPS TO DOING IT
(Rather than just talking about it)

STEP ONE: FIND AN EXPERT
If you can, enlist the help of an expert to get you on track. A reputable gym, for example, should give you a fitness assessment, a tailor-made programme and bags of encouragement along the way. A good yoga or Pilates studio should quiz you on your health and any problems, and give you close supervision. If you can afford one, a personal trainer is a godsend who can design a programme that suits your precise strengths, aims and lifestyle. My trainer really enriches my life – and I miss him when I don't see him. You can share the cost by training with a friend or small group of friends.

If you're on your own then you'll probably need a little trial and error. If you don't like one kind of exercise or routine, or you don't get results after giving it your best shot (it will take six weeks of regular sessions to notice a significant difference), then change. If that doesn't work, change again. Obviously, you need to give the programme a fighting chance, but don't ever force yourself to do something you hate. If exercise is going to work for you, it has to be enjoyable or at least challenging.

STEP TWO: START SMALL

If you haven't exercised before, or for a long time (and especially if you're returning to exercise after pregnancy), take it easy, very easy. Maybe just five minutes a day at the easiest level of the cross trainer or a ten minute swim will be enough. But you'll soon find you can go for longer and work harder – and then you'll get a real buzz out of your improvement. If you can get yourself past the first week, you've passed the period in which half the dropouts occur. If you work out regularly for six weeks, you're likely to have created a long-lasting habit. Grin and bear it for that first week (yes, it will be tough) and then it will start to get easier. The really brilliant part of exercising regularly is that you soon start to notice results. There is nothing more motivating than looking in the mirror and seeing yourself visibly firming up; nothing better than seeing a thigh stop wobbling and start rippling.

STEP THREE: AYURVEDIC BREATHING

If you have ever done an ashtanga yoga class, you will have been introduced to *ujjayi*, the 'victorious' breath. This particular way of breathing (always through the nose) allows yogis to keep going in this extremely tough form of yoga. You can actually use it for any kind of sport or exercise – and will notice a huge difference in your stamina and performance, once you've mastered it. It may seem strange if you are used to gasping in huge gulps of air, but do try it. The only downside is that fellow exercisers may think you have a severe head-cold.

⇢ Breathe in through the nose.

⇢ Breathe out through the nose, slightly constricting the throat so you make a guttural sound – just like Darth Vadar in *Star Wars*. You will feel a sensation in your throat, rather than in your nose.

⇢ Notice that your stomach muscles slightly contract as you breathe out.

You will find at first that, breathing in this way, you can only work for far less time. Don't panic. Just slow down your workout to suit your breath, your body. You will quickly find that, with this form of breathing, you will be able to return to your former fitness levels and even surpass them.

STRETCHING

A stretched body is a healthy body. Stretching is simplicity itself and yet it is a real gift for both body and mind. If you carry out a careful stretch routine, particularly after exercise or sports, you will help to protect your muscles and joints from injury. If you spend your days stuck at a desk or behind the wheel of a car, stretching can release stress and unwind tense muscles. Stretching will also improve your posture and you will be far less likely to suffer neck, shoulder and back pain, or from headaches and bad digestion. Virtually anyone can follow a simple stretch routine. However, if you suffer from a bad back, you should seek professional advice before stretching.

Try to make this routine a daily habit. Practise it in the morning to give your body a wake-up call and also to help you unwind after a long day at work. You can also use it whenever you find yourself feeling tired and stressed. Ideally, wear loose comfortable clothes for stretching – but, if you're stuck for time, simply slip off your shoes and loosen your belt.

SIMPLE STRETCH ROUTINE

Take these stretches slowly and carefully: don't be tempted to over-stretch. The idea is to feel the stretch but not to give yourself any discomfort or pain. Don't 'bounce' the stretch to make it more intense: once in the pose, simply hold it without movement. If you can't make the full stretch, just go as far as you can. With regular practice, you will swiftly increase your flexibility.

You should always warm up before stretching. It needn't be anything fancy, simply get your muscles warm by marching on the spot, swinging your arms briskly, dancing around to the radio or bouncing on your rebounder (if you have one). It doesn't matter what you do but spend at least five minutes getting really warm (particularly if it's cold outside). Then start stretching.

1. CALF STRETCH: Bend your left knee and extend your right leg out behind you into a lunge. Keep both feet parallel, pointing straight ahead. Now, straighten and lower your right leg until your foot is flat on the floor. Shift your hips forward, keeping both feet flat, until you feel a stretch in the calf muscles of the extended leg. Hold gently for a slow count of ten. Now change legs and repeat.

2. QUADRICEPS AND KNEE STRETCH: Keeping one hand on a wall for support if necessary, reach behind your back with your left hand and grasp your right foot by the toes. Keep your supporting knee softly bent, tuck your pelvis forwards and stand up straight. Hold gently for a count of twenty and release. Now, do the same with the opposite hand and foot.

3. GROIN STRETCH: Sit on the floor with the soles of your feet together. Put your hands on your feet and pull your heels in towards your body. This is a strong stretch so don't worry if you can't get very far at first. Now gently pull your body forwards, towards your feet, keeping your back erect until you feel a stretch. Hold for a count of twenty. As you hold the stretch, concentrate on relaxing your arms, shoulders and feet.

4. HAMSTRINGS STRETCH: Still sitting, straighten your left leg out in front of you. Keep your right leg bent as in the groin stretch but now bring the sole of the foot to face the inside of the outstretched leg (as far as you can). Keep the extended leg slightly bent. Now bend forwards slightly, from the hips, with your hands relaxed on the floor next to the extended leg, until you feel an easy stretch. Touch the top of the thigh of your left leg and check it is feeling soft and relaxed. Keep the foot of your left extended leg upright, not turned out. Hold for a count of thirty. Now, release the stretch and repeat with your right leg extended.

5. UPPER HAMSTRINGS AND HIP STRETCH: With your left leg extended in front of you, bend your right leg and bring it up towards your abdomen, cradling it in your arms like a baby. Gently pull the leg towards you until you feel an easy stretch. Hold for a count of twenty, release and then repeat with the other leg.

6. ARCH STRETCH: Sit on your toes (kneeling, but so that you are resting your buttocks on your heels with your toes on the floor). Keep your hands on the floor in front of you for balance. Gently stretch the arches of the feet. Hold for a count of ten.

7. ARM STRETCH: Bring yourself gently to your feet. Raise your left arm up above your head. Grasp it at the elbow with your right hand. Now let your left hand drop down behind your shoulder blade (or as far as you can go). Gently pull the left arm back and in towards the head. Keep your arm, neck and shoulders relaxed. Hold for a count of twenty, then release and repeat on the other side.

8. BACK STRETCH: Sit down and bring your knees up to your chest (with your ankles crossed). Clasp your knees with both arms. Drop your head down to your knees and roll backwards on your spine. Roll forwards and backwards several times.

YOGA – THE MASTER EXERCISE SYSTEM

If you do no other form of exercise, do yoga. Why yoga? Simply because it is the most far-reaching, holistic workout I have ever come across. Yoga has so many benefits that I could write an entire book just about how incredible it is. On a purely physical level, yoga puts pressure on all the different organs and muscles of the body very systematically. As well as toning the outer body (which it does exceedingly well), it tones the whole of the inner body too: liver, lungs, kidneys, spleen, intestines, heart etc. The precise postures of yoga work deep into the body, causing blood to circulate profoundly rather than just around the body's outer edge. It nourishes every organ as well as softening the muscle and ligament tissue.

The deep stretching brings both bones and muscles gently back into their optimum alignment while lubricating the joints. It also fosters that gorgeous, lean, muscled 'yoga body' – you can always tell if someone is using yoga by those long, lean muscles. If you practise yoga regularly, you will almost automatically lose weight and develop a streamlined body shape. Yoga can improve both the oxygenation of your blood *and* its circulation. It is also a superb way of helping your body to detoxify because it encourages lymphatic flow (the 'waste removal' system of the body). Not only does your body detox when you perform yoga: your mind does too. The specific breathing techniques of yoga (*pranayama*) directly affect the nervous system, eliciting the 'relaxation response' in which the parasympathetic nervous system takes over from the sympathetic nervous system. As a result, you feel calm, cool and in control.

Many yoga teachers also find that yoga can help improve willpower: people often find it easier to stop smoking or lose weight when they start yoga. Modern research is now backing up what the yogis have known for five thousand years. A report in *The Lancet,* for instance, describes how yoga relaxation exercises, such *as yoga nidra (*a guided meditative technique), actually alter the neural networks of the brain, inducing deep rest. Yoga is used therapeutically to ease bad backs and to help heal asthma and breathing difficulties. It can be a wonderful form of exercise for mothers-to-be – both before and after delivery (but choose a dedicated class for safety).

Each posture has deep emotional and psychological effects as well as physical benefits. For example, inverted postures, such as shoulder stands, help you gain a different point of view. Bending postures help you to become more flexible in your attitude to life. Twisting postures help you find answers to complex problems. Practise yoga and you feel more at home in your body and more harmonious in your life. You'll sleep better and concentrate more easily, and stress will simply slide over you, gaining no ground.

On a purely cosmetic level, a yoga body is a beautiful body with its long, lean muscles and taut, tight abs, thighs and butt. The increase in circulation brings an inner glow to your skin, makes your eyes shine and your hair gleam. Seriously, grab that mat and get going.

WHICH YOGA WOULD SUIT YOU?

There are so many different types of yoga available that it can be hard to know which would suit. Here are some of the ones you're most likely to come across.

⇢ **Hatha yoga:** the generic name for the physical form of yoga that uses postures – *asanas*. Classes usually include relaxation, warm-up, postures, *pranayama* (breathing techniques) and deep relaxation. Many teachers also include meditation; some will add in chanting and visualisation. Excellent for beginners and the most commonly available.

⇢ **Iyengar yoga:** very focused, precise form of yoga that puts great emphasis on correct posture. Teachers use 'props' such as blocks and belts to help you into position and deepen stretches. Great if you want the physical benefits without too much of the spiritual side.

⇢ **Sivananda yoga:** gentle, laid-back yet pure form of yoga based around twelve key postures. Has a strong spiritual element and usually includes chanting and meditation.

⇢ **Ashtanga vinyassa yoga:** so-called 'power yoga' that uses a sequence of postures carried out at far greater speed than other forms, using a specific breathing pattern (see page 47). An intense workout, not really suitable for beginners or the unfit. Ideal, however, for those who find 'normal' yoga too slow and boring.

⇢ **Dru yoga:** very gentle, holistic approach that includes *pranayama*, visualisation, deep relaxation and meditation. Uses graceful, flowing movement sequences. Said to release negative thought patterns and energy blocks – yoga meets psychotherapy.

⇢ **Vini yoga:** puts emphasis on individual tuition and individual needs with precise focus on the breath. Safe, gentle and ideal for beginners. Often taught on a one-to-one basis.

⇢ **Kundalini yoga:** ancient form of yoga that includes postures, *pranayama*, visualisation, chanting, meditation and *mudras* (hand postures). Aim is to activate the 'serpent energy' coiled at the base of the spine and bring it up through the chakras to awaken divine energy. Gentle, safe, spiritual. Good for beginners.

⇢ **Tantra yoga:** traditional form of yoga including postures, *pranayama*, meditation, visualisation, *mantras* (sacred sound), *yantras* (sacred images) and ritual. Techniques are often chosen to balance your *dosha*. Deeply spiritual form of yoga but safe for beginners.

⇢ **Yoga therapy:** therapeutic form of yoga with a medical background. Yoga therapists usually offer individual sessions or classes for specific problems and conditions, e.g. back pain, arthritis, asthma, pregnancy. The best choice if you have a medical condition.

⇢ **Bikram yoga:** hot, hot, hot! Developed in the 1960s by Bikram Choudhary and the fastest growing form of yoga in the US where it attracts a high celebrity following. Intense and highly athletic, it uses twenty-six postures, practised in the same sequence and in sweltering rooms as hot as 42°C (108°F). You either love it or hate it. Not for those in poor health and particularly not advised if you have a heart condition or high blood pressure.

⇢ **Yogaboxing™:** high-octane fusion of dance, yoga, tai chi and martial arts. Not really yoga as such, but great fun.

⇢ **Partner yoga (or couples yoga):** just as it sounds, you work with a partner (usually someone the same height and sex as you) to help you stretch deeper. Good fun and highly sociable – probably the noisiest yoga class going.

CAUTIONS

As with any form of exercise, yoga can harm as well as heal if you practise it incorrectly. For instance, people with neck problems or whiplash shouldn't be doing headstands.

→ If you are a beginner, always go to a teacher rather than trying to teach yourself from a book or a video. The *asanas* are very precise and you need expert tuition.

→ Find a well-qualified teacher (see the Directory). If you have any health problems (particularly heart conditions and back problems, or if you have had any kind of surgery), you should find a yoga therapist (who has had a strict medical training) rather than a yoga teacher.

→ Don't push yourself beyond your limits. Yoga is not competitive – everyone works at their own pace and within their body's limits. Start small – you will soon find you can stretch further or work harder.

→ Make sure your yoga teacher is aware of any health or fitness problems you have before the class. A good teacher should always ask, but you need to be aware that you have to tell them, too. Then he or she will be able to tell you which postures to avoid and will often give you specific postures to help your condition.

→ If you are pregnant, you will need to avoid certain postures. Again, you should see a yoga therapist or find a class specifically designed for pregnant women – many centres run antenatal classes, and many also run post-natal classes for mothers and their babies.

THE SUN SALUTE – YOUR PERFECT MORNING WORKOUT

The Sun Salute or Salutation to the Sun is a well-known yoga routine. It is perhaps the most effective series of exercises you can do for your body. In ancient India, it was part of daily spiritual practice and was performed in the very early morning facing the sun – the Sun God being the deity for health and longevity.

There are twelve spinal positions and each stretches different ligaments and moves the spine in different ways. At first, this series of exercises will seem jerky and uncoordinated, but persevere. As you learn them, you will find yourself moving ever more fluidly and smoothly from one to another. Start off with just one whole set and gradually build up to doing the exercise the optimum twelve times. You may find it helpful to record the instructions on a tape recorder until you become familiar with them.

POSTURE ONE: Standing upright, bring your feet together so your big toes are touching. Your arms are by your sides. Relax your shoulders and tuck your chin in slightly – look straight ahead, not down at your feet. Bring your hands together in front of your chest with palms together as if you were praying. Exhale deeply.

POSTURE TWO: Inhale slowly and deeply while you bring your arms straight up over your head, placing your palms together as you finish inhaling. Softly look backwards towards your thumbs. Lift the knees by tightening your thighs. Reach up as far as possible, lengthening your whole body. If you feel comfortable, you can take the posture back slightly further into a bend.

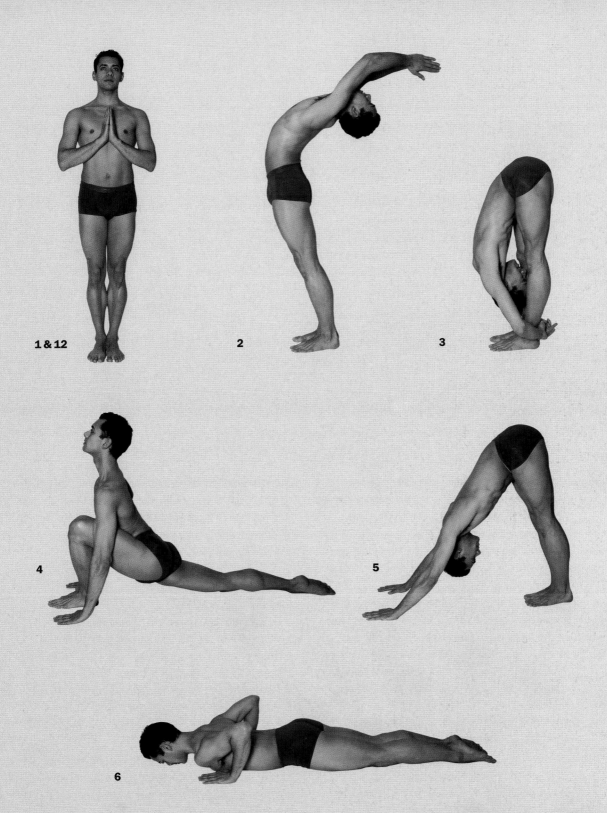

1 & 12

2

3

4

5

6

POSTURE THREE: Exhale as you bend forwards so that your hands are on the floor in line with your feet. Your head should be touching your knees. To begin with, you might find you have to bend your knees in order to reach the floor. Eventually you should be able to straighten your knees into the full posture.

POSTURE FOUR: Inhale deeply and move your left leg away from your body in a big backwards sweep so you end up in a kind of extended lunge position. Keep your hands and right foot firmly on the ground. Your right knee should be between your hands. Bend your head upwards, stretching out your back.

POSTURE FIVE: Exhaling deeply, bring yourself into an arched position. Your arms are in front of your head, palms facing directly in front, arms shoulder-width apart. Your back should be in a straight line with your head in line with your arms. Keep your feet and heels flat on the floor.

POSTURE SIX: Exhale and lower your body onto the floor in a low press-up position (if you do Pilates, it's the Plank). If you're very experienced, you can perform the full *sastanga namaskar* (the eight-curved prostration), so-named because only eight parts of your body are in contact with the floor: your feet, your knees, your hands, your chest and your forehead.

POSTURE SEVEN: Inhale and bend up into the position known as the Cobra. Hands on the floor in front of you, arms straight and bend backwards as far as feels comfortable. Look upwards.

POSTURE EIGHT: Exhale and lift your back once again into Position Five (known as the Downward Dog). Remember to keep (if you can) your feet and heels flat on the floor.

POSTURE NINE: Inhale and return to Position Four, this time with the opposite leg forwards: so, your left foot is in line with your hands while your right leg is stretched back.

POSTURE TEN: Exhale and return to Position Three.
POSTURE ELEVEN: Raise the arms overhead and
bend backwards as you inhale (as for Position Two).
POSTURE TWELVE: Return to a comfortable
standing position, feet together, arms by your sides.
Look straight ahead and exhale. To close, bring
your hands back together in a position of prayer.
As you become more proficient in yoga, you can
extend your practice. Once you have performed
your Sun Salutations, you may like to include
the following postures, all of which will help to
increase your energy, extend your flexibility and
improve your mood. Perform them slowly and
carefully in a controlled manner. Never rush.

THE MOUNTAIN

This seated variation of the Mountain posture
tones your abdominal muscles and improves
your breathing. It can help sluggish circulation
and can also tone the muscles in the back.

1. Sit cross-legged on the floor. Hold yourself
upright and breathe naturally and easily.

2. Inhale and stretch your arms up over your head
to form a steeple shape. Keep the insides of your
arms close to your ears. Bring your palms together
(if you can) as if you were praying.

3. Hold this posture for as long as is comfortable.
Remember to breathe easily and regularly as you
hold the pose.

4. Exhale and slowly lower your arms to your lap.
Rest for a few moments and then repeat.

PRAYER POSTURE

The gentle Prayer posture puts all your internal organs into balance. It encourages deep breathing and helps to align your spine into its optimum position. It is also deeply calming for the mind.

1. Stand with your feet together and parallel. Aim to stand tall without straining – imagine you have a string fastening your head to the ceiling.

2. Check your head – it should be easily balanced on your neck with eyes gazing softly ahead. Your chin should be neither tucked in or jutting out.

3. Tilt your pelvis slightly forwards and keep your knees straight but soft – don't lock them.

4. Now, bring your hands together in front of your chest, as if you were praying.

5. Relax your jaw, your facial muscles and your shoulders. Breathe softly and regularly. You may want to focus lightly on an object in front of you – or you can gently close your eyes.

6. Hold this pose for a few minutes or as long as you feel comfortable. Then, bring your hands back down to your sides and resume your normal stance.

1–3

4–6

1

2–4

5

THE TREE

The Tree position is a well-known yoga posture that is superb for improving your balance, concentration and coordination.

1. Stand up tall and straight. Your feet should be close together and parallel. Fix your eyes gently on a spot ahead and breathe naturally and regularly. You will need to keep your eyes open for this posture.

2. Lift one leg and place the sole of your foot against the inner side of your other thigh. You can use your hands to help. Keep focusing on the point ahead of you.

3. Now bring your hands up in a prayer position in front of your chest.

4. Hold the posture for as long as feels comfortable. Focus on your breathing and think about the strength and poise of a tree – its roots firm in the ground; its branches reaching towards heaven.

5. Repeat the posture on the other side.

CHILD POSTURE

The Child posture looks very simple but has very deep effects. It massages your internal organs, promoting good circulation and helping elimination. It also helps to keep your spine supple and flexible. Use it at any time that you're feeling stressed or tired.

1. Kneel down with your feet pointing backwards and your legs together. Lower your buttocks so you are sitting on your heels.

2. Now, bend forwards slowly until your forehead is resting on the floor before you. You may not be able to get this far – don't worry, just go as far as is comfortable. If it helps, you can rest your head on a cushion.

3. Bring your arms behind you so your hands rest on the floor next to your feet. Relax.

4. Stay in this posture for as long as you feel comfortable. Try to keep your breathing regular and relaxed.

1

2

3–4

OFFICE YOGA

Once you have learned the principles of yoga, you can use it throughout the day to ease tension and keep yourself focused and alert. Most of these adapted variations of yoga exercises are so simple and subtle that you could do them at your office desk without anyone being any the wiser.

NECK ROLLS

This neck-roll sequence will help release tension through the day:

1. Sit at your desk and slowly, and very carefully, roll your head round in a circle: let it drop as far as possible forwards, then circle over to your right shoulder, gently backwards (not too far) and over to your left shoulder.

2. Then, do the same in the opposite direction. Keep breathing.

3. Now clasp your hands behind your back and try to pull your hands away from your back with your arms straight. Hold for a few moments.

4. Next round your shoulders and bring your arms in front of you and clasp your hands. Stretch. Shake out your whole body.

SHRUGGING

Another great stress-buster is shrugging which releases tension in the neck, shoulders and head.

1. Sit at your desk. Breathe in and give your shoulders a really exaggerated shrug, like a cartoon character saying he doesn't have a clue. At the same time, tilt your head back as far as it will go. Really scrunch up.

2. Then, exhale and let it all go suddenly. Let your shoulders drop down as if they were leaden weights. Feel the sense of heat in the back of your neck and shoulders as the blood starts to flow freely there again.

3. Next, gently roll your shoulders in big circles forwards. Let your arms just go floppy. Now, go back in the opposite direction.

JOINT CIRCLING

Joint circling is great if you are working at a computer keyboard all day because it loosens up all your joints, helps to keep them supple and mobile and wards off stiffness. Don't worry if you hear lots of creaking and cracking – it's quite normal. Sit comfortably at your desk:

1. Slowly circle your wrists about five times in each direction.

2. Now, bring your arms up so they are parallel with your shoulders. Bend your elbows so your forearms arms are at right angles to your upper arms, hands facing forwards. Push your hands back and feel the stretch across your upper arms. Next, keep the upper part of your arms still as you bend your forearms slowly forwards and down (still at right angles, but now facing downwards). Push your palms backwards and feel the stretch.

3. Cross one leg over the other and work on the uppermost leg first. Stretch your toes back and forwards. Try to separate your toes if you can. Give them a good wiggle. Now, stretch your heel forward, pulling your toes back – feel the stretch. Circle your ankle slowly, five times in one direction, five times the other. Change legs and repeat with the other leg.

PALMING

Palming is deeply relaxing and soothing – even just ten seconds can help. To someone watching, it looks as if you're sunk in deep thought.

1. Put your elbows on your desk and your face in your hands, cupping your palms over your eyes so that your face is gently supported.

2. Relax your shoulders and sink into the darkness for a few moments.

EYE CIRCLES

Eyes get tired at work, particularly if you're on the computer all day. Try eye circling to soothe and strengthen eye muscles. Keep your head relaxed and in the same position, looking forwards, throughout these exercises.

1. Look upwards, as far as you can, and hold for ten seconds (without moving your head). Now, look downwards and hold. Look to the right and hold. To the left and hold.

2. Next, imagine there is a huge clock in front of your face. Look at the figure 12 (your eyes look up). Then, very slowly, work your way right round the clock, in a clockwise direction, pausing on each number for ten seconds. When you get back to 12, repeat in the opposite direction.

CHILD POSTURE (ADAPTED)

If you're tired and frazzled, this version of the Child posture is truly divine. Duck down behind your desk (you can always pretend you're looking for something on the floor).

1. Kneel down on the floor, with your knees together and your ankles relaxed so the heels fall apart.

2. Allow your upper body to fall forwards onto the floor with your face on the floor and your arms loosely by your sides.

STRETCH HIGH/SWING LOW

This stretching and swinging exercise brushes away the cobwebs and sends a lightning flash of energy right through your body.

1. Stand in a relaxed position, feet shoulder-width apart, arms by your sides. Close your eyes gently, if you like.

2. Clasp your hands in front of you and then slowly bring your arms above your head.

3. As you reach the full stretch, turn your hands so that the palms face upwards. Make sure your shoulders are relaxed. Hold this posture.

4. Stretch as far as is comfortable and breathe in and out deeply through the nose several times. Slowly bring your hands back to Position 1.

5. Now, keeping your eyes open so that you don't lose your balance, clasp your hands behind your back with your palms facing the floor.

6. Slowly, bring your clasped hands up behind your back, as far as is comfortable.

7. Next, bend forwards from the waist so that your back makes a right angle with your legs. Keep your head in line with your back (do not strain the neck by looking upwards). See how far you can stretch your (still clasped) hands above your head.

8. Breathing as slowly and deeply as you can, gently come back to a standing position and let your hands drop back down to your sides.

LEGS UP THE WALL

If it's all too much, slip out and find an empty room (unless you have understanding colleagues) for 'legs up the wall' – a so-simple relaxer and revitaliser.

1. Sit down in front of a wall and shunt your bottom up until it is right up against the wall. Your legs go up the wall (either together or apart – as you find most comfortable). Let your arms rest by your sides. Close your eyes and just let go.

2. Stay like this for as long as you like (or are allowed). It brings blood back to the brain and so sharpens up your mind, making it easier to focus and concentrate. It often changes your perspective, too.

PILATES

If yoga isn't for you, then I'd suggest that you take a look at another great exercise system – Pilates. I have worked with many, many dancers and lots of them use it to keep themselves flexible and in great shape. Pilates aims to put you back in touch with your body. The result is perfect poise, fabulous flexibility and freedom from all manner of aches and pains. You may also come across yoga-Pilates combinations, such as Yogalates™, Yogilates, Pilates Yoga Fusion and Yogamonks. Pilates was developed by the late Joseph Pilates, a German who was interned in Britain during World War I. He wanted a system that would maintain his health and fitness levels (and that of his fellow internees) while they were being held in confinement. Later, he moved to New York and his studio became a magnet for ballet dancers, sportspeople, actors and actresses, amongst other mortals, who all wanted this wonder-workout that gives strength without bulky muscles and promises harmony between mind and muscle. They also loved the way it improves breath control, grace and coordination.

Pilates allies very precise, controlled movements with synchronised breathing. Throughout the exercises, you are encouraged to be aware of your body and what it is doing – it is a kind of moving meditation. Some teachers work from a studio where you use equipment with tensioned springs, but many use a normal exercise space; you simply work out on a mat, using your own body weight and gravity to do the work. Pilates stresses the importance of 'core strength', building up the girdle of postural muscles where your abdominals, lower back, pelvic floor and buttocks meet. Nearly every Pilates exercise starts by telling you to 'pull navel to spine', strengthening the abdominal muscles and protecting your back while you move. Working from this point allows for a very safe form of movement, creating strength, balance and a firm, toned body.

Pilates is wonderful for correcting postural imbalances and bad habits by increasing the mobility, strength and the elasticity of your muscles. Consequently, it is invaluable as rehabilitative exercise after injury and can help prevent old injuries reoccurring. It is a great boon if you have a bad back. It can help prevent the onset of osteoporosis and can even help RSI (repetitive strain injury). Pilates is considered to be one of the safest forms of exercise ever devised (you can even do it while pregnant) and is regularly recommended by osteopaths and physiotherapists. Like yoga, it's a great stress-buster and highly recommended for anyone leading an over-stretched life (so, pretty well everyone, then). Because of its focus on 'core strength', tummies and bottoms automatically flatten. Ideally I'd like you to go to a well-qualified Pilates teacher so that I'm reassured that you will be doing the exercises properly. However, you can try these for a taste of the work.

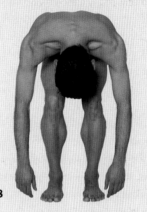

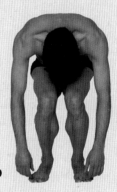

1   **2–4**   **5–8**   **9**

SLIDING DOWN THE WALL

This precise method of 'sliding down the wall' helps to foster flexibility in the spine. It will release tension and help you relax. You need to imagine that your spine is a wheel and that, as you roll and unroll, you are peeling it off the wall, vertebra by vertebra. Repeat this exercise six times.

1. Stand with your feet shoulder-width apart and parallel. You should be standing about 18 inches (45 cm) from a wall with your back to it.

2. Bend your knees and lean back into the wall (as if you were sitting on a stool).

3. Breathe in and feel yourself lengthening up through the spine as the breath fills your lungs.

4. Start to breathe out and gently pull your tummy in, as if you were bringing your belly button back towards the spine. You may feel the small of your back hugging the wall closer.

5. Still breathing out, relax your head and neck so you can let your chin drop forwards. Imagine your forehead has a weight that is pulling it forwards.

6. Now, slowly start to roll forwards. Keep your hands and arms relaxed, your neck and head relaxed. Make sure your bottom stays glued to the wall. Let yourself roll forwards one vertebra at a time, as if you were being peeled off the wall.

7. Go as far as you feel comfortable (eventually you will be able to reach the floor). Now hang in your furthest position and breathe in.

8. Breathe out and pull your belly button to the spine again. Rotate your pelvis so the pubic bone moves towards your chin (remember these are tiny movements).

9. Slowly, vertebra by vertebra, curl your spine back into the wall as you come up.

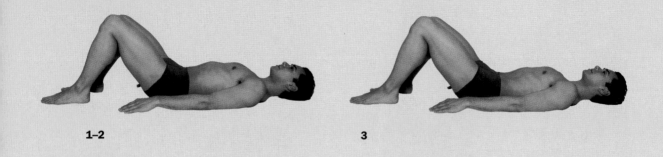

1–2

3

PELVIC TILT

This pelvic-tilt exercise works your abdominal
muscles and stretches your back.

1. Lie on your back with your knees bent and your
feet flat on the floor, about hip-width apart. Arms
rest gently by your sides.

2. Check there is no tension in your neck,
shoulders or face. Your back should be long.
Your head rests easily on the floor.

3. Breathe in. As you breathe out, draw your navel
down to your spine, squeeze your pelvic floor and
lower buttocks, feel your abdomen hollow out. You
need to do all these movements simultaneously,
on the out-breath. Keep your upper body still and
relaxed while you do this.

4. Return to neutral. Now repeat ten times, each
time extending the movement. Eventually your
buttocks will curl up very slightly from the floor.
Remember, keep your lower back on the floor
all the time.

HIP ROLLS

Tension is released from the back and neck through hip rolls.

1. Lie on your back with your knees bent and feet flat on the floor, about hip-width apart. Check you are not holding tension in your neck, shoulders or spine.

2. Breathe in. As you breathe out, draw navel to spine and roll your knees gently and very slowly over towards one side. Take them only as far as they will go without raising your buttocks from the floor (don't be tempted to let them fall onto the floor).

3. Breathe in, and return to centre. Breathe out, and roll your knees over towards the other side. Repeat up to ten times on each side.

PILATES PRANCING

This easy Pilates exercise is a wake-up call to the feet! It increases suppleness in the toes (and is wonderful if you have arthritis) and reaches the calf muscles in a way few exercises can.

1. Stand comfortably with your feet hip-width apart.

2. Lift the toes of your right foot, then your left foot and alternate repeatedly.

3. Once you have established this rhythm, alternate lifting toes and heels. As you lift the toes of your right foot, rise up on the toes of your left foot (so the heel is raised). Then, change sides, lifting up your left toes while rising up on your right toes. (It sounds more complicated in writing than it is in practice!)

4. Once you've got the hang of it, "prance" smoothly for about a minute.

1

2

3

1–2

3–4

5

FOOT CIRCLING

Your ankle joints are kept flexible and supple by foot circling – and your feet will love it!

1. Sit on the floor with your legs stretched out in front of you. They should be a little more than shoulder-width apart with your knees facing up to the ceiling. (**NOTE:** if this feels uncomfortable you can put a pillow under your bottom to tilt you forwards slightly.) Place your hands on the floor beside you for balance.

2. Now, feel yourself lifting out of your hips, keeping your spine straight.

3. Rotate your feet around in outward circles (your right foot will be going clockwise and your left foot anti-clockwise).

4. Keep your knees still and work from your ankles to get a really good range of movement.

5. Repeat with your feet rotating in the opposite (inwards) direction.

6. Repeat the whole exercise ten times.

THE ART AND SCIENCE OF GOOD BREATHING

We take breathing for granted. We all know how to do it and, because we are doing it all the time, we tend to forget about it. However, if you truly want to improve your health, there is no escaping the need for good breathing. Even if you do nothing else for your health, simply taking the trouble to learn how to breathe in the optimum way can have quite amazing benefits for both body and mind.

Why is this? Quite simply, because breathing is the way you pull in oxygen and circulate it around the body to 'feed' each and every cell. Equally, breathing is the way your body pulls out carbon dioxide and waste products, 'cleaning out' each and every cell. You can't overdose on deep, good breathing. The more oxygen you encourage to flow around your body, the better; and the more effectively you clear waste from your body. Breathing fully can do everything including improving your moods, increasing your resistance to colds and illness, fostering better sleep and even helping you resist ageing. It feeds the brain, calms the nerves and has a measurable effect on a number of medical conditions: lowering heart rate and metabolic rate; normalising blood pressure and decreasing the risks of cardio-vascular disease.

Unfortunately, most people breathe too shallowly, almost cautiously, only using a tiny portion of their lungs. It has been estimated that, when you breathe in, you only take in around a tumbler-full of air when you could, in fact, take in at least three times that amount. Why do you need to take in more air? Because the lungs are made up of around 700 million air sacs of which the greater proportion lie in the lower lungs. When you breathe shallowly, you don't ever quite expel all the waste gases and detritus in the lower lungs. You also run the risk of losing vital elasticity in the lower part of our lungs.

Fortunately, there are very simple exercises that can help bring your breathing back to its optimum fullness and freedom. As we've already seen, the yogis developed *pranayama*, the science of breath control and expansion. Research indicates that *pranayama* techniques can affect a huge range of bodily responses, from cardiovascular activity to hormone balance to shifts in the nervous system – and all for the best. **CAUTION:** anyone with chest problems should take these exercises very slowly and carefully, preferably under the auspices of a trained yoga teacher. And anyone with a heart condition, blood-pressure problems or glaucoma should not hold the breath – again, consult a trained teacher.

THE BREATH OF LIFE OR COMPLETE BREATH

For The Breath of Life, first lie down on the floor and make yourself comfortable.

1. Bring your feet close in to your buttocks and allow the knees to fall apart, bringing the soles of the feet together, hands resting gently on the floor. (**NOTE:** this may feel uncomfortable and, if so, you can put cushions under your knees.) This posture stretches the lower abdomen and, in this way, enhances the breathing process.

2. Breathe down into the diaphragm, feeling the abdomen expand and contract. Breathe naturally at your own pace, pausing for a second or two in between each breath.

3. Now, extend the breath so it comes up from the abdomen into the chest.

4. Continue this cycle, pausing slightly between each breath.

5. Finally, bring your knees together and gently stretch out the legs. Allow yourself to relax comfortably on the ground for a few minutes (you may feel more comfortable with a cushion under your lower back or your neck).

ALTERNATE-NOSTRIL BREATHING

The classic *pranayama* technique of alternate-nostril breathing feels rather strange to begin with but, once you become used to it, is very soothing. It is particularly useful if you are feeling stressed or anxious – or if you cannot sleep at night.

1. Sit comfortably in a chair, with both feet on the floor. Don't slouch. Then, gently allow your eyes to close, your body to relax and your mind to still.

2. Place your dominant hand around your nose. If you are right-handed the most natural way to do this will be to rest your right thumb against your right nostril with the rest of the fingers of your right hand lying gently towards your left nostril. The aim is to close off one nostril at a time, comfortably and easily, without constantly moving your hand.

3. Close the right nostril gently, and slowly exhale through your left nostril. Note that you are starting the breath on an exhale. Then, inhale through the same nostril.

4. Swap nostrils by exhaling through the right and inhaling again. Allow your breath to be smooth and relaxed. Don't try to breathe very deeply – keep it natural. You may find you need to blow your nose a lot – don't worry, that's perfectly normal.

5. Alternate between the two nostrils for around five minutes if you can. If you feel uncomfortable at any time, breathe through your mouth for a while until you can go back to the nose.

6. When you've finished, allow yourself to sit and relax with your eyes closed for a while.

THE DETOX BREATH

The Detox Breath is a superb breathing exercise that will help improve elimination of toxins. It strengthens the lungs, massages and tones the abdominal muscles and refreshes the nervous system. **CAUTION:** this should not be used if you have a heart condition, high blood pressure, epilepsy, hernia or any ear, nose or eye problems. Do not use if you are pregnant or menstruating.

1. Choose your position. This exercise can be performed sitting, standing or lying down. Whichever you choose, make sure you are comfortable and relaxed. Breathe regularly and normally.

2. Inhale slowly, smoothly and deeply – but do not strain your breathing.

3. Next, exhale briskly, as if you were sneezing. Focus your attention on your abdomen – it will automatically flatten and tighten as you exhale.

4. Allow yourself to inhale naturally – it will happen automatically following the brisk exhale.

5. Now, continue breathing in this way for a few minutes – or for as long you feel comfortable. It is a brisk technique and very energetic, so don't be surprised if you only manage a minute or so to begin with.

6. Resume normal breathing and relax.

NOTE: if you are pregnant or menstruating, you can use a modified form of this exercise. Instead of the 'sneezing' exhale: pout your lips and allow your breath to come out through them in a steady stream, as if you were blowing out the candles on a cake. This is a much slower technique than the basic detox breath, and is excellent if you need to calm down in a difficult situation.

DANIEL'S STORY

I started seeing Joshi when I decided I'd had enough of feeling run down. I'd always thought I was fairly healthy and exercise was important to me – I'm a regular gym-goer. But I was constantly stressed at work, I suffered from bloatedness, heartburn and flatulence and my skin was always blemished and inflamed. That winter I'd had a permanent cold and I decided enough was enough.

When I visited Joshi he did a blood test and confirmed that I needed to make an immediate effort to get my body back to optimum health. I started the Detox programme right away and also took a course of colonics and Joshi's Lifescience Nutritionals supplements. The first week was tricky but it didn't take long to adapt. I was concerned that giving up things like pasta and sweet things would be hard but I started to feel lighter, healthier and generally better pretty quickly, and the cravings and headaches didn't last more than a week.

By the second week I was noticing big changes. My bloatedness had gone, my skin was calmer, and my heartburn and flatulence were under control. Joshi suggested that I incorporate yoga into my exercise regime and I found that tremendously relaxing and energising. I have stuck to Joshi's Life Plan, not religiously but at least 90 per cent of the time. And I bounce out of bed now, at 6.00am with no puffy eyes or cloudy head. I feel more in tune with my body, with what it needs in terms of fuel and exercise. I no longer rely on protein shakes or weight training to feel good – the whole lifestyle approach has really worked wonders for me.

DANIEL PETERS, 28, WORKS IN FREELANCE MARKETING AND LIVES IN LONDON.

CHAPTER 3
HEALTHY MIND = HEALTHY BODY

YOUR THOUGHTS AND EMOTIONS DIRECTLY AFFECT YOUR HEALTH. AS SCIENTISTS DELVE DEEPER INTO THE NEUROCHEMISTRY OF OUR BRAINS, THEY ARE DISCOVERING THAT OUR MINDS AND BODIES REALLY ARE INTIMATELY CONNECTED. YOUR THOUGHTS CAN HARM, AND YOUR THOUGHTS CAN HEAL. THE HOLISTIC DETOX WAS ALL ABOUT DECLUTTERING YOUR BODY. THE HOLISTIC LIFE PLAN TAKES THAT FURTHER BUT ALSO WORKS ON UNCLUTTERING YOUR MIND. YOU WILL, THEREFORE, NOW BE PAYING AS MUCH ATTENTION TO YOUR THOUGHTS AND EMOTIONS.

DO YOU REALLY NEED TO DETOX YOUR MIND? WITHOUT A SHADOW OF A DOUBT. STRESS AND TOXIC RELATIONSHIPS CAN DAMAGE YOUR HEALTH AS SURELY AS AN OVERLOAD OF ALCOHOL OR BURGERS. IT'S A NATURAL PROGRESSION. I'M WILLING TO BET THAT, WHEN YOU COMPLETE THE DETOX, YOU WILL START TO FEEL MORE ENERGISED AND ENTHUSIASTIC ABOUT LIFE. YOUR MIND WILL FEEL MUCH CLEARER TOO AND YOU WILL WANT TO MAKE FURTHER CHANGES. IT WILL SPRINGBOARD YOU INTO THINKING MORE CLEARLY ABOUT YOUR SITUATION, YOUR WORK, YOUR FRIENDS AND YOUR RELATIONSHIPS. YOU WILL HAVE THE IMPETUS TO CHANGE THE PARTS OF YOUR LIFE THAT JUST AREN'T WORKING. YOU'VE ALREADY SWITCHED FROM EATING CRISPS AND CROISSANTS AND DISCOVERED HOW GOOD THAT MAKES YOU FEEL; NOW , LET'S LOOK AT HOW TO IMPROVE OTHER ASPECTS OF YOUR LIFE. HOW CAN YOU BECOME, NOT ONLY A HEALTHY INDIVIDUAL, BUT A HAPPIER PERSON, TOO?

YOUR HEALTH IS DIRECTLY RELATED TO YOUR AGE, YOUR OCCUPATION, YOUR LIFESTYLE AND YOUR RELATIONSHIPS. I WANT YOU TO REALISE THAT YOUR PHYSICAL HEALTH – YOUR HEADACHES, FOR EXAMPLE, OR NECK PAIN – COULD BE THE RESULT OF PROLONGED TENSION AND ANXIETY AND STRESS. SO MANY PEOPLE LIVE WITH STRESS AND THINK IT PART OF NORMAL LIFE. WE ARE ALL JUGGLERS NOWADAYS – BALANCING HOME, FAMILY AND CAREER IN WAYS OUR ANCESTORS WOULD HAVE BEEN STUNNED TO CONTEMPLATE. OUR EMOTIONS OFTEN RUN OUT OF CONTROL AND STRESS THREATENS TO OVERWHELM US. I WOULD, THEREFORE, ENCOURAGE YOU TO RECOGNISE THAT STRESS NEEDS TO BE DEALT WITH. YOU DON'T NEED STRESS – DEAL WITH IT AND PUT IT AWAY. IT DOESN'T HAVE A FUTURE! IN THIS CHAPTER, I'LL SHOW YOU WAYS TO BEAT STRESS, TO HANDLE TOXIC RELATIONSHIPS AND TO BRING UNRULY EMOTIONS INTO HARMONY. WE'LL LOOK AT HOW TO GET A BETTER NIGHT'S SLEEP – VITAL FOR GOOD HEALTH AND HAPPINESS. FINALLY, WE'LL DISCUSS HOW YOUR ENVIRONMENT AFFECTS YOUR HEALTH – AND HOW TO MAKE CHANGES THAT WILL IMPROVE YOUR LIFE FROM THE OUTSIDE IN.

STRESS – THE MODERN EPIDEMIC

We're suffering a global epidemic of stress. Sixty-four per cent of people in the UK suffer from workplace stress, and some studies suggest that over eighty per cent of people feel stressed in some way. Stress costs British business alone over £400 million a year. Actually, stress, as such, is not dangerous. It's how we react to it that is important. Very simple techniques can make you far more stress-resistant. I suggest these to all my stressed out patients – and strongly advise you to follow them, too. The key to combating stress is realising what pushes your buttons, what causes you stress. We're all very different; what makes one person hot under the collar won't raise a bead of sweat on another. However these strategies should work for everyone.

FIVE SERIOUS STRESSBUSTING STRATEGIES

1. Stress-proof your diet. Eating poorly and on the hoof will, without a shadow of a doubt, increase your stress levels. Following the Life Plan diet will help curtail stress for certain. Many corollaries of stress – anxiety, depression, inability to concentrate, mood swings, forgetfulness, panic attacks and fatigue – can all be triggered by food intolerances or a high-sugar, high-fat, high-junk-food diet.

2. Exercise – strenuously. A tough aerobic workout can boot you out of the twilight zone of high stress arousal, allowing your stress hormones to settle down to normal levels.

3. Delegate. You're not superman, you're not superwoman. You can't do it all and the world will not collapse if occasionally (or frequently) you say 'No'. Take stock of your life and decide what's important and what you can let go. Write a list of everything that causes you stress and consider whether there's anything you can drop or delegate. Stop thinking in terms of 'should', 'ought' and 'must'; if you choose to do something or want to do it that's fine – just remember, it's a choice.

4. Meditate. The supreme stressbuster. We'll discuss this in more depth later. Visualisation is also highly effective. Investigate some of the bodywork therapies we will discuss on pages 86–8. Floatation is also a wonderful stress-relief tool (see Directory for where to find a float tank).

5. Take regular 'time-out' breaks throughout the day – however busy you are. Every hour, give yourself five minutes to meditate, sip water, stretch, do some yoga. You will be far more productive afterwards.

TEN INSTANT STRESSBUSTERS

Sometimes you need some instant stress relief. Try these:

1. Squeeze a 'stress ball' – a hand-sized squashy rubber ball that is available from health or beauty shops. The simple mechanical action of squeezing dampens stress and also massages hoards of acupressure points in the hand.

2. Put a few drops of essential oil on a tissue and sniff throughout the day – or as stress levels rise. Orange and lavender are both effective and easily available (from chemists or health shops).

3. Laugh: it relaxes your muscles and lowers blood pressure. It may even reduce levels of the hormones that create stress. Keep favourite cartoons to prompt you – or just start giggling. It seems false at first but you soon build up speed.

4. Soothe the brain by very gently massaging your third eye (the point above your nose in the centre of the forehead) with sesame oil. Use a very gentle circular movement and keep going as long as possible.

5. Relaxing rapping: using the middle row of the knuckles of one hand, tap the centre of your chest rhythmically. The beat is one heavy tap followed by two lighter taps (ONE, two, three. ONE, two three). Tap for around two minutes. This is known as the 'thymus tap' and is soothing and balancing.

6. Bathe yourself in blue light: colour therapists have found it can help to lower blood pressure and soothe stress. If you don't have a blue light bulb to hand, visualise yourself breathing in blue light, which soothes and calms every part of your body. As you breathe out, visualise all the stress and strain leaving your body.

7. Yawn very widely: it relaxes tension held in the jaw (a common stress spot). Loud groaning or sighing can also help.

8. Any form of deep breathing is excellent. Try the exercises on page 47.

9. Sip a glass of water very, very slowly. Be conscious of the feeling of the water in your mouth – the taste and the temperature. Hold it in your mouth and then feel it slipping down your throat. This is a form of simple mindfulness meditation.

10. Get up and do something physical: run up the stairs, clean the floor vigorously, jump up and down on the spot and stretch.

MEDITATION – THE MASTER STRESS RELIEVER

I grew up doing meditation and I still do it every day. I couldn't imagine living without it. Yet the idea of meditation often fills people with horror. Do you have to spend hours with your legs tied in knots? Do you have to be a bit of a hippie on a spiritual quest? Worst of all, are you going to be singularly bored? Myths, every single one of them. Meditation can fit easily and effortlessly into anyone's daily life. If I can do it, so can you. Not one meditator would ever say that meditation is boring. On the contrary, most insist it has totally changed their lives.

The many benefits of meditation are certainly not all in the mind. Hundreds of scientific studies into TM® (Transcendental Meditation) alone have produced impressive evidence. Researchers have found that it lowers high blood pressure and eases stress. It can reduce the effects of angina, allergies, chronic headaches, diabetes and bronchial asthma and can help wean you off alcohol and cigarettes. The studies (at universities and hospitals all around the world) found that regular meditators see their doctors less and spend 70 per cent fewer days in hospital. Anxiety, depression and irritability all decrease, memory improves and reaction times become faster, thus enhancing sports performance. Meditators, it appears, have more stamina, a happier disposition and even enjoy better relationships than non-meditators. Meditation even seems to reverse the ageing process: after five years of TM®, meditators' brains were found to function as if twelve years younger.

But what *is* meditation? At its heart, meditation is simply the ability to be 'mindful'; to be free of all thoughts, to experience a peaceful awareness of the present moment – free of regrets from the past or fears for the future. This relaxed state helps you remain calm under pressure, more self-confident and free from tension and fatigue. Not bad for sitting still doing nothing.

There are a million and one ways to meditate – the right one is the one that suits you. You don't need fancy tools or clothes or a dedicated meditation room. You certainly don't need to wind yourself into the lotus position. Simply find a place where you won't be disturbed and choose a way of sitting that is really comfortable. That could be cross-legged on the floor (perching your bottom on a cushion or yoga block with your knees on the floor keeps your back straight without strain), but, equally, you could sit upright on a supportive chair with your hands resting gently on your knees. If you are a beginner, it's better not to meditate lying down because it's very easy to nod off. You *can* take courses in meditation (for example, TM® has centres all round the country, however the course *is* expensive), but it is, in fact, very simple to learn at home. Try to set aside a time every day for your meditation. Early-morning meditation is traditional and sets the day off on a great footing. If that doesn't work for you, whenever does is fine. Start off with 5 minutes and gradually extend the time (the optimum is 45 minutes).

HOW TO MEDITATE

Let's look at some simple meditation techniques. Try them and find which work for you:

BREATHING

Most forms of meditation start with the breath. 'Just breathing' can seem almost too easy, yet the challenge is in getting to the point where your thoughts cease to skitter around and become less intrusive.

⇢ Sit comfortably, and gently close your eyes (if you prefer, you can keep them open, softly focused on one spot).

⇢ Start to become aware of your breath. Don't try to control it in any way – just notice how you breathe in, and out, and the pause between breaths. Keep your attention focused on the breath.

⇢ Every time your mind wanders, gently return to the breath. Don't beat yourself up or judge your thoughts – merely let them go.

MANTRA MEDITATION

Through the ages, religions have used sound as a means of meditation. Some forms of meditation chant phrases; others will give you your own mantra or sacred sound. For your own DIY mantra meditation, pick a sound or phrase that appeals to you. OHM is the classic (often taught in yoga classes). Tone it slowly and resonantly with three sounds – AH-OH-MMM. But you can simply use a vowel sound – such as 'aaah' or 'oooh' – or pick a phrase you like, such as 'I am at peace'. Sit calmly and slowly repeat your chosen sound over and over. Keep your attention on the sound: if it wanders, gently bring it back.

COUNTING MEDITATION

This counting meditation is deceptively simple but, in practice, very challenging. All you do is to count very slowly from one to ten in your head, keeping your attention on each number. At any point, if you feel your attention wandering (and undoubtedly it will, often before you reach three!), go back to one and start again.

CANDLE MEDITATION

Candle meditation is a very ancient and rather beautiful meditational form that has a strong sense of the sacred. Sit down comfortably in front of a lighted candle. Focus your eyes on the flame and watch it. Notice the way it moves, the colours within it. When your attention wavers, or your mind starts jumping, gently bring it back to the flame.

AMBIENT SOUND MEDITATION

The practice of ambient sound meditation is for you if you want to bring meditation into everyday life. Instead of trying to shut out external sounds, allow your mind to notice them – whether they be the sound of birdsong or the screech of car brakes. Don't make judgments about the sounds and don't become involved in them, only notice them. If your attention lapses, gently bring it back.

WALKING MEDITATION

The ancient practice of walking meditation takes a little time to master. Your aim is not to get *to* somewhere but to be fully present in every part of every step.

1. Start by standing still. Become aware of your body, your posture and how you stand on the earth.

2. Next, walk very slowly, so slowly that you can pay attention to every part of every step. Say 'lifting' as you lift up your foot; 'moving' as your foot moves through the air; 'placing' as you place your foot down on the ground; 'shifting' as you shift your weight onto that foot.

3. Repeat with the other foot and continue in this way. Yes, it's really slow. Again, if your attention is distracted, bring it back to the walking.

VISUALISATION

Visualisation is the next technique that I frequently advise my patients to use. It has been shown to be a powerful way of stimulating the immune system and galvanising the body into health – and all through the power of the mind.

Psychoneurimmunology (PNI) is the mind's ability to effect change in the body. Eastern therapies have accumulated a vast reservoir of evidence linking the powers of body and mind, connecting immunology and neurology, and have developed specific techniques for activating that link. Now, Western research is recognising it too. Visualising yourself in a calm, beautiful place is one of the key strategies suggested by organisations such as the American Institute of Stress.

Visualisation is, in fact, the major technique in PNI. Patients are taught to focus their minds to visualise healing energy flowing into ailing organs so as to dissolve tumours, repair tissue and so forth. PNI works best if the image used has some meaning for you. One young boy with cancer imagined jet fighters zooming into his body to bomb the tumours. His strategy worked: the tumours shrank and disappeared without recourse to chemotherapy, radiation or surgery. Others have helped themselves through chemotherapy by visualising increased blood cell production while they are having the treatment. Furthermore, studies have shown that if people with broken bones visualise the bones mending and regrowing, it actually speeds up the healing process.

Of course, visualisation isn't just for serious illness. You can use it for any condition or problem, whether physiological or psychological. It is a superb stressbuster and can also help with emotional issues, such as difficult relationships.

SAFE-PLACE VISUALISATION

Visualising yourself in a safe place is an excellent way to begin your practice. It is supremely soothing and relaxing – and highly effective. If you practice it regularly, you will find that you can put yourself into an instant state of calm anywhere, at any time, simply by recalling the visualisation. Ideally, for the first few times, you should practice this technique when you are not stressed so you can build up the relaxed atmosphere. Thereafter, it is a superb mental detoxer.

1. Find somewhere quiet where you will not be disturbed. Make yourself comfortable – you can either lie on the floor (covered with a blanket if it is cool) or sit in a comfortable chair.
2. Close your eyes gently and allow yourself to breathe deeply. As you breathe in, your abdomen pushes outwards; as you breathe out, it comes back in. Allow as much air as possible to flow into your lungs – be aware of it filling them up right down to the very bottom.
3. Next, take twelve conscious breaths. Each time you breathe in, imagine you are also breathing in total relaxation and calm. As you breathe out, imagine that all the stress and strain, all the anxiety and irritation of everyday life, is leaving your body.
4. When you have completed your twelve breaths, relax for a minute and sense how much more easy and calm your body and mind feel.
5. Now, think of a wonderful place in which you feel completely safe and very happy. It might be an actual place or an imaginary ideal retreat. It could be anywhere: a cosy room with an armchair and a fire; a beautiful desert island with the sun warming your body; a dappled glade in a cool forest.

6. Make this place as real as possible. In your mind's eye, explore all around it: not just seeing it, but also hearing the sounds (waves, birdsong, the crackling of logs?); smelling the scents (salty tang, resinous pine, wood smoke and coffee?); and experiencing the feel of it (the warm sun on your skin, the rough texture of bark, the slight roughness of a wool blanket?).

7. This is a place of inner peace and inner healing. Anything can happen here. Feel all the stress and strain – and all your negativity and morbid thoughts – simply evaporating as you sit here quietly. Feel your body become lighter, softer, warmer, more peaceful.

8. The next step is to bring healing into your body and into your life. Become aware of the area around your heart. Gradually, it is becoming suffused with light – with healing energy. Feel the light spreading out through your whole body (you may feel warmth or coolness or a kind of tingling).

9. The light pinpoints any areas that need healing and you feel your body respond and change. Stay here, in your special place, as long as you like. You may want to meditate quietly or just sit and enjoy the relaxation. This place is always available for you and you can come here at any time.

10. When you are ready, slowly bring yourself back to waking reality. Become aware of the room around you. Become aware of your body lying on the floor or sitting on the chair. Start to move your fingers and toes. Give yourself a good stretch. Slowly open your eyes. Rest for a few minutes before you race back to normal life.

CONFIDENCE VISUALISATION

You can also use visualisation to build up your confidence and self-esteem. Use this technique when you have a difficult situation coming up (but give yourself as much time beforehand as possible).

1. Once again, sit or lie in a comfortable position. Check through your body to ensure that you aren't holding any tension. Spend a few moments softly following your breath.

2. Now, imagine you are going into that difficult situation. However, this time, you are totally in control. You are holding yourself in a positive way – your posture is upright and confident – and you make easy, strong eye contact. You look great!

3. Next, go through the situation in the way it would ideally happen. You can do nothing wrong. You say exactly what you want to say in exactly the way you want to say it. People are impressed, you can hear them whispering how wonderful you are. Maybe they applaud or pat you on the back.

4. If, at any time, you find this hard, think what a favourite hero or heroine would do if faced with this tricky situation. How would they tackle it? Now, take that behaviour as your own.

5. Repeat this several times until you can feel the confidence brimming inside you.

CUTTING TOXIC TIES

While it is good and necessary to have loving links with people, all too often we are bound to others by less healthy emotions. Many of us are tied by guilt, duty, lust or habit. Still others have even more destructive relationships based on fear, power or anger. The following visualisation can help you release yourself from dependent or destructive relationships. Note that it need not *end* your relationship – but may well transform it.

1. Sit quietly and become aware of your breathing. Imagine yourself inside a bubble of pure white light – let it extend to about six feet around you. While you are inside this protective bubble, nothing and no one can hurt or harm you.

2. Think about the person from whom you need to release. You may feel uncomfortable or uneasy – just stay with that feeling, knowing you are safe. Visualise a second bubble of light – some distance from yours. The other person is inside, kept firmly in place by the bubble.

3. Observe the person – what are they doing? Are they trying to talk to you? What are they saying? Remember that you are in control. If you want to talk to this person, to understand them better or to state your case, take it in turns to speak. Remaining inside their bubble, they will listen to you (whether or not they would in real life). Say what you feel, what you have always wanted to say.

4. Notice, now, that there is a thin silver cord that stretches from your solar plexus (just below your ribcage) to the other person's solar plexus. Give it a small tug and see the other person lurch towards you slightly. This is the source of your attachment.

5. The time has come to cut this attachment, to release both of you from this form of relationship. Remember, it does not mean that you cannot have a relationship – if you wish to you can build a new one based on equality and fairness.

6. Visualise yourself picking up a pair of silver scissors. Send love and forgiveness and understanding (as far as you are able) to the other person. Then cut the cord. The cord shimmers and is absorbed back into your solar plexus. Now you both stand free in your bubbles.

SLEEP HYGIENE

Good sleep is vital. I see so many patients who are burning the candle at both ends, skipping sleep in order to cram more into their days. It's counterproductive. If you don't sleep properly, and for the optimum amount of time, you simply won't function so well. If you're stressed, you'll only increase your stress; the production of cortisol (one of the key stress hormones) only stops when we sleep. Lack of sleep is blamed for up to 40,000 road crashes a year, bad decision-making in business and even for such disasters as the Challenger space shuttle, the Three Mile Island nuclear power accident and the Chernobyl disaster.

How much sleep you need will depend entirely on you. The majority of people function best with 7–8 hours; however, some quite happily manage on 5 or 6 while others feel lousy with less than 9. It's very individual; there is no one-size-fits-all prescription.

The kind of sleep you get is as important as how much sleep you get. Sleep is divided into three types: light, deep and REM (or dreaming) sleep. If you lessen your hours of sleep, your body will automatically compensate – first by cutting down on light sleep and then, if necessary, REM sleep, too. Because REM sleep is when you dream, psychologists consider it to be an absolutely essential process.

Sleep is the time when your body rests, repairs, balances and regulates. Lose sleep, and your immune system is lowered, your mental alertness dives and your mood plummets. Research even shows that your sex life will suffer because sex hormones are suppressed when we're deprived of sleep. You will also notice the effect in the mirror when your skin loses its bounce, dark circles appear under your eyes and your face looks grey, stressed and lacking in tone. They don't call it beauty sleep for nothing!

SOLVING INSOMNIA –
WITHOUT SLEEPING PILLS

Most of us have the odd night when we can't sleep (transient insomnia), usually brought on by a change in routine such as jet lag or switching shifts. However, according to the World Health Organisation (WHO), up to a third of all people suffer from persistent insomnia, Sometimes, there are very simple causes – too much caffeine or alcohol that disrupt sleep, or not enough physical exercise so that your body simply isn't tired. However, much chronic insomnia is caused by stress, anxiety or depression. Try these steps to root insomnia out:

1. Look for any underlying psychological causes behind your insomnia and, if necessary, seek appropriate help (e.g. counselling, stress management etc.).

2. Keep your room cool and airy. Make sure your bed is comfortable and right for you.

3. Avoid caffeine, alcohol and heavy meals – especially in the evening. But don't go to bed hungry; low blood sugar can cause insomnia.

4. Ensure that you get enough aerobic exercise, but avoid exercising too late or it will rev you up.

5. Have a warm (not hot) bath, adding restful aromatherapy oils to maximise the effect. Lavender, chamomile and neroli relieve anxiety, are calming and balance the mind and emotions. Bergamot is good for insomnia linked to depression. Benzoin is handy when external worries are causing sleeplessness. Clary sage is effective for deep relaxation (not to be used with alcohol). Marjoram, sandalwood, juniper and ylang-ylang are all warming and comforting. A neutral (body temperature) bath can be helpful, too.

6. Try a milky drink before you sleep, or else brew up a naturally relaxing and soporific herbal tisane. Look for those containing valerian, passiflora and hops.

7. A massage (ideally, before bedtime or else in the late afternoon) will often work wonders. The same oils given for your bath would be great, diluted with a carrier oil.

8. Homeopathy can often cure insomnia. If the insomnia is chronic, a homeopath will take all factors of life into account before prescribing a personalised remedy. For acute conditions, try Aconitum when kept awake by a sense of fear and panic, Arnica when overtired both mentally and physically, or Coffea when wide awake with an active mind (all in potency 6).

9. Acupuncture can help with insomnia and has been known to cure unpleasant dreams and nightmares.

10. If stress is stopping you sleeping, write down all your worries and anxieties in a notepad before you go to bed. And there they will remain until you pick it up again in the morning.

HANDLING YOUR EMOTIONS

In this country, nobody teaches you how to keep control of your emotions. In the same way that many people have no knowledge of how to look after their bodies, so the majority haven't the faintest idea of how to keep on an even emotional keel. This matters because toxic emotions, such as anger, fear, guilt and jealousy, can seriously damage your life. For some people, these emotions are deep-seated and have their roots in childhood, and this may make the idea of working with them feel uncomfortable or threatening. If so, you might consider working with a trained professional – a psychotherapist or counsellor (see the Directory). If you do not like the idea of talking about your emotions, bodywork therapies could be very useful (we'll look at those later in this chapter). However, many toxic emotions appear simply because we are not able to express our honest needs and desires. We lack the confidence and the self-esteem to stand up for what we want, and this results in anxiety and resentment or inappropriate anger. Often, a greater sense of self-awareness and some simple techniques can help enormously.

Emotions can become a habit. Our minds get into ruts and we trot out the same unnecessary responses time and time again. Once you become aware of how futile many negative emotions are, you can deliberately choose not to let them run away with you. Pause, assess and decide how to act. Yes, it really can be that simple. These exercises might act as a starting point:

AUDIT YOUR EMOTIONS

Start keeping a journal. Psychologists recognise that writing without censoring what you say in any way can be incredibly useful in uncovering toxic emotions. There are no rules except that you should aim to be as honest as possible. If you find it hard to get started, just write about anything that runs through your head – you'll soon find your subconscious will move onto the relevant information. Alternatively, give yourself trigger sentences such as:

I always wanted to . . .
My deepest fear is that . . .
If I could change anything, I'd . . .

If you know you have a problem with a particular emotion, you could start with something like:
I get angry when . . .
I am so jealous that . . .
The worst thing that could happen would be that . . .

Make a pact to write in your journal every day, or several times a day, and to be totally truthful. Remember, don't censor what you're saying, just let it all hang out. Nobody reads this except you. If you find writing hard, you could talk into a Dictaphone. Otherwise, maybe try painting your feelings – again, it doesn't have to be Monet, just an honest expression of how you feel. What does your painting tell you about yourself?

EXPRESS YOUR FEELINGS

Of course, there are occasions when it is wise to suppress or hide your true feelings. However if you continuously stifle them – suppress all displays of anger, hide your fears and swallow annoyance – it can trigger all kinds of health problems from headaches to cardiovascular difficulties. The best course of action is to be as honest and assertive as humanly possible.

→ Take responsibility for your feelings – remember you have control over the situation and can decide whether to be angry or not, or whether to be jealous or not.

→ Deal with minor irritations and resentments as and when they arise rather than letting feelings fester and build up to boiling point.

→ Don't simply turn fear into anger by screaming and yelling. The best response is to be assertive, not aggressive. Be honest and say what you mean: 'I'm really scared of that,' or 'I feel very depressed right now,' or 'I feel unloved when
you do that.' However you express it, the key is not to deny your feelings and not to develop the habit of hiding them from others. Be clear about how you feel.

→ Check whether anger, jealousy or irritation is hiding a deeper emotion, such as grief or hurt. Ask yourself: 'What does my anger remind me of? Does it have links with my past?'

TOXIC RELATIONSHIPS

Relationships don't have to be physically abusive to be toxic; they can be emotionally toxic. By toxic, I mean any relationship that puts you down, that doesn't let you grow, that doesn't nurture you. Emotional relationships directly affect your mind and body. Relationships are reflected in the way you carry yourself – your posture – and in the way you look. Think about it – when you're in love, you have a glow around you. Something about you changes – whether it's your aura or your energy. Your eyes have a sparkle, you have a smile on your face – in fact your whole face looks relaxed because the tension is gone.

Certain people, even just the thought of them, puts a little sparkle in our eyes. They are good for us, they invigorate us, they create a positive nurturing universe for us. On the other hand, we all know people who make us feel bad. Again, even the mere thought of them makes us feel exhausted. We have to face it: some people are just not good for us. I find it incredibly stressful having meetings with certain people because they are so draining. This isn't nonsense – trust me. If you want to feel better, you have to cut out toxic people, just as you have already cut out junk food. Make a list of all the people you know. Divide them into three columns – those that make you feel good; those that make you feel bad; and those who don't really have any noticeable effect on you (neutral). Now, figure out how much time you give these people. I'm willing to bet that the toxic people are demanding a lion's share of your time – so, you are spending huge amounts of time with people who make you feel lousy and not enough with those who make you feel good.

Now you have a choice. You can either:
1. Stop seeing the people who drag you down.
2. Alter the relationship so it's no longer toxic.

Sometimes an address-book cull can be the best option. You don't have to be cruel. Most relationships will wither and die with benign neglect. It's important to recognise that friendships don't always last forever. We change, other people change, and there is no shame in admitting that you have outgrown a relationship. Bless it and let it go.

However, there are relationships that aren't so easily discarded. We can choose our friends, but not our family, for instance. Equally, friends may be going through a tough time and you don't want to leave them in the lurch. Furthermore, you might be in a toxic relationship that's bound by children or some other 'situation'.

The most important point to recognise and take on board is this: you cannot change anyone else. You can only change yourself. By developing good self-esteem, by recognising and asserting your own needs, you can stop being a victim in a toxic relationship. Of course, this can be a tough, complicated process and I cannot go into it in the necessary depth in this book (but I have included useful resources in the Directory at the back). Do get help if you need it. Don't fight your battles alone. There are support groups and counselling services around the country that can help.

BODYWORK

I am a fervent believer in the power of bodywork, not just for solving physical ailments (though it's wonderful at that) but for unravelling psychological tension, too. Emotions, thoughts and memories aren't held purely in the brain, they are also contained in the soft tissue and skeletal structure of the body. By releasing old patterns and strictures, the body can release past trauma and pain. It sounds bizarre but our bodies really do know the truth, and the truth can be stretched, squeezed, manipulated or simply touched out of you. Virtually every bodywork practitioner – from osteopath to zero balancer, from reflexologist to shiatsu practitioner – affirms that touch (whether deep or light) seems to draw psychological material from the body.

It was the biochemist Dr Ida Rolf who, in the mid-twentieth century, discovered that manipulating the fascia (the connective tissue of the body) could bring about profound changes to both body and emotions. By manipulating and stretching the fascia back to their original position, she could reprogramme neurological pathways and return her patient to alignment and, eventually, physical comfort. However, she also found that, when she changed the body on a physiological level, her patients changed on a mental and emotional level as well. I would urge you to consider bodywork while on the Life Plan, particularly if the 'talking therapies' are too confrontational. Bodywork offers the chance to relieve emotional distress without having to say a word.

There are so many different types of bodywork that you should be able to find one that suits you. Here, briefly, are some of those on offer:

--> **Aromatherapy:** wonderful 'feel-good' therapy using essential oils that work directly on the chemistry of the body and can even bring out hidden memories. Great for those new to bodywork as usually very gentle. Make sure, however, that your aromatherapist is fully qualified – many beauty salon therapists are not. Certain aromatherapy oils are contraindicated if you are pregnant, or if you have high blood pressure, epilepsy or other health conditions. A good therapist will take a case history and ask these vital questions.

--> **Biodynamic massage:** unique form of deep, powerful massage aimed at releasing emotional blocks. The therapist gauges the effect of the bodywork by listening to your stomach through a stethoscope – the rumblings indicate how the therapy is working. Can be quite painful.

--> **Bowen technique:** brisk, down-to-earth therapy that manipulates muscles and connective tissue (fascia). It's firm but not painful. Performed through clothing.

--> **Chavutti thirumal:** the ultimate massage, but not for the faint-hearted. You lie naked on a mat while the therapist (using a rope for balance) massages you with his or her feet. It's deep yet subtle bodywork and totally divine.

--> **Chiropractic:** pragmatic, down-to-earth system that adjusts, manipulates and realigns the spine which, in turn, helps muscles, nerves, joints and ligaments to work better. The clunks and clicks can be a bit of a shock to the system but aren't really painful.

--> **Cranial osteopathy/cranio-sacral therapy:** very subtle, gentle techniques that help to correct the flow of the cerebrospinal fluid. Work is carried out on the head and lower spine (the sacrum). Cranio-sacral therapy is more spiritual than cranial osteopathy in its approach.

--> **Manual Lymphatic Drainage (MLD):** very gentle massage technique that encourages the elimination of toxins by stimulating the lymphatic system. Has wonderful cosmetic effects too – reducing puffiness and the appearance of scar tissue.

--> **McTimoney Chiropractic:** very gentle form of manipulation that uses small but effective manipulations. The major technique is called the 'toggle recoil', which feels as if your spine is being flicked. Network Chiropractic is another gentle form of chiropractic.

--> **Osteopathy:** system of massage and manipulation that aims to bring the whole structure of the body back into balance. Modern osteopathy uses a wide variety of techniques: manipulation and stretching, massage and gentle touch. In addition, osteopaths often advise on posture, diet and exercise.

--> **Reflexology:** therapists manipulate the feet, working on the theory that different areas of the feet and toes correspond to different body systems and organs. Sometimes delicious, sometimes painful. There are some schools of Reflexology, such as Morrell Reflexology and Soft Touch Reflexology that use a much softer (though still effective) touch.

⇢ **Rolfing/Hellerwork:** similar systems that focus predominantly on the connective tissue (fascia) of the body. Usually taken as a course of ten or eleven sessions, this is very deep bodywork that can be quite uncomfortable at times but the results are wonderful – both physiologically and psychologically.

⇢ **SHEN®/Kairos Therapy:** scientifically researched forms of energy healing that focus on releasing emotions trapped in the body. You lie, clothed, on a special 'cradle' (rather like a camp-bed on top of a standard massage couch) and the therapist holds various parts of the body until normal energy flow is restored. Painless.

⇢ **Shiatsu/acupressure:** ancient forms of bodywork that aim to balance the body's vital energy by stimulating acupuncture points in the body. Shiatsu is performed, through clothing, on a mat on the floor; for acupressure you usually lie on a couch.

⇢ **Thai massage:** strong bodywork, often called 'passive yoga' because you are flexed into positions you would never manage on your own. You stay fully clothed (loose-fitting clothes) for this. The therapist uses hands, feet and elbows to release blockages in your energy flow. Highly energising but quite tough.

⇢ **Trager®:** very gentle system of bodywork that uses rocking, rolling, bouncing and shimmering (swift and soft stroking movement) plus gentle stretching. Sets out to make your body feel lighter, easier and happier. Supremely relaxing to the central nervous system.

⇢ **Watsu/Jahara Technique/WaterDance:** deep, powerful massage and manipulation techniques, carried out in a warm swimming pool. The therapist holds you, moving and deep-stretching your body to release tension and old emotions. You usually wear a swimming costume.

⇢ **Zero Balancing:** works on the bone structure and the energy systems of the body. The touch is deep but not painful and works equally on the physical and emotional levels. You wear clothes.

DETOXING YOUR ENVIRONMENT

The sad truth is that there are as many external toxins as there are internal ones. You could eat a perfect diet yet still inhale toxins from the air you breathe, and even from your home and office. We are exposed to up to 300 volatile organic (carbon based) compounds within our homes alone, indoor air pollutants that can wreak havoc on our health. That's not taking into account the pollution from exhaust fumes, factory emissions and cigarette smoke.

'Biomonitoring' of blood samples from people all over the UK has shown that every person tested so far has traces of an average of 27 different chemical toxins. Even chemicals that were banned back in the 1970s, such as PCBs (linked to hormonal problems, nervous and immune system problems and suspected carcinogens) and HCBs (linked to damage to the adrenals, blood, bone, brain and immune system) still lurk in our bodies.

Don't panic. It's easy to get paranoid about our toxic world. If your immune system is working at the optimum and your lungs are well exercised by good breathing, you can put up a good fight. Of course, the other side of the equation is to lessen your toxic load wherever you can. There's not a lot you can do about outdoor pollution levels, but you can take stock of what goes on inside your own home.

1. Don't add to the toxins. Synthetic materials are packed with chemicals so, whenever you redecorate or refurnish your home, choose natural alternatives. Think about pure wool carpets or natural floor coverings (sisal, coir etc.). Choose eco-paints and varnishes – they now come in a huge variety of colours and finishes. Go for recycled floorboards rather than laminates; real wood (non-tropical) instead of plastic or MDF for furniture or shelving. And use all-natural fabrics, please, for curtains and soft furnishings.

2. If you have an open fire, have the flue swept regularly. Service all heaters and boilers on a regular basis. The fuels we use for heating can all release harmful by-products into our air.

3. Keep electrical appliances unplugged when not in use as they emit electro-magnetic radiation. Never ever go to sleep with the TV on. Avoid electric blankets for the same reason – get out the hot-water bottle instead.

4. Replace any fluorescent bulbs (linked with nausea, eye strain, headaches, depression and even panic attacks). If possible, use daylight bulbs – particularly if you suffer from SAD (seasonal affective disorder).

5. Call in the professionals for the safe removal of any old lead paint and/or asbestos (found in insulation, roofing and even in old curtain fabrics) in your home. Don't even think about doing this yourself.

6. Allow fresh air into your home to help flush out toxic build-up – fling open the windows for at least 15 minutes twice a day. So simple, so effective.

7. Dry-cleaned clothes should be left outside (with the plastic covers off) for at least 30 minutes before you bring them in.

8. Buy household cleaners from your local health store which should have non-toxic alternatives. Synthetic polishes, fabric and carpet cleaners and air fresheners often contain potentially harmful VOCs (volatile organic compounds), which release vapours into the air. Burn aromatherapy oils or naturally scented candles rather than use synthetic air fresheners.

9. Turn your garden organic and so wean yourself off toxic pesticides and fungicides. Pest-control products are amongst the most toxic chemicals known – causing irritation, allergic reactions, rashes, sore eyes and throats. Some have been linked with cancer, genetic mutation or birth defects.

10. Fill your home with cleansing plants (which can mop up chemical pollutants from the air). The most effective include peace lilies, *sansevieria* (mother-in-law's tongue), spider plants, golden pothos (*scindapsus aureus*) and philodendrons.

11. Take a long hard look at your cosmetics and beauty products. Even those purporting to be 'natural' are usually stuffed full of potentially toxic chemicals. Hypoallergenic products leave out about sixty known allergens but can't seem to cut out all of them. Even products for babies and young children still contain potentially toxic chemicals. Read labels carefully – and don't believe the hype. Good choices include Dr Hauchska, Weleda, Spiezia and REN.

12. Install a water-purification system (as discussed in the Holistic Detox). If your water supply is unfiltered, take warm baths or cool showers rather than piping hot showers. Many water-polluting chemicals can be vaporised in a hot shower and
you could absorb up to one hundred times more pollutants by breathing the air around a shower than by drinking all the water passing through it.

13. Keep leftovers in glass or ceramic containers, rather than plastic, to prevent contamination by chemicals. Don't microwave food in plastic (in fact, preferably don't microwave at all) as this encourages chemicals to leach into your food.

14. Eliminate damp. Mould spores in the walls of damp houses can release toxins. If you habitually dry your clothes inside, use a dehumidifier to remove water vapour.

15. Look out for untreated cotton bed linen – most is finished with formaldehyde! Wash all new bed linen at high (60°C/140°F) temperatures to help remove the finish.

MICHAEL'S STORY

I knew I was desperately overweight but I was still horrified when Joshi weighed me on my first visit to his clinic and told me I was 21 stone! I had gone to see him on the recommendation of a colleague who was looking fantastically well after a bout of treatment with Joshi. I knew that although I needed to change my lifestyle, I just wasn't going to manage it without support.

The situation had got really serious over the course of a few years. I used to be fairly slim but a diet of red meat and gluten-rich carbs, a lot of alcohol and cigarettes had taken its toll. Essentially I was heading for heart failure unless I made some drastic changes. I began on the Detox Programme and aside from some abdominal pains I suffered no side effects. Acupuncture needles in my ears dealt with cravings and I very quickly started to feel better. In fact, I know it's a cliché, but I honestly do feel like a different person. I've stopped smoking and drinking and I don't miss either at all. In six weeks I lost three and a half stone and

I am now on the Life Plan and fully intending to stick to it. The benefits really have been incredible, for my mental wellbeing as well as my physical health. I'm much calmer, and more balanced, which means no more erupting moods. I feel more in control and more able to cope with stress and the quality of my sleep has improved dramatically. I also feel that my brainpower has improved – my ability to retain data has increased ten-fold.

One of the best things has been the way the improvement in my health has affected my relationships. My wife and children have all started to eat what I'm eating and are also feeling the benefits. I've always loved to cook but now I have a whole new lease of creativity in the kitchen. The Life Plan really has affected every aspect of my life, for the better.

MICHAEL JOBSON, 40, IS THE MANAGING DIRECTOR OF A MUSIC PRODUCTION COMPANY. HE IS MARRIED WITH THREE CHILDREN.

CHAPTER 4
PREVENTING ILLNESS AND TREATING AILMENTS WITH COMPLEMENTARY MEDICINE

THE HOLISTIC LIFE PLAN IS BUILT ON A FIRM FOUNDATION OF COMPLEMENTARY MEDICINE. COMPLEMENTARY MEDICINE ENCOMPASSES A WIDE RANGE OF HOLISTIC THERAPIES. THESE THERAPIES DON'T SEPARATE MIND AND BODY BUT RECOGNISE THEY ARE INTIMATELY CONNECTED. COMPLEMENTARY MEDICINE IS ALSO PREVENTATIVE MEDICINE. THE SINGLE MOST IMPORTANT THING YOU CAN DO IF YOU WANT TO LIVE A HEALTHIER, HAPPIER LIFE IS TO REALISE THAT YOU HAVE TO TAKE RESPONSIBILITY FOR YOUR OWN WELLBEING. THAT MEANS EVERYTHING FROM SHIFTING TO THE VERY BEST DIET TO FINDING AN EXERCISE SYSTEM THAT FITS IN WITH YOUR LIFESTYLE; FROM LEARNING HOW TO KEEP STRESS UNDER CONTROL TO SAVING YOUR BODY FROM THE STRAINS CAUSED BY BAD BREATHING AND POOR SLEEP. A GOOD NATURAL-HEALTHCARE PRACTITIONER SHOULD BE ABLE TO ADVISE YOU IN ALL THESE AREAS. IN ADDITION, HE OR SHE SHOULD BE ABLE TO ASSIST WITH ANY HEALTH PROBLEMS YOU HAVE – IF NECESSARY, IN CONJUNCTION WITH YOUR PHYSICIAN.

CONSULTING A COMPLEMENTARY THERAPIST DOES NOT MEAN YOU HAVE TO GIVE UP YOUR DOCTOR – FAR FROM IT. GOOD THERAPISTS WILL HAPPILY WORK ALONGSIDE YOUR GP OR CONSULTANTS AND MANY ORTHODOX DOCTORS ARE NOW RECOGNISING THE BENEFITS OF THESE GENTLE FORMS OF HEALING. HOWEVER, YOU MAY WELL FIND THAT YOU DON'T SEE YOUR DOCTOR SO OFTEN ONCE YOU START DOWN THE COMPLEMENTARY-MEDICINE PATH.

COMPLEMENTARY MEDICINE NURSES YOU BACK INTO TUNE WITH YOUR BODY. PRACTISED PROPERLY, IT DOESN'T JUST ATTACK THE SYMPTOMS; IT ROOTS AROUND FOR THE CAUSE. THIS IS THE REASON WHY HOLISTIC THERAPIES ARE NOT USUALLY A QUICK FIX. ALTHOUGH AN OSTEOPATH, FOR EXAMPLE, WILL OFTEN GIVE YOU SWIFT RELIEF FROM A TWISTED MUSCLE OR PAINFUL JOINT, HIS OR HER TRUE INTENT WILL BE TO BALANCE YOUR WHOLE BODY IN ORDER TO COAX YOU BACK TO MAXIMUM STRENGTH AND VITALITY, AND TO PREVENT THE PROBLEM REOCCURRING.

DON'T, THEREFORE, EXPECT AN INSTANT CURE. SOMETIMES MIRACULOUS THINGS DO HAPPEN VERY QUICKLY, BUT THAT IS NOT USUALLY THE CASE. BEWARE OF ANY PRACTITIONER WHO SWEARS HE OR SHE CAN 'CURE' SERIOUS DISEASES. NO ONE CAN PROMISE TO CURE CANCER, OR AIDS, OR MULTIPLE SCLEROSIS JUST LIKE THAT. CERTAINLY, THERE HAVE BEEN DOCUMENTED CASES OF SPONTANEOUS REMISSIONS, OF WONDROUS CURES, OF SEEMING MIRACLES, BUT PLEASE DON'T PIN YOUR HOPES ON THE CLAIMS OF SOMEONE WHO OFFERS THEM AS A MATTER OF COURSE.

AS YET, FEW NATURAL THERAPIES ARE REGULATED BY LAW AND SO YOU DO NEED TO EXERCISE A LITTLE CAUTION WHEN CHOOSING A PRACTITIONER. MOST GOOD, WELL-QUALIFIED, ETHICAL THERAPISTS BELONG TO SOCIETIES AND ORGANISATIONS THAT MONITOR STANDARDS. IF YOU ARE UNSURE ABOUT HOW GOOD THE ORGANISATIONS THEMSELVES ARE, CHECK WITH UMBRELLA BODIES SUCH AS THE INSTITUTE FOR COMPLEMENTARY MEDICINE OR THE BRITISH COMPLEMENTARY MEDICINE ASSOCIATION (SEE DIRECTORY).

COMPLEMENTARY MEDICINE – THE GOOD GUYS

I've already talked about bodywork in the last chapter. Now let's look at some of the other best-known and most widely available therapies.

AYURVEDA

The 'mother' of all medicine, Ayurveda, has been practised for over five thousand years. Ancient practitioners had detailed knowledge of paediatrics, psychiatry, surgery, toxicology, geriatrics, general medicine and other specialties. Practitioners aim to balance both body and mind, nipping any problems in the bud and returning you to full health.

Treatment usually involves diet, lifestyle shifts, exercise and breathing. Herbal preparations are often used, as are massage, manipulation and cupping. Ayurveda does demand a commitment in time and effort but can have wonderful results with a wide range of chronic conditions, including those involving the digestive system, the skin, joints, the heart, allergies and gynaecological disorders. It can also help with such psychological problems as insomnia, addictions, anxiety and depression.

HOMEOPATHY

Homeopathy can be quite mind-boggling for many people – how can a pill that doesn't contain even a molecule of its original substance possibly help cure an illness? The jury is still out but it seems as though homeopathy is working at an energetic, rather than a purely physical, level. However, what is clear is that it can have remarkable results. Homeopathy is particularly useful for babies and young children. It is a very gentle, safe form of medicine that can help avoid the necessity for frequent antibiotics, steroids and other powerful drugs during delicate young years. Homeopathy is excellent for acute conditions such as allergies, eczema, colds, burns and stings but works equally well in chronic, long-standing complains. It can be particularly useful for the treatment of anxiety and some other psychological problems.

HYPNOTHERAPY

Hypnotherapy is a precise form of psychotherapy in which a hypnotherapist leads the client into a state of deep relaxation. From there, the therapist may only offer positive statements to the subconscious mind or he/she may involve the client in a more dynamic experience – exploring feelings, re-enacting situations or going back into dreams to uncover their meaning. Contrary to popular belief, you are always in control and aware of what is happening. Clinical hypnotherapy (which is a million miles away from stage hypnosis) is very useful for a variety of issues, including weight control, addictions, depression, anxiety, low self-esteem and relationship issues.

MEDICAL HERBALISM

Medical herbalists use the same diagnostic protocol as doctors and so, if you are new to complementary medicine, you will feel on home ground here. However, the herbalist will be seeking not just to soothe your symptoms but to balance your whole body and restore you to full health. Expect to be given a combination of herbal tinctures to take on a daily basis and also to be ready to make any necessary changes to your lifestyle (diet, exercise and stress are all scrutinised). Detoxing is commonly deployed because the body needs to be cleared before it can be balanced and strengthened. Herbalism can help a vast variety of chronic complaints and has particularly good results with rheumatic and arthritic conditions and psychological issues.

NATUROPATHY

Naturopathy is a complete system of natural healthcare that includes diet, exercise, hydrotherapy (water treatments) and osteopathy. Some naturopaths also use homeopathy, herbalism and acupuncture. Virtually all chronic diseases respond well and it has particular success with rheumatic and arthritic conditions, hypertension, allergies and fatigue problems. However, be prepared to make some sweeping changes in your diet and lifestyle and your whole attitude towards your health. Some of the treatments are quite stringent.

PSYCHOTHERAPY

The 'talking cure' – psychotherapy – aims to make you feel better about yourself and to help you get the most out of your life. People usually go because they want to shift some form of negative behaviour or pattern of thinking, or because they feel they could benefit from uncovering toxic patterns from the past. There are as many different forms of psychotherapy as there are days in the year – so you are bound to find something to suit your personality and your pocket.

However, be aware that psychotherapists aren't gods – they can't wave a magic wand and make you better. They are not there to give you the answers on a plate, but to help you find the answers yourself. Psychotherapy can be very useful when such problems as depression, anxiety, panic attacks fail to respond to nutritional changes. It can also help if you have low self-esteem or recurrent negative emotional patterns, such as abusive relationships, inappropriate anger or chronic people-pleasing.

TRADITIONAL CHINESE MEDICINE (TCM)

There's much more to the Chinese tradition than becoming an acupuncturist's pincushion. A good practitioner will use a barrage of techniques from herbalism and massage to diet therapy and exercise. As with naturopathy and Ayurveda, this is a system designed to overhaul your entire life – so expect to make some quite far-reaching changes. TCM has a favourable effect on most chronic conditions. Acupuncture, in particular, is beneficial for emotional and psychological problems, for addictions and for achieving weight/smoking control. It has been proven to relieve pain and has been used with great success during childbirth. There is evidence that it can help with fertility problems, and Chinese herbalism is famed for its success with skin problems.

SAFEGUARDING YOURSELF FROM KNOWN RISKS

If, when you look back over your family health history, you discover that a high proportion of your blood relatives suffered from, or died from, the same illness, you might consider taking further steps to minimise your risk of developing these illnesses. First and foremost, do talk to your doctor to ensure you are properly screened and tested. However, there is a lot you can do to help yourself. Let's take a look at four of the most common chronic diseases – all of which respond well to the preventative approach. Again, you'll see many of the factors we've already discussed in the Life Plan coming up again and again. Merely by following this book you will be giving yourself a firm helping hand.

CANCER

1. Eat a well-balanced, healthy diet that is high in fruit, vegetables, whole grains, nuts, seeds, oily fish, lean white meat and the omega-3/-6/-9 oils. Drink adequate clean water.
2. Boost your diet with anti-cancer foods. Have a serving of cruciferous vegetables (broccoli, cabbage, kale etc.) every day and a clove or two of garlic. Add shiitake mushrooms to salads and turmeric to stews, soups and stir-fries. Make soya products, including tofu, a part of your diet.
3. Achieve, and maintain, your ideal weight. Being overweight creates twice the risk of developing cancer and is linked, in particular, to breast, colon, endometrial (lining of the womb) and prostate cancer.
4. Cut out (or down on) alcohol. Heavy drinking is linked to a variety of cancers. Combined with smoking, it can be even more deadly.
5. Stop smoking. Lung cancer is the single most preventable cancer known to our society.
6. Avoid chemicals – preservatives, additives, pesticides, nitrates and nitrites. Most non-organic and processed food is stuffed with them and they contribute a serious risk factor for cancer. Avoid mouldy food. Avoid barbecuing or burning food, and any fried food.
7. Try to avoid environmental chemicals too. Detox your home as suggested in Chapter Three.
8. Exercise regularly – it can help protect you from many forms of cancer.
9. Cut out caffeine and, instead, drink green tea (super-high in antioxidants). Do not drink green tea if you are pregnant. Cat's claw tea is another excellent anti-cancer option but, again, not suitable if you are pregnant.
10. Have regular screening – discuss with your doctor.

HEART DISEASE

1. Lower your lipids (a fancy name for fats). Cut out saturated and hydrogenated fats and don't fry your food.
2. Eat plenty of fruit, vegetables, wholegrains, fish, nuts and seeds – all high in the nutrients that help prevent heart disease.
3. Balance the ratio of omega-3, omega-6 and omega-9 fatty acids in your diet. The Life Plan does this automatically but you may like to supplement your diet with oil blends that combine all three types of omega fatty acids (available from health shops) – use in salad dressings or drizzle over vegetables.
4. Check out the glycaemic load of the food you eat and aim to keep it low. Foods with a high glycaemic index raise blood-sugar level fast, whereas foods that release energy slowly have a beneficial effect on plasma glucose and insulin response.

5. Check your level of homocysteine (an amino acid in the blood implicated in heart diseases). If it is high, boost your intake of vitamins B6, B12, folic acid and trimethylglycine under the auspices of a nutritional therapist.

6. Exercise. People who exercise regularly have fewer heart attacks. Aim for 30 minutes of brisk exercise (a smart walk would do it) five times a week.

7. Stop smoking.

8. Take steps to get stress under control – try meditation, visualisation and the tips in Chapter Three. The yogic Sun Salute helps to strengthen the heart and is an excellent preventative. Breathing exercises, particularly *ujjayi* (see page 47) are also helpful.

9. Keep your weight under control – being overweight is a risk factor for heart disease. Your Body Mass Index (BMI) should be less than 25kg per metre squared. See pages 142–3 for how to test yours.

10. Keep alcohol consumption strictly limited – no more than one small drink a day. If you feel the need to drink any more, you must address the underlying factors motivating you. Deal with any stress or anxiety.

DIABETES

1. Eat low-glycaemic-load foods that release energy slowly – wholegrains, lentils, pulses, and raw or lightly cooked vegetables. These foods are also high in soluble fibre, which is important. Severely limit or cut out refined and processed carbohydrates that cause blood sugar to spike.

2. Have protein with every meal or snack, e.g. a few nuts or seeds with a fruit snack.

3. Boost your diet with foods that help to stabilise blood sugar levels, such as garlic, kelp, soya, vegetables, berries, fish, eggs and spirulina.

4. Exercise – regular exercise can prevent or delay adult-onset diabetes. Research shows that more vigorous exercise is the most effective.

5. Reach your ideal weight and maintain it. Obesity can trigger diabetes if you are genetically susceptible, and over ninety per cent of non-insulin-dependent (Type II) diabetics are overweight.

6. Cut out or cut down alcohol – it causes blood-sugar imbalance.

7. Boost your diet with the omega-3/-6/-9 oils – in oily fish, nuts and seeds – or buy special blended oils for use in salads or to add to vegetables (don't heat).

8. Consider a chromium supplement – check with a nutritional therapist. Chromium increases the efficiency of insulin, the hormone that controls blood glucose. Do not take chromium without checking with your doctor if you are already taking medication for diabetes and go for the polynicotinate variety.

9. Stop smoking.

10. Have regular blood checks if diabetes runs in your family. Also have your blood pressure checked – the two often run hand in glove.

ARTHRITIS

1. Keep your diet predominantly alkaline at all times. Monitor your pH levels regularly because acid-forming foods are strongly related to arthritic conditions. Sulphur-containing foods (such as asparagus, eggs, garlic and onion) are anti-arthritis superfoods; so, too, are green leafy vegetables, other veg, non-acidic fruits (especially fresh pineapple), whole grains, oatmeal, brown rice and fish.

2. Ensure you get enough protein, zinc and folic acid in your diet – deficiencies are linked to arthritis.

3. Avoid the nightshade family of vegetables (potatoes, peppers, aubergine, tomatoes) as they contain solanine, to which many people with arthritic tendencies are highly sensitive.

4. Check out food allergies and intolerances. The most common associated with arthritis are gluten and dairy.

5. Boost your diet with the omega fatty acids – natural lubricants. Seeds, nuts, oily fish are all excellent. However, to ensure the right mix and quantity, it may be advisable to take a supplement.

6. Avoid saturated fat, dairy produce, red meat, salt, caffeine, paprika, citrus fruits, alcohol and tobacco.

7. Have hair analysis to check for toxic metals in your body.

8. Avoid excess iron. Do not take iron supplements or multi-vitamins containing iron – check with a nutritional therapist. You can obtain adequate iron from the balanced Life Plan diet.

9. Exercise regularly, but choose low-impact forms that don't put undue strain on joints – swimming is superb, rebounding is good. Walk briskly rather than run; choose low-impact rather than high-impact aerobics.

10. Spend time outdoors in the fresh air so your body can synthesise vitamin D, essential for proper bone formation.

DEALING WITH SPECIFIC PROBLEMS – NATURALLY

Of course, not all health problems are chronic or severe. Sometimes the most distressing problems are the least dangerous. Think of this section as your family's natural health-problem solver, offering simple, effective cures for everyday ailments. I discussed numerous solutions in my first book, *Joshi's Holistic Detox*; here are many more. If any problem persists, please consult your doctor. If you are pregnant, breastfeeding, or are taking medication (whether orthodox or herbal) please consult your doctor or a complementary-health practitioner before taking herbs or using essential oils.

The homeopathic remedies mentioned should, ideally, all be taken in 30c potency (if 30c is not available, use 6c). Follow the instructions given on the pot.

ACNE

Acne has a variety of causes, including hormonal changes, stress, and exposure to chemicals or infection. Following the Detox Plan will undoubtedly help most cases of acne by cleansing your colon and liver. Avoid alcohol, caffeine, fried foods, sugar and animal protein.

Aloe-vera juice can help – mix with fresh fruit juice if you dislike the taste. Drink a spice tea made up of equal amounts of cumin, coriander and fennel. Stress is such a common cause that it's well worth trying visualisation – relax and visualise yourself looking in the mirror and seeing your face clear and blemish-free; or visualise yourself directing healing light to the cells of your skin.

Homeopathy has many remedies for acne but you would need to consult a homeopath to find the exact one for you.

ASTHMA

Asthma is on the increase and is incredibly distressing. It can even be life threatening. Check for any root cause. Food intolerances are common in asthmatics, with gluten and dairy being the most common culprits. Try the NAET method of allergy testing (see Chapter 1) if you don't want to do the elimination diet. Environmental pollution and chemical products can be another cause – eliminate as much environmental toxicity as possible and use natural cleaners, washing powder, bed linen etc. Check for pet allergies. Stress is another factor – review your stress levels and take steps to keep them under control (see Chapter 3).

Increase your breathing capacity through breathing exercises and other exercise (see Chapter 2). The Buteyko method of breathing can be very helpful (see Directory). Essential fatty acids are invaluable – omega-3/-6/-9 oil, flax seeds, oily fish (but not tuna). A tea made of half licorice and half ginger can prevent asthma (avoid licorice if you have high blood pressure). Another helpful method is to bake two large onions, extract the juice and mix with a teaspoon of manuka honey and a pinch of black pepper.

Complementary therapies that have good success rates with asthma include Ayurveda, homeopathy, medical herbalism and TCM (Traditional Chinese Medicine).

ATHLETE'S FOOT

Itchy and unpleasant, athlete's foot is caused by a fungal infection. Soak your feet in a basin of water to which you have added 15 drops of grapefruit-seed extract (a powerful anti-fungal) for 5 minutes. Avoid sugary and fermented foods because they feed fungal infections, and eat natural live yoghurt each day (or take a probiotic supplement). You can also try mixing a teaspoon of aloe-vera gel with half a teaspoon of turmeric and applying this to the affected area at night (wear a pair of old socks as otherwise it will stain the sheets). A mixture of neem and tea-tree oil can also be effective – and less messy!

BACKACHE

Your first step should be to book an appointment with an osteopath. Back pain has a variety of causes: muscle strain; poor posture; a trapped nerve or a slipped disc; osteoporosis or even an underlying infection. A good osteopath (or chiropractor) can usually pinpoint the causes of your backache and either offer relief or refer you to a specialist. They will also show you how to avoid many problems in the future. You should, now, pay attention to your posture – Alexander Technique and Feldenkrais Method are both superb ways of learning how to work with your body to avoid injury or discomfort. Take a series of lessons and feel the difference. Massage and bodywork can also ease the misery of a bad back.

On a very practical level, check your bed: if your mattress is too old, too hard or too soft, that can contribute to back pain. Ask your osteopath for advice. If you constantly wear high heels, maybe it's time to give the Manolos a break and swap them for some gorgeous flatties, instead. Equally, do you regularly carry a heavy bag on one shoulder? It might not be the fashion, but a backpack or dinky trolley (providing you don't have to stoop to push it) would be kinder to your back; otherwise, split the load between two bags – your perfect excuse for buying another! Yoga and Pilates also come into their own if you have chronic back pain. Their deep stretching is incredibly therapeutic.

BAD BREATH

Bad breath is usually a sign of poor digestion, indicating either that your intestines are overloaded with toxins or that you have indigestion or malabsorption. Gum or teeth infection can be another cause – get a check-up at the dentist. If the back part of your tongue is coated, the problem is likely to be an excess of mucus and toxicity. Undertaking my Detox should already have helped with this. You can also use a tongue scraper, daily.

Chewing cardamom seeds makes the breath smell sweeter and improves digestion, or you could try chewing a teaspoon of roasted fennel and cumin seeds after meals. Aloe-vera juice can also make your breath fresh.

BALDING

There are many reasons for balding. Sometimes it's purely the (bad) luck of your genes. However it can be caused by infection, by nutritional deficiencies, or be a symptom of some other problem. It would be worth having a check-up from a naturopath, Ayurvedic physician or medical herbalist. Indian head massage is wonderful for stimulating the scalp. In Ayurvedic terms, hair loss is considered to be caused by excess *Pitta dosha*, so drink aloe-vera juice three times a day for about three months; and rub your scalp and feet with coconut oil at bedtime (wear socks and wrap your head or pillow in a towel to protect the bed linen). Yoga postures can also help by relieving tension in the neck and encouraging blood flow to the scalp. Inverted postures, such as shoulder-stands and head-stands, are particularly good.

BITES/STINGS

If you are allergic to bee venom, a sting can be literally life threatening. However, for most of us, bites and stings are annoying but unavoidable parts of life, particularly in the summer. Fortunately, there are remedies that can soothe the irritation. Diluted feverfew tincture or a vinegar/water mix are natural insect repellents.

If you are stung, remove the sting carefully with a clean pair of tweezers. Neem is a natural antidote to most insect stings – use either a paste made from neem powder and water, or dab herbalised oil directly on the bite. Also effective is mixing together equal amounts of turmeric and sandalwood powder with a little water and applying.

Homeopathic Apis is superb for most stings and bites where the bite is red, hot and swollen. Treat animal bites with Hypericum (but also consult a doctor). Midge bites, which are painful to the touch, respond well to Staphysagria.

BLOATING AND FLATULENCE

Uncomfortable and embarrassing, bloating and flatulence can be caused by fluid retention, fungus in the gut, food intolerances, constipation or trapped wind. The Life Plan will undoubtedly ease many cases of bloating and flatulence by soothing digestion and reducing constipation. By following the Detox as an elimination diet, you will also have uncovered any underlying intolerances that may be causing the problem (wheat is the usual culprit) – or try the NAET method of allergy detection. Exercise (particularly yoga and Pilates) can help enormously.

Ensure that you're drinking enough *still* water – fizzy water will just make the problem worse. Watch out for excess salt in your diet, and eat plenty of leafy green vegetables to help boost your potassium intake. Chew your food *really* well to increase enzyme production.

Charcoal tablets can help prevent flatulence as can Triphala (an Ayurvedic combination of herbs).

Homeopathic Lycopodium can help when your bloating is accompanied by stomach rumblings, and can also regulate bowels that alternate between diarrhoea and constipation. Apis encourages the elimination of excess fluid in pre-menstrual bloating.

BUNIONS

Try soaking your feet in warm water containing about three tablespoons of Epsom salts, and do this every night for at least three weeks. Wear less tight-fitting shoes and avoid pointed styles.

BURNS

Serious burns need urgent medical attention. Hold minor burns or scalds under the cold tap for several minutes and then use one of the following methods to speed healing and minimise the pain. Lavender oil (10 drops mixed in a little sweet almond oil) is soothing; so, too, is a tablespoon of turmeric powder mixed in aloe-vera gel. Take homeopathic Arnica for the shock, followed by Urtica urens for minor burns that are red, burning and blistered. Arsenicum is useful for deep burns that are slow to heal.

CELLULITE

Cellulite is usually a clear sign that your system is toxic and in need of a clear-out; the bottom line is that you've been consuming too much alcohol, caffeine, red meat, sugar, fatty and junk food. Diet really is the answer here, and following the Detox and then the Life Plan will help enormously. Make sure you're drinking enough water and exercising (swimming, rebounding and yoga are particularly helpful). Skin brush daily before your bath or shower (always working towards the heart). Most forms of massage can help by stimulating the lymphatic flow – endemology, aromatherapy and MLD (manual lymphatic drainage) are superb. Otherwise, massage yourself using a mixture of sesame and mustard oil (half and half). Don't waste your money on fancy anti-cellulite creams, lotions and potions – sorry, but it's hard work alone that shifts cellulite.

COLDS/FLU

The Life Plan helps to build up your immune system so you will be far less likely to catch colds or flu once you're in peak condition but, every so often, one sneaks through.

Herbal Echinacea fights viral infections stoutly by balancing the immune system. Goldenseal and grapefruit-seed extract are also good herbal allies (but check with a herbalist before taking). Ginger is also a great cold and flu fighter. Drink plenty of ginger tea and also plain hot water to flush out toxins. You can also try steaming – put a few drops of ginger essential oil in a bowl of freshly boiled water. Place a towel over your head and the bowl and inhale to relieve congestion. **CAUTION:** don't take medicinal doses of ginger internally with aspirin as they both thin the blood.

At the first sign of a cold, take homeopathic Aconite (throat feels hot and dry, you're thirsty and you feel feverish). If your face alternates between being pale and flushed, try Ferrum phos instead. Once a cold is established, there are two great homeopathic remedies: Belladonna for colds that come on suddenly where everything feels hot and red. Natrum mur is worth trying for colds where your nose alternates between running copiously and feeling blocked.

Above all, rest. Don't soldier on when you've got a cold or flu – give your body time to rest and recover (and avoid spreading your germs to your colleagues as well).

CONSTIPATION

If you want to stay healthy and beautiful, keep your bowels moving! You should already have noticed an improvement after doing the Holistic Detox, and the Life Plan diet naturally shifts even the most stubborn cases of constipation by upping your intake of complex unrefined carbohydrates (whole grains, pulses, vegetables and fruit). Make sure you're drinking enough water – around seventy per cent of constipation cases are caused by dehydration. Many people also get constipated when they're stressed, and so a soothing abdominal massage – using a blend of fennel or marjoram oils diluted in sweet almond oil – can help enormously.

Ayurvedic Triphala is an excellent cure. Laxative foods include prunes, figs, raisins, pineapple, peaches and ripe bananas. You could also try a teaspoon of ghee (clarified butter) in a cup of hot milk at bedtime (but not if your predominant *dosha* is *Kapha*).

Homeopathic Bryonia eases the kind of constipation that is combined with a headache and dry mouth; Nux vomica can help if you've been overdoing the party lifestyle – drinking too much, sleeping too little and eating rich fatty foods.

COUGHS

Coughing is our bodies' way of ridding the lungs of congestion. Try massaging the chest with a blend of tea-tree or eucalyptus essential oils added to sweet almond oil. You can also steam using a few drops of either essential oil to ease the congestion.

An Ayurvedic cure is to chop a clove of garlic and boil it in a cup of milk. Take off the heat, add a large pinch of turmeric, stir, and sip slowly. Black pepper works well for loose, productive coughs –

mix half a teaspoon of powdered black pepper with two teaspoons of manuka honey. Take it with meals throughout the day.

Homeopathic Bryonia is useful for coughs that are dry and tickly with an accompanying headache; Pulsatilla is good if your cough is dry at night but loose in the morning; Hepar sulph for coughs with a hoarse sore throat; Phosphorus for coughs that get worse in the evening with a burning sensation in the chest. If your cough persists, see your doctor.

DERMATITIS AND ECZEMA

Many skin conditions clear up as if by magic when you uncover underlying food intolerances. Chemical sensitivities can also cause these distressing conditions so it's worth turning detective to see if there is anything in your lifestyle or environment that could be responsible for the problem. Cosmetics, bath and skin products might be the culprits. Check out your household cleaning materials, rubber gloves, jewellery and perfume. Some people are acutely sensitive to animal hair, dander or saliva – check these, as well. Even handling foods (potatoes, citrus fruits and tomatoes in particular) can trigger an allergic response.

Boosting your immune system on the Life Plan will help, as will getting stress under control with the suggestions in Chapter 3.

Homeopathic Graphites may help weeping eczema. Arsenicum can ease eczema that alternates with asthma (a common pattern). Rhus tox soothes patches of highly itchy skin (blisters that weep and crust over after scratching). However, for best results you should consult a professional homeopath. TCM also has good results with skin problems.

DIARRHOEA

Diarrhoea is usually your body's way of saying you have eaten something that doesn't agree with you. It can also be caused by stress and anxiety.

An Ayurvedic cure is to cook two apples until soft, then add a pinch of nutmeg and a pinch of cardamom. Eat slowly. Another option is to blend together equal amounts of natural live plain yoghurt and water, adding a little (about a quarter of a teaspoon) freshly grated ginger. Sip slowly.

Homeopathic remedies usually work a treat. If the diarrhoea has been caused by food poisoning (often accompanied by vomiting), take Arsenicum. If it's the result of anxiety about an upcoming event, try either Gelsemium or Arg nit. If you only experience it on waking, try Sulphur. The homeopathic remedy China (*China officinalis*) will be effective in helping you get over the tiredness that a bout of diarrhoea often causes.

Don't be tempted to stop drinking – your body loses a lot of fluid through diarrhoea and you need to keep it hydrated.

FATIGUE

A common problem nowadays, and one that doesn't have a simple solution, fatigue is often not only physical but also mental, and frequently comes from an overloaded, over-stressed life style. It can be caused by anaemia, poor adrenal function, poor liver function, sluggish digestion, viruses or an under-functioning immune system (in other words, toxicity). The Life Plan will probably go a long way to easing or eliminating the majority of cases of fatigue by supporting the detox systems of the body and also uncovering any food intolerances (another cause of fatigue). Surprisingly, exercise usually makes you feel more energised, not more tired – so don't shy away

from it. Yoga and *pranayama* are especially helpful for fatigue. Pay particular attention to Chapter 3 and make meditation and visualisation a part of everyday life.

If you are still exhausted after following the Life Plan, then you should see your doctor to rule out any other underlying causes (such as anaemia, Epstein-Barr virus, thyroid imbalance, diabetes etc.). Complementary therapies can help enormously – consult a homeopath, naturopath or nutritional therapist, or a TCM or Ayurvedic practitioner.

GUM PROBLEMS

Ayurveda has a host of cures for common gum problems. Neem is a wonderful herb for general mouth hygiene and health – you can buy neem toothpaste and mouth washes from health shops. Receding gums are treated by warm sesame oil. Just before bed (after your usual brushing), swill a mouthful of sesame oil around your mouth for about two or three minutes. Spit it out and massage your gums with your index finger.

Triphala is useful if you have bleeding gums or gingivitis – use a tea mixture as a mouthwash.

Clove and tea-tree essential oils can help infected gums – put one drop on the problematic area or else dip dental floss in the oil just before you floss.

Keeping your diet healthy and high in bioflavonoids (found mainly in fruit, especially berries) will also help.

HANGOVERS

Of course, if you're following the Life Plan you won't get hangovers! But we're all human and fall by the wayside from time to time, so I'm just being realistic by including this information.

Rehydration is of key importance – drink plenty of water and freshly squeezed fruit or vegetable juice. One particular cure is to drink a glass of natural water to which you have added a tablespoon of lime juice, a teaspoon of sugar, a pinch of salt and half a teaspoon of baking soda. This soothes *Pitta dosha*, which is aggravated by excess alcohol. Cat's-claw tea can help, too. Some nutritional therapists recommend taking doses of vitamin C and glutamine every two hours until you have relief.

Next time you're tempted to overdo the alcohol, just think what you're doing to your poor liver – and slow down.

HEADACHES

The causes of headaches are extremely varied. Some can be brought on by poor posture, neck or eye strain or by working too long in front of a computer. Eye and ear problems can cause headaches, as can insomnia, food intolerances, blood sugar imbalances, hangovers or dehydration. Ayurveda also recognises three distinct kinds of headaches, each caused by an imbalance in one of the three *doshas*. *Vata* headaches tend to be at the back or left side of the head and are usually aggravated by stress, anxiety, constipation or muscular tension. This type of headache may well lessen once you follow the Life Plan. Make sure you are drinking enough water – dehydration is a common problem for *Vata*. Make a paste by mixing a quarter of a teaspoon of ground nutmeg in a little water; apply it to your forehead and leave for about half an hour. As a preventative, massage your feet and the top of your head with a little sesame oil before bedtime.

Pitta headaches tend to sit in the centre of the head, behind the eyes or around the temples. They are commonly provoked by alcohol, junk food, and overly spicy or fatty food. Hot sun or getting overheated can also be a cause. The aim, here, is to cool the body, so try taking aloe-vera juice internally and putting aloe-vera gel on your forehead. Alternatively, make a paste from one teaspoon of sandalwood powder mixed with a little water and apply to your forehead and temples – leave for about half an hour. Also, try eating something sweet – ripe fruit or fruit ice cream.

Kapha headaches are usually in the front of the head and around the sinus areas and are often brought on by poor digestion and sinus congestion. A eucalyptus steam often eases sinus headaches. A warming paste can also help – mix one teaspoon of powdered ginger with a little water and apply to your forehead, cheekbones and across your nose. Leave for half an hour.

Homeopathic Bryonia eases throbbing headaches that are made worse by the slightest movement. Nux vomica helps hangover/overindulgence *Pitta*-type headaches. Lachesis can ease migraines accompanied by feelings of dizziness. Chromium polynichotinate will help regulate blood sugar levels and headaches or migraines brought on by hypo-glycaemia.

Osteopathy and chiropractic can be useful in relieving neck and shoulder tension, as can massage and, in particular, Indian Head Massage. Many people who suffer from chronic headaches find the Alexander Technique very useful. SHEN and Kairos Therapy have a reputation for being able to stop headaches and even migraine.

HEARTBURN/INDIGESTION

Most people with heartburn and indigestion reach for antacids, but these aren't the answer. If your stomach becomes too alkaline, you simply won't be able to digest your food properly and the problem will exacerbate. Once again, the Life Plan will sort out most problems of indigestion and heartburn as it avoids their major causes: alcohol, caffeine, food additives, hydrogenated fat, red meat, dairy, sugar and sweeteners, wheat and stress. Drinking plenty of water helps and adding aloe-vera juice to your daily diet will soothe the gut. Papaya juice (with a pinch of extra cardamom) is also soothing. These are predominantly *Pitta* conditions so also avoid hot spicy food, pickles and fermented food, and cut down on citrus and sour fruits.

Stress and diaphragm tension can cause acid reflux. A good cure for this is diaphragm breathing exercises or massage. You can alleviate the problem yourself by working on a pressure point at the bottom of your breast-bone on the V that's formed by the base of your ribcage. Gently push your fingers into that spot and try to breathe normally. It may feel tender and uncomfortable but those feelings will subside as your diaphragm relaxes.

Homeopathic Arsenicum can relieve burning pains with queasiness; Lycopodium helps stress-related acid reflux and heartburn linked with bloating and gurgling; while Bryonia is very useful for the heavy feeling in the stomach that comes with heartburn, acidity and a desire for cold drinks.

If you still experience heartburn or indigestion after you have completed the Life Plan, consult a nutritional therapist or naturopath who can test for further food intolerances, stomach acid and digestive enzyme levels, and mineral deficiencies (zinc levels, for instance, will often be found to be low).

IBS

IBS (irritable bowel syndrome) is a catch-all name for a wide variety of digestive problems including heartburn, indigestion, flatulence, irregular bowel movements (often alternating between diarrhoea and constipation), bloating and cramping.

Stress is considered the major trigger for IBS, so it's vital that you pay serious attention to the strategies outlined in Chapter 3. Yoga is invaluable, as are breathing exercises (*pranayama*). Undertaking the Detox will have ironed out food intolerances, and these can also exacerbate IBS. Wheat, sugar and dairy are very often found as underlying causes, but other foods can also trigger it so it might be worth having yourself tested for intolerances and allergies with the NAET Method.

Homeopathy can be very helpful, but you would need to consult a trained practitioner. Ayurveda, TCM and naturopathy are also valuable complementary therapies.

Depending on your symptoms, check the other entries in this section (constipation, bloating, indigestion etc.).

JET LAG

Ayurveda sees jet lag as resulting from too much *Vata dosha* in the body. An hour before you fly, take ginger (either capsules or tincture – but not if you're taking aspirin on a regular basis). While on the flight, drink plenty of still water and avoid alcohol or caffeine (so you don't get dehydrated). When you arrive, drink a mug of hot milk to which you have added a pinch each of nutmeg and ginger powder. Rub a little warm sesame oil on your feet and the top of your head.

Homeopathic Arnica is useful for jet lag in general. If you have a sense of paralysis, try Gelsemium. Cocculus is excellent for balancing disturbed sleep patterns. If you suffer extremely badly, consult a nutritional therapist who could prescribe the hormone melatonin.

An interesting cure involves balancing the flow of *prana* or *qi* (vital energy) throughout the body. Clasp the thumb of your left hand with the fingers (but not thumb) of your right hand. Hold until you detect a slight but noticeable pulse. Then, move on to the index finger and then, in turn, on to the other fingers of the left hand and repeat the procedure. Do not move on to the next finger until you have received the pulse. Then switch hands and repeat on the right hand.

LOW LIBIDO

A host of factors can depress your sex drive, but the causes are usually just as likely to be psychological as physiological. Stress, in particular, can have a hugely negative effect on hormone balance and therefore, following the anti-stress plan in Chapter 3 should help enormously. Good nutrition can also play a part so the Life Plan is bound to give you a boost in bed – as well as everywhere else – by upping your levels of the essential B vitamins and the vital 'sex mineral' zinc. Make sure you add such supersex foods as almonds, apples, dates, figs and honey to your diet. Ensure you're not constipated (see the earlier entry for advice on this).

It's also worth taking a good honest look at your relationship: are there stresses and strains that need addressing? It's hard to feel desire if you're angry or resentful.

Ashwagandha is a good herbal tonic for men. Muira puama (from a small Amazonian tree known as 'potency wood') can help women with low libido as it tones the female sex organs. However it is best to consult a medical herbalist, naturopath or Ayurvedic practitioner.

Homeopathy has good results with low libido but, ideally, you should have a full consultation. However, you could try Causticum (loss of libido following period, vagina feels sore); Natrum mur (loss of libido caused by grief or suppressed emotions); Pulsatilla (loss of libido plus depression and weepiness); Sepia (irritable, indifferent to sex, chilly, exhausted).

NAUSEA

Ginger is the anti-nausea spice *par excellence*. It can help nausea brought on by travel sickness, food poisoning, toxicity and even morning sickness in pregnancy. Again, don't take ginger if you already take aspirin to thin your blood. Nausea is usually caused by excess *Pitta dosha*, so keep away from hot, spicy or fermented foods. Chewing a couple of cardamom seeds can help, as can drinking cranberry juice with a little squeezed lime juice.

Homeopathic remedies include Nux vomica (for nausea combined with stress and tension); Pulsatilla (superb morning-sickness remedy, where you can't face fatty foods, in particular); Sepia (nausea made worse by the sight, smell or even thought of food).

If nausea follows a trip abroad, you may have picked up a micro-organism – see your doctor or a nutritional therapist who can run tests. If nausea continues with no obvious cause, consult your doctor.

SINUS PROBLEMS

The sinuses consist of cavities in the skull that lie behind the eyes and cheekbones. They can become blocked and inflamed (usually following a cold) and then give rise to intense pain or great discomfort. If you suffer from chronic sinus problems, you need to look to your diet. As you will have discovered from doing the Holistic Detox, foods that increase mucus production (such as dairy and sugar) need to be avoided. The Life Plan diet is really an excellent anti-mucus formula, so it will inevitably help. Eat plenty of fresh garlic and lots of fresh vegetables and fruits to boost your immune system and help fight infections. Add turmeric to your cooking. Other herbal antibiotics include neem, goldenseal, echinacea and the Ayurvedic combination remedy Trikatu. Decongesting steams (use eucalyptus oil) can ease the discomfort and congestion.

Homeopathic remedies include Hepar sulph (for congestion with thick yellowish-green mucus, worse for cold air); Kali bich (for sinus pain across the bridge of the nose with stringy green mucus); and Pulsatilla (for sinus congestion after a cold, usually accompanied by a cough, with thick green mucus).

SORE THROAT

A sore throat is a clear sign of infection and often a warning of a cold to come.

An Ayurvedic remedy is to gargle with warm water to which you have added half a teaspoon each of sea salt and turmeric powder. A soothing tea for sore throats combines equal amounts of ginger, cinnamon and licorice. **CAUTION:** avoid licorice if you have high blood pressure.

Or take homeopathic Belladonna at the first inkling of a sore throat – particularly if the throat appears red and you have a temperature. Lachesis works well for left-sided sore throats (or where the pain moves from left to right). Hepar sulph is the remedy when you feel as if something is stuck in your throat, usually accompanied by swollen glands.

SPRAINS/STRAINS

A sprain affects the ligaments and, Ayurvedically speaking, is a *Pitta* condition. A strain, on the other hand, affects the muscles and is considered a *Vata* condition. Drink pineapple and/or pomegranate juice; both are natural anti-inflammatories that promote healing. Then, make a paste out of a teaspoon each of turmeric powder and sea salt (add enough water to make a stiff paste – if it's a sprain use cold water, if it's a strain, use hot). Apply to the injury to reduce swelling.

Homeopathic Arnica will reduce swelling, too. Rhus tox is good for sprains that are relieved by gentle movement. Bryonia should be taken after Arnica for strains that are better for rest and worse for movement. Ledum helps strains that are soothed by cold water.

Sprains also respond well to being soaked in hot water into which you have placed a muslin bag containing two teaspoons of brown mustard seeds).

SUNBURN

You've read all the warnings – if you want to keep your skin beautiful and youthful (and avoid skin cancer), keep yourself covered up and use a strong-factor suncream for any bits that are on show. But if the worst happens and you burn, you need to bring down the inflammation as fast as possible. Aloe-vera gel is incredibly soothing; so is cold milk, yoghurt, and/or coconut oil. You could also bathe in a cool bath to which you have added 10 drops of lavender essential oil. Homeopathically, take Belladonna for dry, hot, red and throbbing skin. If the sunburn is severe, take Cantharis. Drink plenty of water to rehydrate the body.

WARTS

Warts are the outward signs of, firstly, a virus in the body and, secondly, a compromised immune system unable to cope with the problem. The Life Plan diet will boost your immune system and may well help the problem by improving your immune function and upping vitamin C levels (warts don't like a vitamin C-rich environment). Garlic is a powerful antiviral – so include plenty in your diet.

There are very many homeopathic specifics for warts, but you would need to consult a trained homeopath to discover the best for you. However, it may be worth self-treating with Thuja: take the tablets internally and also apply Thuja mother tincture (the original, undiluted, plant-extract solution – available from homeopathic chemists and good natural health stores) directly onto the wart.

YOUR NATURAL FIRST-AID KIT

Complementary medicine offers very practical and effective alternatives to many common problems. A basic, home first-aid kit would include the following:

⇢ Arnica cream or ointment: for bruises, muscle aches, painful joints. Don't use on broken skin.

⇢ Arnica tablets: for any shock or accidents. To bring out a bruise.

⇢ Aconite tablets: take at the very first hint of a cold. Also good for harsh, dry coughs.

⇢ Arsenicum tablets: useful for suspected food poisoning.

⇢ Nux vomica tablets: for overindulgence in rich food or alcohol.

⇢ Calendula cream or ointment: healing and soothing for cuts, grazes, athlete's foot, itchy skin.

⇢ Aloe-vera gel: for acne, bites, stings, burns, cuts, sunburn, itchiness.

⇢ Ginger powder: eases nausea, sickness and travel sickness.

⇢ Echinacea lozenges: great for sore throats, mouth ulcers and sinus problems.

⇢ Echinacea tincture or tablets: useful for all infections, colds, flu, earache, catarrh etc. Can be taken alongside antibiotics and helps reduce their side effects.

⇢ Probiotic supplement (acidophilus/Bifido bacterium): take after any course of antibiotics to restore beneficial bacteria in the gut.

⇢ Lavender essential oil: soothes headaches, insomnia, tension. Rub on temples or add to baths (don't take internally).

⇢ Tea-tree oil: natural antiseptic useful for foot infections and acne. Burn in an aromatherapy burner to ward off colds. Don't use internally.

⇢ Garlic capsules: use for any form of infection. Powerful anti-fungal, hence useful as a douche for thrush.

SARAH'S STORY

I had been trying to get pregnant for some time but my husband and I were having problems conceiving. I was about to undergo my first round of IVF treatment and I wanted to maximise my potential success rate by detoxing and cleansing my whole body before I started treatment. I was also looking for ways to relax, as it was a particularly stressful time.

Joshi put me on the Detox Programme and I have to say that despite my motivation, I found it quite hard not being able to eat as I usually did. Initially I felt weak and drained and suffered from headaches and cramps. I stuck at it though and the various extra treatments I had such as cupping and acupuncture and colonics really helped to alleviate both cravings and stress.

I felt that I had more energy as a result of following the Programme, and I lost some weight, but most important of all, I conceived the very first time of trying, eight weeks after completing IVF and Joshi's Detox Programme. I absolutely believe that it was the combination of approaches that enabled me to get pregnant and of course my life has been changed in the most wonderful way – we now have a healthy baby boy!

SARAH OWEN, 36, IS THE DIRECTOR OF A PR AND MARKETING COMPANY. SHE IS MARRIED WITH ONE SON AND LIVES IN LONDON.

CHAPTER 5
HOLISTIC BEAUTY

THE HOLISTIC LIFE PLAN IS NOT JUST A HEALTH PLAN; IT'S A BEAUTY PLAN, TOO. THE DIET, EXERCISE, MEDITATION AND VISUALISATION TECHNIQUES ALL COMBINE TO MAKE YOU STUNNING, FROM THE INSIDE OUT. HAVING DONE THE DETOX, YOU WILL ALREADY HAVE NOTICED THAT YOUR SKIN IS MORE RADIANT AND CLEAR, YOUR EYES HAVE REGAINED THEIR SPARKLE, YOUR HAIR IS SOFTER AND SILKIER. THE LIFE PLAN ISN'T ABOUT EXPENSIVE CREAMS OR FANCY FACIALS – YOU DON'T NEED TO SPEND A FORTUNE MASKING A POOR SKIN. IT'S ABOUT CREATING THE PURE, NATURAL, RADIANT BEAUTY THAT COMES WHEN YOU GIVE YOUR SKIN, HAIR, EYES, NAILS AND TEETH THE EXACT NUTRIENTS THEY NEED TO LOOK THEIR GORGEOUS BEST. IT'S ABOUT USING STORE-CUPBOARD INGREDIENTS TO MAKE YOUR OWN PRODUCTS – PRODUCTS THAT WILL WORK FAR BETTER THAN MOST LUXURY SKINCARE RANGES.

MY MOTHER AND AUNTS WOULD LAUGH OUT LOUD AT THE IDEA OF BUYING FACE CREAMS, TONERS OR SHAMPOO – THEY SIMPLY MAKE THEIR OWN. I GREW UP WATCHING MY MOTHER AND SISTER MAKING THEIR BEAUTY PREPARATIONS ALL THE TIME. THERE WERE CERTAIN SEEDS YOU WOULD BOIL TO MAKE INTO A SHAMPOO, FLOURS AND SPICES YOU'D MIX TOGETHER TO MAKE A MASK. JUST NATURAL THINGS THAT WERE HANGING AROUND. FOR EXAMPLE, GRAM FLOUR MAKES A GREAT EXFOLIATOR AND MASK. THE DAY BEFORE PEOPLE GET MARRIED IN INDIA, THEIR WHOLE BODIES ARE WASHED WITH GRAM FLOUR AND TURMERIC. ITS PURPOSE IS TO PURIFY THE BODY AND ALSO TO GIVE A GORGEOUS GLOW TO THE SKIN.

MY AUNTS ALL HAVE AMAZING WHITE TEETH BECAUSE THEY USE A PARTICULAR PASTE THAT HAS BEEN MADE FOR YEARS AND YEARS – WOOD IS BURNED TO CHARCOAL, THEN GROUND AND MIXED WITH OIL AND SANDALWOOD. THEY RUB THE POWDER INTO THEIR GUMS AND TEETH AT NIGHT AND IT PREVENTS GINGIVITIS AND GIVES THE TEETH A NATURAL BLEACHING.

THE BEAUTY PLAN, LIKE THE LIFE PLAN, FOLLOWS THE PRINCIPLES OF AYURVEDA – PRACTICES THAT HAVE BEEN TESTED AND REFINED OVER FIVE THOUSAND YEARS. AND, JUST BECAUSE IT WON'T COST YOU AN ARM AND A LEG, THAT DOESN'T MEAN IT ISN'T LUXURIOUS. THIS CHAPTER WILL OFFER YOU THE CHANCE TO ENJOY YOUR PERSONAL SPA, TAILOR-MADE FOR YOUR SKIN, IN THE PRIVACY OF YOUR OWN BATHROOM.

I INTEND TO PAMPER YOU TO THE HILT. YOU WON'T BELIEVE HOW GOOD YOU CAN LOOK. IT'S NOT AN INDULGENCE – YOU NEED TO GIVE TIME TO YOURSELF. CLEANSING YOUR FACE, DOING YOUR NAILS, MAKING SURE YOU COMB YOUR HAIR ARE ALL REALLY IMPORTANT BECAUSE THEY SHOW THAT YOU LOVE YOURSELF, THAT YOU CARE ABOUT YOURSELF AND YOUR APPEARANCE. YOU CAN THEN BE THE BEST YOU CAN POSSIBLY BE.

WHY FANCY CREAMS AREN'T GOOD FOR YOUR SKIN

The beauty business is a multi-million-pound industry, founded on our perfectly reasonable desire to stay looking young and beautiful. But the side effects of many products can be far less glamorous. You could be putting on your face such unappetising ingredients as human urine and placental tissue, animal hormones and sheep fat plus a witch's brew of chemicals to make them look pleasant and smell good. I've lost count of the number of my patients who are allergic to the common ingredients in cosmetics and beauty products, even such everyday items as shampoo, soap, after-shave and antiperspirant. Even tiny amounts of their ingredients might cause eczema and acne, asthma and dermatitis. Hypoallergenic products usually leave out around sixty of the ingredients most likely to aggravate allergies; however, they can still cause allergic reactions. Cosmetics make you toxic – they get stuck in your fat cells.

Creams and lotions are packed full of chemical preservatives, synthetic perfumes and colourants – all of which can cause sensitivity and toxicity. Even the active ingredients that are supposed to take care of skin 'problems' can themselves cause damage. Many products stop the skin doing what it wants to do naturally. For example, if you strip the skin of all its natural oil, you panic the skin and make it produce even more oil. If you drive acne further into the body, it will cause permanent problems. People who say they have sensitive skin actually have sick skin – sick of the things that are being put on it. The skin simply can't get rid of complicated fragrances or fat-soluble preservatives and so it stores them up for a while and then gets dry or develops a rash.

What we often forget is that the skin will absorb anything we put on it; within a very short amount of time that substance will be circulating through the blood stream to every cell in the body. In the case of beauty products, the substance could be bovine-tissue extracts, liquid plastics, paraffin and even acids that, outside the beauty industry, are used for etching metal. The World Health Organisation (WHO) found that many of the colourants used in lipstick, rouge and eye shadow are unsafe. The American Government Accounting Office found that 884 chemicals that were available for use by the cosmetic industry were on a federal toxic-substances list. For example, formaldehyde, used in skin products as a preservative and disinfectant, is a suspected carcinogen. Coal tar, listed as FD&C or D&C colours, is a common ingredient in cosmetics, hair dyes and dandruff shampoos. It is also a known carcinogen and has been linked to frequent allergic reactions including asthma attacks, headaches, nausea, fatigue, nervousness and lack of concentration. I could go on and on.

Watch out, too, for 'natural' products. Something can be labelled 'natural' if it is, for example, just two per cent natural and ninety-eight per cent petroleum and chemicals. Even products high in natural ingredients need preservatives. Some use natural preservatives (such as grapefruit-seed extract, tea-tree oil and other essential oils) but they usually still need at least one of the synthetic preservatives for the product to 'keep'. Of course, not all chemicals are dangerous – but do you really want them on your skin?

BACK TO BASICS

Could there be a simpler, easier, *safer* way to a healthy, beautiful skin? Yes, yes and yes. Stop spending a fortune and take your skin-care regime right back to basics: thorough cleansing and nourishing plus a great, healthy lifestyle. Remember that real beauty does come from within – people like Gwyneth and Cate really take care of themselves. They have a good diet, they drink plenty of water, they have massage and they do everything that promotes good skin. You'll find that most actresses don't put much at all on their skin.

Given the right raw ingredients, our bodies have the power to heal themselves. This doesn't just apply to our internal organs but also to what we often forget is our largest organ – the skin. Nowadays, of course, natural healing is a tough job for the body: however healthy we try to make our lifestyle, we are battling against an ever-more-polluted environment and ever-more-polluted food and air. Our skin needs extra help in sloughing off toxins, gaining essential nutrients and protecting itself against the ravages of modern living. Unfortunately, as we've seen, many of the high-tech, highly expensive beauty products are not helping the skin but actively hindering it.

Skin-care products are essentially food and nourishment for the skin; so, why not treat the skin, our largest organ, with the same care that we give to the inside of our bodies? Having detoxed your body, it's now time to detox your dressing table and your bathroom shelf. I'm going to show you how to put together your own totally natural and wildly effective products for the face, body and hair – and to do it using mainly store-cupboard ingredients.

However, as you know, I'm pragmatic and know that not all of you will have the time or inclination to make your own products all the time. So, let's look, first of all, at how to minimise the dangers of store-bought skin care:

→ Look carefully at the products you use, particularly if you have 'sensitive' or problem skin. If the product does not list all its components, ask the company for full label disclosure. A reputable company will happily tell you precisely what is in its creams and lotions. If you're not sure what an ingredient is, ask. Cosmetic language is designed to confuse – for instance, they itemise 'aqua' instead of water. However, in general, if it's too long and difficult to pronounce, it's probably too unpleasant to put on your skin.

→ Be particularly wary of highly perfumed or coloured products. The chemicals used to make products look and smell nice are often the most problematic. Remember, too, that lots of bubbles mean lots of chemicals.

→ Be wary of products that offer a quick fix. If you force your skin to do anything fast, it will undoubtedly rebound on you. And beware of products that claim to be able to 'force' or 'push' wonder ingredients such as Vitamin C or collagen into the skin.

→ If you regularly dye your hair, use natural hair colourings – e.g. henna. Dark hair dyes, in particular, have been linked with increased cancer risk. Highlights are safer than all-over dyes because they don't soak the scalp.

→ Be gentle with your skin: don't rub it and don't vigorously exfoliate it. The outer layer of the skin is there for a reason. Treat it carefully. A gentle, once-a-week exfoliation – using my natural recipes – is fine.

→ Make sure your skin is really clean. Adopt a thorough but gentle cleansing routine morning and night (see page 125). Avoid products that strip the skin of its natural oils.

→ Don't use a heavy moisturiser at night – it won't allow the skin to carry out its natural nightly detox, rest and repair. Use a light cream, a herbal gel or the natural nourishers I suggest.

→ Moisturise your skin from the inside by drinking two litres of fresh water a day (it also helps the skin eliminate toxins). Caffeine dehydrates the skin – instead, drink either green tea (packed with antioxidants) or fruit, spice or herbal tisanes.

→ Get your antioxidant fix by eating tons of fruit and vegetables (rather than using artificial products containing them). Invest in a juicer and enjoy skin-boosting juices such as orange, grape, papaya, mango, guava, carrot or celery. See Superfood Skin Boosters on the next page.

→ Of course, make-up is equally full of chemicals. Holistic skin-care ranges do exist but don't usually have the high performance of high-tech make-ups. Try to limit the time you wear foundation, in particular, and make sure you always take all make-up off thoroughly.

→ Exercise regularly: lack of exercise can lead to your muscles deteriorating which, in turn, can affect the tone and firmness of your skin. Yoga poses, in particular, take blood all round the body that nourishes your skin and hair. In addition, sweating helps to unblock your pores, cleanse the skin and rid the body of toxins.

→ Stress, tension and tiredness all take their toll on your skin. Follow the exercises given in Chapter 3. Practise meditation – serene bliss for skin.

SUPERFOOD SKIN BOOSTERS

What you put inside your body is just as important as what goes on the outside. Yes, you *can* eat yourself beautiful. These are the beauty foods with which to plump up your diet *and* skin.

⟶ **Carrots:** sky-high in antioxidant beta-carotene, carrots help prevent your skin ageing and can even reverse some of the damage already incurred.

⟶ **Eggs:** high in lecithin, one of the primary building blocks of cell walls; high levels of lecithin protect your skin from ageing. Eggs are also a vital source of coenzyme Q10; this heightens your levels of squalene that, in turn, keeps your skin hydrated and supple. Do try to eat more of the whites than the yolks though – this will maintain a good acid/alkaline balance and reduce cholesterol.

⟶ **Green tea:** as your skin cells get older, they aren't renewed so often; so, dead skin cells sit around creating a dull, tired complexion. Green tea helps your cells live longer, making your skin look and act younger than it is. Green tea has also been shown to help collagen fend off free radicals (that cause ageing) and to protect against UV damage.

⟶ **Olive oil and olives:** rich in oleic oil that plumps out skin cells and so makes wrinkles and lines less noticeable.

⟶ **Pomegranate:** one of my favourite fruits, packed with ellagic acid which makes your skin heal swiftly. It is also a natural internal sunscreen – drink pomegranate juice and you increase your protection from UV light by twenty-five per cent. You can also add the juice to your sunscreen and boost its SPF by a further twenty per cent. Pomegranates have also been shown to be one of the most powerful natural antioxidants.

⟶ **Raisins:** red grapes are packed with resveratrol, a specific antioxidant that slows down the speed at which your skin cells age.

⟶ **Turkey (organic):** a great source of carnosine, an amino acid that protects collagen and keeps it elastic and supple thus helping to prevent wrinkles, lines and sagging.

WHAT IS YOUR AYURVEDIC METABOLIC SKIN TYPE (AMST)?

I don't look at your skin and think 'dry, oily or combination' – rather, I would say you had *a Vata*, *Kapha* or *Pitta* skin. Just as your body type is determined by the three *doshas*, so, too, is your skin. Common beauty problems (dry flaky skin, spots, rashes, grease etc.) are simply signs that one of your *doshas* is out of balance. Instead of suppressing the symptoms (as most high-tech products do), I aim to balance your skin from the inside out, to get to the root of the problem once and for all.

Once my patients start following the correct Ayurvedic beauty regime, their skin becomes clearer and healthier. Even such persistent problems as acne, eczema and psoriasis disappear.

It is likely that your skin type is the same as your overall ruling *dosha*; however, this isn't always the case. Start, now, to find your AMST (Ayurvedic metabolic skin type). You will need to look carefully at your face – using a magnifying mirror, if possible. You may need to tick off more than one response on the skin-analysis checklist, or the question may not apply – in which case, just ignore it.

SKIN CHECKLIST

1. Is your face: a) small, thin, long, oval; b) large, round, or square with soft contours; c) average, triangular with sharp contours.

2. Does your skin feel: a) dry, thin, rough, cold; b) oily, moist, thick, cold; c) slightly oily, soft, hot

3. Would you describe your skin tone (not skin colour) as: a) bluish; b) yellowish; c) reddish

4. Are the pores on your face: a) small and fine; b) large and open; c) large on your nose and chin but small and fine elsewhere.

5. Do you have: a) fine lines, prominent veins; b) blackheads, excessive oiliness; c) broken capillaries, freckles and/or moles.

6. Do you have any discolouration such as: a) dark pigmentation on the cheeks; b) white or brown pigmentation; c) reddish pigmentation all over.

7. Is your skin prone to: a) dryness and dehydration, especially in cold weather; b) acne and pimples, especially around your mouth, chin or neck; c) inflammation, rashes and sunburn, especially in hot weather

8. Is your hair: a) dry, thin, coarse, curly, frizzy, wiry, scanty, dark; b) thick, oily, abundant, wavy, dark or light; c) moderate, fine, soft, golden or reddish, prematurely grey or balding.

9. Are your lips: a) thin, dry, long, irregular; b) thick, large, even, firm; c) average, soft, red.

10. Are your fingernails: a) dry, small, crooked, brittle, rough, discoloured; b) thick, oily, smooth, white, strong; c) soft, medium, pink.

YOUR RESULTS

Add up the number of answers you checked in each column, a, b and c.

a:_____   b:_____   c:_____

⇢ If your highest score is in column a, your AMST is Vata

⇢ If your highest score is in column b, your AMST is Kapha

⇢ If your highest score is in column c, your AMST is Pitta

According to your AMST, you will need to use different ingredients for your skin-care products – another reason why ready-made products just don't hit the spot.

YOUR BEAUTY STORE CUPBOARD

Let's look at some of the prime ingredients you will be using to make up your beauty products. Most can now be easily obtained from health stores, corner shops or even supermarkets. A few might be harder to find (depending on where you live). I've given mail-order suppliers in the Directory.

ALMONDS: soothing, revitalising and nourishing; ground almonds, almond milk and almond oil are frequently used in natural cosmetics as they make excellent emollients. The nut is packed with protein and vital skin vitamins. **CAUTION:** avoid almonds if you suffer from nut allergies.

ALOE VERA: the juice and gel are cooling, soothing and healing, and hence very useful for troubled or sunburned skin. They are also used in hair masks to promote growth. Buy the juice and gel from health shops or else keep a plant on your window ledge and harvest the occasional leaf. Dab it on spots and acne or on chapped and sore lips. It also makes a great after-shave soother.

AVOCADO: well known as a beauty aid, avocado pulp makes a great face mask and a fabulous hair conditioner. The oil is packed with antioxidant vitamins (E, C and beta-carotene) and the B vitamins plus linoleic acid, lecithin and natural fatty acids, all of which give it moisturising, nourishing, rehydrating and soothing qualities.

BANANAS: high in antioxidants and potassium, bananas are superb for rehydrating masks and also help stimulate hair growth. They can soothe acne and spots and nourish dry frizzy hair.

COCONUT: used widely in Ayurveda, coconut oil and milk are nourishing, soothing and detoxifying. They are used in face and body creams and lotions, shampoos and hair treatments, and massage blends. Because coconut is cooling, it is particularly useful for *Pitta* skin.

CUCUMBER: packed with vitamins and minerals, including potassium, silicon and sulphur, cucumber can help keep skin cells healthy and elastic. It also works as an anti-bacterial to combat spots and acne. Its intense cooling properties make it a wonderful ally for hot, sore *Pitta* skin.

EGGS: eggs are the ultimate store-cupboard beauty aid, full of vitamins, minerals, protein and lecithin; nourishing and conditioning for both skin and hair. Don't use with warm ingredients, though – or you'll end up with scrambled eggs.

FRANKINCENSE: a wonderful beauty-enhancing essential oil used for treating wrinkles and mature, dry or chapped skin. It is deeply soothing, anti-inflammatory and regenerating. Used for facial steams or added to creams and massage blends.

GRAM FLOUR (CHICKPEA FLOUR): the basis of a huge number of Ayurvedic scrubs, masks and rubs. Chickpeas are packed with antioxidants and also make a gentle yet effective exfoliator.

HONEY: honey has been used as a beauty product for thousands of years all over the world. It's full of antioxidants, minerals and B vitamins and has powerful anti-bacterial and antiviral effects. It's deeply healing, moisturising, nourishing and cleansing for the skin and hair. Choose organic, cold-processed, clear honey.

LEMON: Antiseptic and astringent, lemons are also prized for their stimulating, rejuvenating and balancing properties. They can counteract the oiliness of *Kapha* skin and hair, and help beat spots and blemishes. **CAUTION:** may irritate sensitive skin. Do not use if you are going into the sun or about to use a sunbed (hopefully you would not do the latter). Do not put lemon juice on broken or irritated skin.

OATS: oats are supremely soothing and healing and also act as natural exfoliators. Choose finely ground oatmeal for face masks and exfoliators, while a coarser oatmeal works well for body scrubs. A handful of oatmeal in the bath is nourishing and healing for troubled skin.

PAPAYA: a superb exfoliator, thanks to the natural fruit acids and enzymes it contains. It's also packed with antioxidants. Puréed papaya makes a great body and face mask – you can even use it (carefully) around the sensitive eye area to soften wrinkles. **CAUTION:** may irritate very sensitive skin – try a patch test before using.

PINEAPPLE: full of vitamins, minerals and fruit acids, fresh pineapple is a great exfoliator, cleanser and rejuvenator. It is ideal for oily or acne-prone *Kapha* skins. It's also a natural anti-bacterial so can help banish spots. **CAUTION:** may irritate very sensitive skin – try a patch test before using.

POMEGRANATES: the juice is highly astringent and packed with antioxidants and fruit acids, so is often used as a mask to close pores and calm very oily skin. The juice is also used to treat hair, leaving it shiny and glossy. In addition, as we've already seen, pomegranate juice is also a potent protector of your skin from the sun.

SALT (SEA): deeply detoxifying, sea salt has been used in thalossotherapy (sea water therapy) spas for centuries. Salt not only draws out toxins from the skin, it is also an effective exfoliator, sloughing off dead cells.

SANDALWOOD: sandalwood is prized for rehydrating dry sensitive skin and for calming oily skin and cooling irritated skin – so it is invaluable for all the *doshas*. It is used widely in face and body masks, hair conditioners and as an after-shave soother. Its intense, warm, woody scent is supremely soothing, sensual and relaxing, and so the essential oil is often used in massage and bath blends.

TURMERIC: you've already met turmeric as a wonder spice for your diet but it's also a powerful ally in your beauty process. Turmeric boosts the circulation, making skin literally glow. It's used widely in nearly all beauty products – not just for skin and body, but for hair as well. In India it's thought to bring divine energy to the wearer and is also strongly purifying and anti-inflamatory.

YOGHURT: natural live yoghurt is nourishing, softening and hydrating for the skin and hair. It is cooling, and so useful for overheated *Pitta* skins. Its natural 'good' bacteria can help acne or blemish-prone skin. It is commonly made into a paste with dry ingredients. Milk and cream are alternatives.

YOUR TWICE-DAILY BEAUTY RITUAL

I know you're busy, and I promise that you won't need to spend masses of time on your everyday beauty regime. Five minutes twice a day (first thing in the morning and last thing at night) will do – although, if you can give yourself longer, your skin will appreciate it.

Beauty is not rocket science – you really only need two simple basic steps – cleanse thoroughly then nourish appropriately. Could it be simpler? However, by turning your cleansing and nourishing from a chore to a ritual, you can also make it into a mini-meditation and lower your stress levels while you're making yourself look gorgeous.

Be aware of each step of the process. Tell yourself, 'Right now I'm cleansing my face' (or whatever you are doing). Feel the touch of your fingers, feel how your face responds. Be aware of every move you make. You can also use the power of visualisation – imagine yourself becoming more beautiful with every stroke of your fingertips, visualise those lines softening, wrinkles fading away.

Use the very gentlest of touches when you work on your skin – so never scrub it, rub it or pull it, or you are likely to stretch it.

This is your two-step ritual . . .

STEP ONE: CLEANSE

First remove every last trace of make-up. You can either use ghee (clarified butter) or, if that feels too heavy, an organic, cold-pressed vegetable oil that suits your AMST. *Vata* should use warming sesame oil, *Kapha* should use light safflower while *Pitta* should go for cooling almond or sunflower. Use a little on a cotton-wool ball and wipe very gently. Do not pull the skin, particularly around the eyes.

Now, cleanse your skin very thoroughly using the cleanser recipe suited to your AMST. (See pages 121–2.) It is vital to cleanse well because your skin needs to be clean and free of all dirt or old make-up in order to soak up the gorgeous ingredients you're going to put on it next. If you live in the city, you may need to spend extra time on this stage. You can also use a deeper cleanser or exfoliator once or twice a week (see the recipes on page 127). If you like, you can cleanse your skin while having your shower or bath. This would be a good moment to do some facial exercise to tone the facial muscles and improve sagging skin. Make large movements with your mouth and repeat the vowels five times with a large yawn to stretch the jaw and the front of the neck muscles between each set.

STEP TWO: NOURISH

Having achieved the cleanest possible skin, it's time to feed your face. Here, in the West, moisturising creams are commonly used but, in India, it is a part of everyday life to massage blends of essential oils mixed with water into the skin.

Clean skin can easily absorb their nutrients which are pulled deep into the skin tissue, plumping, rehydrating and balancing. Don't panic if your skin is oily; you will be using oils that will actually counteract the oiliness – even though that might seem a little odd. Follow the oil blends given for your AMST and, trust me, you will notice wonderful results.

Your skin needs to be wet. So spend a little time gently splashing water onto your face (*Vata* and *Kapha* should use warm water, *Pitta* suits cool water better). If you like, you can use a pure flower water, such as rosewater or orange-blossom water. Don't use toners; they are too harsh and can strip the skin.

Now, massage the oil into your skin working generally upwards and outwards: from the centre of your chin to the side of your face; from the edge of your nose to the side of your face; up your nose to the point between your eyebrows; from the centre of your forehead out to your temples. Massage around your eyes in a circular movement, from the outside corner of the eye to the inner edge, with the very gentlest of touches. Allow a few minutes for the skin to settle before putting on your make-up.

Your beauty regime includes no moisturisers, no eye creams, no neck creams, no toner. Truly, you don't need them. I would ask you to try this system while you are on the Life Plan and, at the end of the four weeks, see how your skin looks and feels. You may find there is a settling-down period, in the first week or so, while your skin adapts to being able to breathe properly and detoxes from all those chemicals. Bear with it, any side effects will be temporary and the results will be well worth it.

THE BASIC RECIPES

VATA CLEANSER
1 TSP CRUSHED ALMONDS
½ TSP POWDERED MILK
PINCH OF SUGAR OR JAGGARY (AYURVEDIC SUGAR)
1 TBSP FRESH MILK

Mix the first three ingredients together, then moisten with the fresh milk to make a paste. Use warm water to splash off after cleansing.

VATA NOURISHER
2 FL OZ/50ML SESAME OIL
10 DROPS GERANIUM ESSENTIAL OIL
5 DROPS SWEET ORANGE ESSENTIAL OIL
5 DROPS FRANKINCENSE ESSENTIAL OIL

Mix all the above together and store in a glass bottle or pot and put out of the light. Shake gently each time before use. Put 3 drops onto the palm of your hand and add about 6 drops of water. Blend together and apply to your face.

KAPHA CLEANSER
1 TSP FINELY GROUND OATMEAL
½ TSP POWDERED MILK
1 TSP GRATED LEMON PEEL
1 TBSP ORANGE-BLOSSOM WATER

Mix the first three ingredients together, then moisten with enough orange blossom water to make a paste. Use warm water to splash off after cleansing.

KAPHA NOURISHER
2 FL OZ/50ML SESAME OIL
10 DROPS LAVENDER OIL
5 DROPS CLARY-SAGE OIL
5 DROPS BERGAMOT OR LEMON OIL

Follow instructions as for *Vata* nourisher using above ingredients.

PITTA CLEANSER
1 TSP CRUSHED ALMONDS
½ TSP POWDERED MILK
½ TSP FINELY GROUND CORIANDER SEEDS
½ TSP GROUND ORANGE PEEL
1 TBSP ROSEWATER

Mix the first four ingredients together, then moisten with enough rosewater to make a paste. Use cool water to splash off after cleansing.

PITTA NOURISHER
2 FL OZ/50ML SWEET ALMOND OIL
10 DROPS SANDALWOOD OIL
5 DROPS FRANKINCENSE OIL
5 DROPS ROSE OR VETIVER OIL

Follow instructions as for *Vata* nourisher using above ingredients.

FACIAL TREATS

When you have more time, you might like to try some of these treats for your face. Don't overdo them – once a week is usually quite enough (if you can use a recipe more often, I have indicated this).

GRAM FLOUR AND TURMERIC FACIAL MASK

This simple mask softens your face and gives it an incredible glow. Use once or twice a week.
1 TBSP GRAM FLOUR
1 TBSP GROUND TURMERIC
ENOUGH LIVE NATURAL YOGURT TO MAKE A PASTE

Mix together and spread over your face and neck. Relax for 20–30 minutes and then splash off.

FIRMING MASK

Does exactly what it says in the title!

1 TBS GRAM FLOUR
2 TSP ROSEWATER
½ TSP RUNNY ORGANIC HONEY

Blend into a creamy paste and pat onto the face. Relax for 15 minutes and then rinse off.

AVOCADO MASK FOR MATURE SKIN

This nutrient-rich mask really revitalises and plumps out the skin.

1 RIPE (SOFT) AVOCADO
1 TBSP RUNNY ORGANIC HONEY (MANUKA IS IDEAL)
1 TSP EVENING-PRIMROSE OIL (OR SQUEEZE OUT TWO CAPSULES)

Mash the avocado until it's a slushy pulp. Mix in the honey and oil. Press all over your face and neck and relax for 20–30 minutes. Rinse off with water or wipe off with cotton-wool balls soaked in rosewater or orange-blossom water.

PAPAYA EXFOLIATOR

Papaya will gently exfoliate your skin, smoothing it and combating any oiliness (so it's well suited to *Kapha* and *Pitta* skin in particular).

1 RIPE PAPAYA

Simply mash up the papaya, drain off the excess juice (drink!) and smooth it all over the skin. Leave for 10 minutes and then wash off.

GENTLE EXFOLIATOR

2 TSP FINELY GROUND OATMEAL
2 TSP ORGANIC DOUBLE CREAM

Mix together and apply to your skin with a gentle circling motion (using just the tips of your fingers). Rinse off.

FRUIT PEEL

½ PINEAPPLE, PEELED, CORED AND MASHED (MAKE SURE THERE ARE NO ROUGH BITS LEFT)
1 TBSP FINELY GROUND OATMEAL OR ALMOND MEAL

Mix the two ingredients together. Pat onto your face and neck (avoid eye area) and relax for 10 minutes before washing off.

HEALING SPOT VANISHER

2 TSP ORGANIC RUNNY HONEY
1 TSP TURMERIC
¼ TSP CRUSHED SEA SALT

Mix all ingredients into a paste and apply to spots for 30 minutes (you can do this every day until they vanish). It's best used in the evening.

SOOTHING EYE MASK

½ CUCUMBER
1 TSP POWDERED MILK

Grate the cucumber (you need about two teaspoons of 'grated' juice). Mix the juice with the powdered milk. Close your eyes and apply carefully all over your eyelids and under the eyes. Relax for 10 minutes and then carefully remove using dampened cotton wool. You can use this several times a week, as necessary.

BODY TREATS IN YOUR BATHROOM SPA

Fancy spas are lovely but you can do so much in the privacy of your own bathroom – at a fraction of the cost. Do spend time making your bathroom as gorgeous as you possibly can. Clean it thoroughly from top to toe and consider a fresh lick of paint if it's looking dingy. Re-grouting tiles can make a huge difference. If it's a tiny room, put up a big mirror to make it look bigger and more glamorous. Invest in decent storage so you're not pampering yourself amidst piles of old toiletries, half-empty bottles and children's bath toys.

Buy up the best-quality scented candles you can afford – or choose plain candles and burn aromatherapy oils instead. Indulge yourself with beautiful fresh flowers (keep a few aside so you can float petals in your bath). Big fluffy towels, a thick bath mat and a snuggle-into bathrobe – and you're all set.

OILING AND MASSAGE

Ayurveda uses oil liberally to keep skin smooth and supple. You don't need clever techniques: the most common practice is simply oiling – getting oil all over the body. However, add some simple massage strokes and the benefits increase exponentially. Massage has a huge array of benefits: it opens and cleanses the pores, increases blood circulation, reduces fat, rejuvenates the skin, calms the nerves and soothes the psyche. It even helps strengthen bones. Of course, it also feels fantastic. Ideally, find someone to massage you – it is far more relaxing that way. I advise my patients to do this all the time, particularly in relationships where love is fizzling out. People need to be encouraged to touch more. The human touch, particularly with your partner, is incredibly important. Holding hands, massage, cuddling up in front of the TV, scrubbing each other's backs – it's all quite essential. Physical interaction recreates the intimacy.

If you don't have a partner, trade massages with a friend. And even if you're on your own, it's still quite possible to achieve good results with a self-massage.

Pick your oil according to your AMST. *Vata* in particular, will benefit from oiling and massage as often as possible. *Pitta* skin loves a cooling weekly or twice-weekly massage. *Kapha* skin doesn't tolerate oil so well and should be massaged (using only a small amount of oil) no more than once a week. If you wish, you can add a few drops of your favourite *doshic* essential oils (but check with an aromatherapist if you have any chronic health condition or if you are pregnant).

BASE OILS:
- **VATA:** sesame, olive, sweet almond, wheat germ.
- **KAPHA:** sesame, safflower, mustard.
- **PITTA:** coconut, sweet almond, sunflower, pumpkin seed.

ESSENTIAL OILS:
- **VATA:** bergamot, chamomile, cinnamon, cypress, frankincense, geranium, ginger, lemon, orange, rose, ylang-ylang.
- **KAPHA:** basil, bay leaf, black pepper, cinnamon, eucalyptus, ginger, patchouli, peppermint, rosemary, sage.
- **PITTA:** chamomile, cardamom, coriander, frankincense, geranium, lavender, rose, sandalwood, vetiver.

HOW TO MASSAGE

1. Choose a warm, comfortable room for your massage, free from clutter and drafts. Place a large, warmed towel on the floor and ask your subject to lie on their front. Ideally they should be naked (oil will stain clothes); if modesty dictates, suggest that they wear (old) pants or a piece of muslin as a loin cloth. You may want to cover the parts not being massaged with towels. If you are massaging yourself, it may be easier to sit upright.

2. Warm the chosen oil to body temperature (by placing in a *bain marie* of hot water).

3. The most usual Ayurvedic massage touch is light, rhythmic and repetitive. As a general rule of thumb, use circular movements over rounded areas such as joints and straight strokes over straight areas such as the arms, legs, neck. There's no need to learn a whole battery of techniques – you're simply aiming to get the oil all over the body and for the process to feel great.

4. Start with the head and massage the oil gently into the scalp and down the neck.

5. Continue down the back and onto the hips and buttocks. Keep your touch light and rhythmic. Work down each leg in turn and pay particular attention to the feet (these can take a firmer pressure,

and be sure you massage between each toe).

6. Move back to the shoulders and work down each arm – making sure every inch is covered with oil – and on down to the tip of each finger. Take your time – don't rush.

7. Quietly, ask your subject to turn over. Massage the arms, legs, abdomen and chest. Traditional Ayurvedic massage always includes massaging a woman's breasts but it's not advised for amateur masseurs; also, I suspect many Westerners would feel distinctly uncomfortable with this.

8. Finish with the neck and face. Pay particular attention to every part of the face, making your movements very gentle. Pull the ear lobes (give them each a firm tug) and massage gently inside the ear (but don't poke – keep your fingers on the first ridge of the ear). Work gently inside each nostril.

9. End up by spending quite some time (at least 5 minutes) gently massaging the third-eye area (just above and between the eyebrows) with your thumb.

10. Make sure your subject is warm (it's probably a good idea to cover them with old towels or blankets) and leave them to relax for between 15 and 30 minutes.

BATH-TIME

A quick shower does the basics but, for deep beauty results, you need a good long soak. There are three basic steps: exfoliate, soak, and replenish. **NOTE:** full body exfoliation is not advised during pregnancy. So, first off, some delicious recipes for exfoliators…

SIMPLE OATMEAL EXFOLIATOR

Exfoliating boosts the circulation, loosens dead skin cells and moisturises the skin. This one is simple to make and gentle yet effective.

2 TBSP FINELY GROUND OATMEAL
1 TBSP SWEET ALMOND OIL

Combine the two ingredients into a stiff paste. Stand on the floor or in the empty bath and rub the oatmeal scrub into your skin – first over your body, then onto arms, legs, neck, face and even behind your ears. Your skin should become warm and pink. Pay special attention to hard skin on elbows, knees, soles and heels – the scrub will soften them. Massage the paste into your finger and toenails, working right into the cuticles. Shower the paste off before you run your bath.

SALT AND PEPPER SCRUB

This is a tougher scrub that packs a serious punch. It is intensely warming and so *not suitable* for *Pitta*.

2 TBSP SEA SALT (THE FINE VARIETY, NOT THE COARSE GRAINS)
1 TBSP FRESHLY (AND FINELY) GROUND BLACK PEPPER
2 TBSP SESAME OIL
FRESHLY SQUEEZED JUICE OF ½ LEMON
5 DROPS CINNAMON ESSENTIAL OIL

Combine all the ingredients. Take a quick shower to dampen the skin. Then, massage the scrub all over your body, always using a circular movement and moving towards the heart. You can be quite vigorous over your thighs, buttocks and upper arms. Take your time over this scrub – spend about 15 minutes really massaging it into the skin. Shower with warm (not hot) water to rinse away the mix.

SOOTHING FRUIT BODY MASK

This body treatment uses soothing and cooling aloe vera plus powerful, natural fruit acids to make it both gorgeous-smelling and powerful-acting. It is especially suitable for *Pitta* skin. It is important to use really ripe fruit to gain the maximum benefit.

1 RIPE PAPAYA, PEELED
1 RIPE PINEAPPLE, PEELED AND CORED
2 TBSP ALOE-VERA GEL (OR FRESH ALOE-VERA JUICE, IF YOU HAVE A PLANT)

Blend the fruits together and add the aloe-vera gel or juice. Smooth the mask all over your body. Wrap yourself up in a plastic sheet (available from hardware stores) and then cocoon yourself in warm towels. Relax for about 20 minutes.

TURMERIC AND SANDALWOOD BODY PASTE

3 TBSP GRAM FLOUR
2 TBSP GROUND SANDALWOOD
2 TSP GROUND TURMERIC

Mix the ingredients together and moisten with 1 tbsp milk (*Vata*), or the juice of a lemon (*Kapha*) or a small tub of natural live yoghurt (*Pitta*). Rub the paste all over your body as you did for the Salt and Pepper scrub. Relax for 5 minutes. You may wish to lie on a plastic sheet or old towel because this paste will stain.

SOAKING

The simplest bath involves adding 10 drops of your choice of essential oils (those that suit your *dosha*) to two tablespoons of base oil or milk. Swirl them around the water (after you have filled the bath, not while it is running), get in, lie back and relax. Your bath temperature should be quite hot for *Kapha*, warm for *Vata* and cooler for *Pitta*. Add a few flower petals for maximum effect. However, your bath can be as fancy as you please. Here are a few ideas to get you started.

WARMING GINGER BATH

Great for chilly *Vata* and for energising sluggish *Kapha*, but too hot for *Pitta*. This ginger bath stimulates your circulation and encourages your body to detox. It also helps combat aches and pains – and may well see off a cold.

Simply grate two large pieces of fresh ginger root. Place in a piece of muslin (from chemists or baby stores) and squeeze out the juice. Add the juice to your bath (it needs to be pretty hot). Tie up the muslin and let it float in the bath to increase the ginger zest.

AYURVEDIC FIVE-NECTAR BATH

In Ayurveda, there are considered to be five 'nectars' for the body: milk, honey, ghee (clarified butter), yoghurt and bananas. This luxurious bath is soothing and rejuvenating for all the *doshas*.

1 BANANA, MASHED
2 TBSP MILK
1 TBSP GHEE
1 TBSP YOGHURT
1 TBSP RUNNY ORGANIC HONEY

Combine all the ingredients and plaster all over your body. Massage into your skin and then get into a warm bath. Don't rub off the mixture, just allow it to melt into the water. Relax for about 20 minutes. You can gently remove any excess mixture at the end of this time but don't scrub your skin. This bath is best taken straight before bed.

'SAUNA' SALTS BATH

Epsom salts make you sweat like fury and help release toxins. It's strong medicine, so use it as a stand-alone bath without any pre-scrubbing or after-massaging. Ideally, have it just before bed. Perfect for *Kaphas*; *Vatas* should use it with caution; *Pittas* will probably find it too heating.

CAUTION: do not use this bath if you have heart trouble, are diabetic or are feeling weak or under par.

→ Run a warm bath and dissolve about 450g of Epsom salts into it.

→ Lie back and relax for about 20 minutes. If you want to increase the perspiration effect, sip a cup of hot peppermint tea.

→ Be careful as you get out of the bath – you may feel light-headed.

→ Don't rub yourself dry. Instead, wrap yourself up in several large towels and go straight to bed. Wrap your feet up snugly.

→ In the morning, have a shower or sponge yourself down with warm water. Rub your body vigorously dry.

DEEP DETOX MINERAL BATH

Most spas offer mud and/or mineral baths and you can easily duplicate these at home (and far less expensively) as most health stores now stock bath preparations such as Austrian Moor 'mud' or Dead Sea Mineral bath. Simply follow the instructions on the product and wallow for at least 20 minutes. Pat yourself dry (don't rub), wrap yourself up in towels and take to your bed.

Once again, this is a bath to have right before bedtime – or on a day when you can have a long sleep afterwards.

REPLENISHING TREATMENTS

The simplest way to moisturise your skin after a soak is either to enjoy a luxurious, leisurely full body massage (pages 130–1) or just to oil your skin with the suitable base oil for your *dosha*. However, here are a couple of alternatives.

BEESWAX BODY TREAT
10G BEESWAX
10G COCOA BUTTER
3 TBSP SWEET ALMOND OIL
6 TSP ROSEWATER
2 DROPS EACH OF YOUR FAVOURITE DOSHIC ESSENTIAL OILS

Melt the first three ingredients in a *bain marie* and stir continuously until totally melted. Remove from the heat and mix in the flower water – just a drop at a time and stirring continuously. Add the essential oils. Put into a sterilised dark glass jar and allow to cool. Massage into damp skin. Any left over can be kept in the fridge for a week or two.

CUCUMBER COOLING BODY LOTION
SOOTHES PITTA SKIN AND IS USEFUL FOR ANY SKIN THAT GETS SUNBURNED OR OVERHEATED.
1 CUCUMBER (BLENDED WITH SKIN ON)
2 TBSP ALOE-VERA GEL (OR FRESH ALOE-VERA JUICE)
1 TBSP COCONUT OIL
2 DROPS OF CHAMOMILE ESSENTIAL OIL

Sieve the cucumber pulp and mix with the other ingredients. Plaster all over your body.

HAIR TREATS

The women in my family have always had gorgeous, lustrous hair – in common with most Indian women (and men, come to that). Their secret, once again, lies in age-old traditions, not in super-dooper fancy hair products. First and foremost, the key to stunning hair lies in head massage. I grew up thinking that head massage was the norm. In India, children are massaged from birth by their mothers and learn, early on, how to give massages to the rest of the family. My nephew and niece are learning right now. By the time you reach adulthood, it's a well-established ritual: women have head massage to keep their hair beautiful and glossy; men have it to prevent them going bald. Everyone enjoys it as a supreme stressbuster and as a subtle way of keeping the family close and loving.

Once again, of course, the practice comes from Ayurveda and was originally used therapeutically: it can cure eye-strain and headaches, remove tension, soothe sinus pain and can even improve concentration. However, over the years, it has been adapted for everyday family life and loved for its amazing beauty benefits. Massage stimulates the circulation of the scalp, and this, in turn, nourishes the hair roots. The oil improves the texture of the hair and gives it a wonderful gleam. Massage can help to prevent hair turning grey and can even stop it falling out.

CAUTION: do not have head massage if you have a skin condition such as weeping eczema or psoriasis, or if you have any open cuts or sores on your head, or if you have recently suffered a head injury.

GET A HEAD START AT HOME

Head massage is one of the simplest techniques of massage to learn. You can easily give a highly effective treatment by following these simple instructions. A head massage should ideally last around 20–30 minutes.

Depending on whether you use soft or vigorous movements, it will either relax or energise your subject. Before you start, make sure your hands are well washed and your nails scrupulously clean. Ask your subject to remove glasses, contact lenses and any jewellery. Your subject does not need to undress for the massage but, if you are using oil, they may want to wear an old loose top or wrap up in a large towel.

Although you can perform this massage without oil, for the very best effects you should use oil (it will shampoo out quite easily). Sesame oil is good for *Vata* and *Kapha*; coconut for *Pitta*. You can add a few drops of essential oil if you like. The oil should be warm but not hot, so stand it on or near a radiator for around half an hour, or place it in a microwave for around 30 seconds. Be careful – it may be hot so check with a finger before taking a handful.

1. Have your subject sit upright in a straight-backed chair. Gently, lay your hands on the crown of your subject's head and just hold them there for around 30 seconds. Slowly, begin to massage the scalp with the pads of your fingertips. If you are using oil, apply it now – you don't need to drench the hair: use just enough to lubricate the scalp itself.

2. Now, support the head with one hand. Using the palm of your other hand employ a swift rubbing motion, as if you were buffing a window. Start behind the ear, go around it and then away from the ear. Then repeat on the other side of the head. This relaxes and warms the muscles.

3. Next, support the head with one hand while the other gently strokes the top of the head. First, use long sweeping movements, then 'comb' the hair, running your fingernails through the hair in long strokes. Work all the way around the head, swapping hands where necessary. This stimulates blood flow through the scalp and gives the head a lovely tingly feeling.

4. Take the weight of your subject's head on your arm. Now, starting at the top of the neck (where it joins the cranium), massage down either side of the spine, using small circling movements of the thumb and middle finger. Go carefully and be aware of how your subject reacts – don't press too deeply. This stroke soothes and calms the brain itself.

5. Massage the temples using gentle, circular movements – use the tips of the index fingers. Then support the back of the head with your hands and use a firmer (but still soft) pressure, massaging the temples with your thumbs.

6. Now concentrate on the neck and shoulders. Imagine you are ironing the shoulders, using the heel of your hand to roll forward over the shoulder from the back to the front. Start from the outside edge of the shoulder and move in towards the collarbone. If you are performing the massage on someone much taller than you, press across and over the shoulder with your forearm, using your body weight for pressure. This is wonderful for releasing tension in the shoulders and neck.

7. Put both hands around the head like a cap. Squeeze, lift and let go for several repetitions. You can use this movement alone to combat headaches.

8. Now stroke the face lightly with your whole hands (with the palm against the face), moving gently down from the forehead to the chin. Repeat as much as you like. Then cover the eyes with your palms. Press very gently on the eyeballs. If you are performing the massage before bedtime, this is the best place to end as it will send your subject gently off to sleep. You can use this part alone to help insomnia.

9. However, if your subject wants to feel energised, use a brisk rubbing motion, back and forth across the scalp. Vary this with a fast scratching action, using your fingernails. Both can be quite firm and deep – gauge your subject's tolerance level. Finally, finish by pressing firmly but carefully on the crown, as you did at the beginning.

If you can, try to leave the oil in the hair for as long as possible – an hour is good but if you can leave it overnight (wrapped in a towel) you will give your hair a really deep conditioning treatment. To wash out, put on your shampoo *before* wetting the hair and then work well into the hair before washing off with warm water.

CLEANING YOUR HAIR

Given the huge number of shampoos, conditioners, treatments, gels, mousses and so on, you'd think hair care was an incredibly complex, scientific process. Absolutely not. In fact, by lathering on tons of 'product', you are probably creating far more problems than you are solving. Modern hair is heavy with residues and so easily becomes 'weighed down', dull, heavy and lifeless.

Finding a shampoo that isn't packed with chemicals is tough because shampoo needs them to make the bubbles that create the froth we're accustomed to. But do you really need it? No, not really. However, I suspect I might have a problem weaning you off shampoo so my suggestion is to buy the gentlest shampoo you possibly can (if it doesn't lather up, that's a good sign) and then deal with the chemical residues. This is simplicity itself: simply dissolve half a cup of baking soda in a cup of warm water and pour it over your hair after shampooing. If you have been using a lot of hair products for a long time, you will need to do this about once a week for a month or so. After that, you can shift to a gentler method, rinsing with water to which you have added a few tablespoons of fruit or cider vinegar. Not only will this take away the last vestiges of shampoo, but it will give your hair a gorgeous shine and softness (it helps restore the pH balance to hair).

BEAUTIFYING YOUR HAIR

These delicious treats are guaranteed to restore lustre and shine. Once your hair is really clean of residues, it will responds fantastically to some beautifying.

CHAMPAGNE HAIR TREAT

This is an old French secret for giving your hair a gloss. If you're blonde, it will also bring out any natural highlights. Above all, it feels deliciously decadent to toss champagne over your hair!

Mix a cup of leftover champagne with a cup of hot water. Apply after washing and rinsing the hair – and leave in.

EGG-YOLK DEEP CONDITIONER

Variations of this exist all over the world, from Russia to Japan. It really is a superb treatment for all kinds of hair, leaving it looking and feeling thick, luxuriant and simply gorgeous.

2 EGG YOLKS
1 TBSP OIL (ALMOND FOR VATA, SAFFLOWER FOR KAPHA, COCONUT FOR PITTA)
2 DROPS OF ESSENTIAL OIL (LEMON FOR VATA, ROSEMARY FOR KAPHA, SANDALWOOD FOR PITTA)

Mix all the ingredients together – a whisk works best. Dampen hair and towel dry. Massage the mixture into the hair and scalp. Wrap your head in a towel and (preferably) have a long soak in a warm bath. For best results, keep on for an hour or two. Rinse your hair in warm water then shampoo and rinse again.

SPICY, SHINING TREATMENT

This really brings a gloss to your hair.
2 TBSP OF ALMOND (VATA), SAFFLOWER (KAPHA) OR COCONUT (PITTA) OIL
½ TSP EACH OF BLACK PEPPERCORNS, CORIANDER SEEDS, CUMIN SEEDS, CARDAMOM SEEDS AND CLOVES
2 DROPS SANDALWOOD ESSENTIAL OIL

Grind the spices together (use a pestle and mortar, or the grinding tool on your food processor). Put the oil into a *bain marie* and mix in two teaspoons of the spice mixture. Heat very gently until warm, but not so hot it burns. At the last minute, add the essential oil. Massage into dry hair and cover with a plastic head-cap and towels. Leave for about 30 minutes and then shampoo off.

BEATRICE'S STORY

I went to see Joshi last year, having read his first book. I have suffered from severe eczema all my life and I was desperate to find something that would alleviate my symptoms. It was particularly distressing for me because the eczema was on my face and hands, which meant I was always self-conscious about it.

Having read that Joshi's Holistic Detox could be very beneficial for patients with skin problems I decided to give it a go, and although I thought I could follow the programme on my own, I wanted to have a one to one to really explore what the diet could do for me. I didn't find the Detox too hard to stick to, apart from having to give up fruit – I had major apple cravings! I did experience headaches and stomach cramps in the first week but Joshi assured me that this was perfectly normal and they quickly cleared up. Joshi also used cupping and acupuncture to treat me. The cupping was initially a bit scary because the marks on my back took a while to fade (a sign that my body was full of toxins) but subsequent sessions were fine, and I absolutely loved the acupuncture and found it very beneficial.

Within three weeks the eczema on my hands started to heal. Around my eyes it took longer – about three months, but my skin is now completely clear. And a welcome additional benefit is that I have loads more energy than I used to have.

I have pretty much stuck to the diet, and even going out to eat in restaurants or with friends has never been a problem. Besides, I only need to look in the mirror to be reminded of the difference that the programme of treatment has made, so I don't feel any need to go back to eating 'normally'. I feel amazing. I'm no longer embarrassed to shake hands, I can wear make-up and jewellery and I've discovered a new self-confidence as well as a sense of calmness.

BEATRICE MAYFIELD, 38, IS AN ARTS ADMINISTRATOR FOR AN ARTS CHARITY.

CHAPTER 6
THE FOUR-WEEK PROGRAMME

ARE YOU READY TO START A BRAND NEW LIFE? DO YOU FEEL EXCITED ABOUT THE POSSIBILITY OF A BRAND-NEW YOU? YOU SHOULD DO. YOU ARE ABOUT TO LAUNCH INTO FOUR WEEKS THAT COULD TOTALLY TRANSFORM YOUR LIFE – PHYSICALLY, MENTALLY AND EMOTIONALLY. AS YOU'VE SEEN, THE HOLISTIC LIFE PLAN IS NOT SOME ARCANE, MYSTERIOUS, DIFFICULT PROCEDURE. IT'S SIMPLE, STRAIGHTFORWARD AND DESIGNED TO FIT IN WITH BUSY MODERN LIVES. IF I CAN DO IT AND MY PATIENTS CAN DO IT, YOU MOST CERTAINLY CAN DO IT, TOO. YOU ARE JUST FOUR WEEKS AWAY FROM ABUNDANT HEALTH, OVERFLOWING ENERGY AND RESTFUL SLEEP. JUST FOUR WEEKS AWAY FROM BEAUTIFUL SKIN, BRIGHT EYES AND GLOSSY HAIR. JUST FOUR WEEKS AWAY FROM A CLEAR, CALM FOCUSED MIND AND THE POSSIBILITY OF SUPPORTIVE, HONEST RELATIONSHIPS. HOW GOOD CAN IT BE? EXTREMELY GOOD, I PROMISE.

I HAVE ALREADY GIVEN YOU A HOST OF INFORMATION ON HOW TO MAKE YOUR LIFE AS HEALTHY AS POSSIBLE. MAYBE YOU'RE FEELING A BIT OVERWHELMED AND WONDERING HOW YOU CAN POSSIBLY INCORPORATE IT INTO YOUR LIFE? THIS CHAPTER BREAKS IT DOWN INTO MANAGEABLE, BITE-SIZED CHUNKS. YOU WILL BE TAKING 'BABY' STEPS EACH WEEK – WORKING WITH DIFFERENT ELEMENTS OF THE PLAN – UNTIL IT ALL BECOMES SECOND NATURE.

FIND YOUR MOTIVATION

Before you start, I would like you to think about why you want to go on the Life Plan. To help you do that, the best place to start is where you are right now. Fill in the first column of the Progress Chart and remind yourself of how you *don't* want to feel any more. This chart will also help you see, as the weeks go by, how you are improving. That, in itself, is a huge motivation. Once you start feeling good and losing the symptoms of poor health, it can be hard to recall just how bad you once felt. The Progress Chart will remind you; and, by making sure you notice your visible improvement, week by week, it will keep you well on track.

Now, think about how you would like to feel, how you would like to look. What are your goals? Try writing down the goals you would like to achieve while on this Plan – and beyond. Psychologists say that, for goals to be effective, they need to be specific, measurable, achievable, realistic and time-defined. So, be very clear about what you want. Don't just say, 'I want to lose weight,' or 'I want to get fit,' or 'I want to be self-confident,' or 'I want a better relationship' – define *exactly* what you mean by that. You could decide, for instance, that you would like to shed eight pounds; or be able to run up the stairs at work in one go without puffing; or give a short speech feeling cool, calm and in control; or be able to communicate with your partner without shouting. Do you get the idea?

Next, project yourself into the future and see your ideal life. How do you look? How do you feel? What are you doing? Realise that you *do* have the power to change. The beauty of the Life Plan is that it automatically sets you on the road to achieving – not only short-term, but long-term life-shifting – goals.

As I keep saying, this is not a quick fix. It's not a get-thin-quick diet or a plaster-over-the-cracks programme – it is about longevity, about sustainable, achievable, life-long change. That's why I call it the *Life* Plan.

PROGRESS CHART

Score points from 1 to 5 and complete the chart at the beginning of each week of the Life Plan.

1 = very frequent/severe symptoms
2 = regular/bad symptoms
3 = fairly regular/tolerable symptoms
4 = infrequent/manageable symptoms
5 = rare/minor symptoms

	Week One	Week Two	Week Three	Week Four
Bloating	☐	☐	☐	☐
BMI score	☐	☐	☐	☐
Constipation	☐	☐	☐	☐
Energy levels	☐	☐	☐	☐
Exercise (frequency)	☐	☐	☐	☐
Headaches	☐	☐	☐	☐
Heartburn	☐	☐	☐	☐
Indigestion	☐	☐	☐	☐
Insomnia	☐	☐	☐	☐
Lethargy	☐	☐	☐	☐
Menopausal hot flushes	☐	☐	☐	☐
Mental clarity	☐	☐	☐	☐
Mood swings	☐	☐	☐	☐
Motivation/willpower	☐	☐	☐	☐
Self-confidence	☐	☐	☐	☐
Skin problems	☐	☐	☐	☐
Sugar cravings	☐	☐	☐	☐

YOUR BODY MASS INDEX

Another factor we will be keeping an eye on is your Body Mass Index (BMI). This indicates whether you are underweight, normal weight, overweight or obese. It will also help you see how your weight balance shifts (for the better) as you go through the Plan. You will be familiar with it from my first book. It's a more meaningful measure of weight than mere pounds or kilograms. You should work out your BMI before you go on the Life Plan and once a week (no more) during the plan, recording your scores on your Progress Chart.

BMI = a person's weight in kilograms divided by height in metres squared.

BMI metric formula

BMI = Weight [in kilos] divided by
(Height [in metres] X Height [in metres])
or:

BMI Pounds/Inches Formula

BMI = Weight [in pounds] x 704.5 divided by (Height [in inches] x Height [in inches])

BMI examples

You are 63 inches in height.
Your weight is 135 pounds.
Your Body Mass Index is 24. (normal weight)

You are 66 inches in height.
Your weight is 161 pounds.
Your Body Mass Index is 26. (overweight)

You are 64 inches in height.
Your weight is 174 pounds.
Your Body Mass Index is 30. (obese)

BMI results

18.5 or less = underweight
18.5 – 24.9 = normal weight
25 – 29.9 = overweight
30 – 34.9 = obese
35 – 39 = very obese
40 plus = dangerously obese

BODY MASS INDEX CHART

Height / Weight in Pounds

Height	19	20	21	22	23	24	25	26	27	28	29	30	31	32	33	34	35	36	37	38	39	40
58"	91	96	100	105	110	115	119	124	129	134	138	143	148	153	158	162	167	172	177	181	186	191
59"	94	99	104	109	114	119	124	128	133	138	143	148	153	158	163	168	173	178	183	188	193	198
60"	97	102	107	112	118	123	128	133	138	143	148	153	158	163	168	174	179	184	189	194	199	204
61"	100	106	111	116	122	127	132	137	143	148	153	158	164	169	174	180	185	190	195	201	206	211
62"	104	109	115	120	126	131	136	142	147	153	158	164	169	175	180	186	191	196	202	207	213	218
63"	107	113	118	124	130	135	141	146	152	158	163	169	175	180	186	191	197	203	208	214	220	225
64"	110	116	122	128	134	140	145	151	157	163	169	174	180	186	192	197	204	209	215	221	227	232
65"	114	120	126	132	138	144	150	156	162	168	174	180	186	192	198	204	210	216	222	228	234	240
66"	118	124	130	136	142	148	155	161	167	173	179	186	192	198	204	210	216	223	229	235	241	247
67"	121	127	134	140	146	153	159	166	172	178	185	191	198	204	211	217	223	230	236	242	249	255
68"	125	131	138	144	151	158	164	171	177	184	190	197	203	210	216	223	230	236	243	249	256	262
69"	128	135	142	149	155	162	169	176	182	189	196	203	209	216	223	230	236	243	250	257	263	270
70"	132	139	146	153	160	167	174	181	188	195	202	209	216	222	229	236	243	250	257	264	271	278
71"	136	143	150	157	165	172	179	186	193	200	208	215	222	229	236	243	250	257	265	272	279	286
72"	140	147	154	162	169	177	184	191	199	206	213	221	228	235	242	250	258	265	272	279	287	294
73"	144	151	159	166	174	182	189	197	204	212	219	227	235	242	250	257	265	272	280	288	295	302
74"	148	155	163	171	179	186	194	202	210	218	225	233	241	249	256	264	272	280	287	295	303	311

DEALING WITH CRAVINGS

The good news is that, having detoxed before starting the Life Plan, you should not suffer horribly from cravings. Once your body has lost its addiction (and it is a very real addiction) to sugar, alcohol, caffeine, chocolate and fatty foods, you simply won't want or need those foods any more. They just won't have that hold over you.

However, don't let your guard down. It can be tempting to think, 'Oh, a little bit of this or that won't do any harm now'. In theory that's true, and I always say that it's better to have a *little* of what you fancy (a square of seriously good chocolate, for example) rather than reaching the point where all your resolve caves in (and splurging on a whole bar of nasty cheap stuff). However, you have to recognise that, once you reintroduce the bad guys, they can easily regain their control over your eating habits. Everyone is different – some of us can cope with a bit of sugar or the odd coffee and keep it as a one-off treat. Others are like ex-smokers – one puff and we're hooked again.

Keep your willpower, keep your determination. What is more important – your health and your looks, or the momentary pleasure of a bit of sugar?

By now, you should find you are far more attuned to your body's needs – as distinct from your wants. You will recognise thirst – and give your body the water it needs (not the soda or double espresso). When you're tired after exercise, you'll know your body needs to replace some salt and so will reach for some slightly salted seeds or nuts, or a handful of corn chips, rather than a chocolate bar. You'll know that eating small, nutritious, balanced meals is the best way to keep going all day. If you suddenly crave something sweet, you'll reach for a banana or make yourself a herbal tea with a spoonful of honey.

Remember, your aim is to get your body off that roller coaster of soaring and plummeting blood-sugar and salt levels. Balance, balance, balance all the way. You can do it.

EATING SOCIALLY

The Life Plan is not like the Detox. Your range of foods is much wider and I wouldn't for one moment expect you to stay home like a hermit for a month! In fact, I'd say it's essential to get out and eat out, whether in restaurants or with friends. This Plan is a blueprint for healthy living forever, so it wouldn't work if you couldn't go to your favourite restaurant. Don't go mad, though. Let's look at some healthy choices for eating out.

THE TEN GOLDEN RULES FOR EATING OUT

1. Choose your restaurant with care. Pick places that cook food freshly and so will be willing to adapt recipes for you. Don't be scared of asking what's in dishes and where they come from. A good restaurant will be delighted to tell you and happy to help. If they're not helpful, vote with your feet and go elsewhere.

2. Order without looking at the menu! You know the food you need. Zero temptation – and you will get a perfect Life Plan meal. Again, good chefs will have no problem with this.

3. Hold the dressings and sauces. Take away the heavy and rich sauces and salad dressings and, ten to one, you have a healthy meal.

4. Ask for food to be grilled or baked, rather than fried. You can eat your fill of steamed vegetables and salad (but watch out for 'salads in sauces' such as coleslaw, potato salad, Caesar salad etc.). Ask for plain vinaigrette, on the side.

5. You don't need three courses – honestly. Try sharing starters and don't even think about pudding until you have eaten your meal . . . and had a herbal tea . . . and waited at least ten minutes – and you will probably find you're too full to eat it.

6. If you really truly crave something sweet, go for fruit salad, or share a sorbet or ice cream, or – if you must – take a spoonful of someone else's Death by Chocolate. Cheese is not a good option – it's very fatty and mucus forming.

7. Drink tea (herbal teas are even better) with your meal rather than wine or water. It will help your digestion.

8. If you really must drink alcohol, try diluted drinks – white-wine spritzers, for example, or a very tall vodka and pomegranate juice. Skip the ice – very cold drinks will stop digestion in its tracks. Drink a glass of room-temperature water for every alcoholic drink.

9. Avoid the nibbles that come with restaurant meals – crisps, bread, *amuse-bouches* – all very tempting, all very calorific and all not good for your body. Just say 'No'. Nibble on a few olives, instead.

10. Eat slowly and stop when you're full. Just because it's on your plate, you don't have to eat it. Listen to your body.

WHAT TO EAT WHERE

FRENCH: the danger here is in the sauces and the liberal use of fat and butter. Even vegetables can come drenched in creamy sauces. Soups can make a good starter, providing they are not swimming in cream. Ask for simple, grilled chicken or fish and plain vegetables or salad. French cuisine always has a good selection of vegetables, so stock up on those. Avoid the *frites*!

ITALIAN: there's more to Italian cooking than pizza and pasta. Minestrone makes a good starter (providing you're not wheat intolerant), as does mozzarella tricolore salad (mozzarella is buffalo cheese and far less mucus-forming than most cheeses) or avocado. Fresh fish and grilled chicken are usually good choices, accompanied by a fresh salad or grilled or steamed vegetables (spinach, broad beans and cavalo nero – black cabbage – are delicious). Risottos make a good choice for vegetarians. If you aren't gluten intolerant, a few breadsticks are fine.

CHINESE: Chinese food is often steamed or stir-fried – great news for the Life Plan. However, the starter section is a minefield. Steer clear of anything deep-fried or cooked in batter, such as pork balls, deep-fried spring rolls, fried seaweed, or prawn crackers. Soups are great. So are most vegetable dishes. Avoid sticky sweet-and-sour sauces and gloopy, MSG-laden sauces in general. Choose plain rice or noodles (if you can tolerate them) rather than fried. Crispy duck and pancakes are OK as a treat. All the chicken and vegetable stir-fries are fine, and the beansprouts, water chestnuts and mushrooms that are used are packed with nutrients. Steamed fish is delicious, too. Eat with chopsticks – it takes longer and you fill up quicker!

THAI: a healthy choice on the whole, although the creamy coconut sauces do pile on the calories. Avoid the prawn toasts and deep-fried spring rolls, though. Rice-paper rolls filled with salad, beansprouts and sometimes chicken are a good alternative. Chicken satay is delicious and good for you – but don't overdo the fattening peanut sauce. The soups are fabulous and so are Thai salads. Steamed fish is great as are the stir-fried vegetable and chicken dishes. Avoid the very spicy curries as they are very acid forming. And veer away from the pork, duck and beef dishes as they are heavy and hard to digest.

INDIAN: choose your dishes with care and you can eat like a King or Queen with any form of Indian cuisine. *Paneer*, sautéed spinach, or chicken *tikka* make excellent starters. For main courses, baked or grilled chicken and fish dishes are best – *tikkas*, *tandooris* or anything 'dry' cooked, rather than creamy sauces (*korma, masala* etc.) and dishes cooked in lots of oil (e.g. *birianis*). Remember that there is more to Indian cuisine than just 'curries' – check out delicately spiced grilled fish, chicken or vegetarian dishes. Avoid deep-fried dishes such as onion *bhajis*, and also the breads and *poppadoms*. Ask for your *poppadoms* to be grilled if you really love them. *Dahls* (curried lentils) are delicious and perfect for the Plan, and experiment with the many varied vegetable dishes, too.

MEXICAN: not a great choice for Life Plan eating because it is so heavy on the red meat, cheese and oil. Also, the heat of the spices is too much for most constitutions (particularly *Pitta*). Salsa is fine, though, served with fresh vegetables – or plump for gazpacho. Avoid the nachos and tortillas and go for something like *arroz con pollo* (chicken with rice) for your entrée.

JAPANESE: on the whole, a very healthy cuisine packed with fish, vegetables, seaweed and mushrooms – high in glyconutrients, and so perfect for the Life Plan. There's a huge choice – salads, *yakitori*, *sushi*, *sashimi*, *ramen* (noodle soups), *bento* boxes are all superb and delicious. There are really only a few dishes you should avoid – deep-fried *tempura* dishes, *gyoza* (dumplings) and *don buri* (vegetables or meat coated in breadcrumbs and deep-friend).

AMERICAN: portion size is your major problem, here, plus a reliance on red meat, deep-frying and chips. However, on the plus side, American cooking does great salads (remember, keep that dressing on the side), and can also offer excellent grilled fish and chicken. Steer clear of Tex-Mex and Southern cuisine if you can (they pile on the fat) and opt for Californian-style dishes – often with healthier Asian influences.

MIDDLE EASTERN/GREEK/TURKISH: piles of choice here, especially if you go for the mezze – small dishes that you share amongst you. Hummus, *tzatziki* and *baba ghanoush* are all delicious and you will usually be given pitta bread (OK if you're not gluten-intolerant) and a pile of crisp vegetables for dunking. *Falafel* and *dolmades* are delicious too. These cuisines excel in wonderful chicken kebabs and grilled chicken and quail, while grilled fish is another good option. Steer well clear, however, of the fried pastries and sickly sweets and puddings. Peppermint tea is a good accompaniment.

ENCOURAGING YOUR FAMILY

The Life Plan is not a diet, and you shouldn't feel you have to eat separately from your family. In fact, the best thing you could do is encourage them to eat with you in this new, healthy way. Given the incidence of obesity amongst our children, you could be giving your children the best possible start in life. Use the recipes at the back of this book to whet their appetites. Encourage them to read this book, too. Use carrots, not sticks – older members of the family could dwell on the fact that eating this way will add years to their lives, and could prevent them getting chronic illnesses. Obviously you won't want to scare children but, by explaining how food works, and what different foods do to their bodies, you can often coax them into healthy eating without any trouble at all. Children are naturally competitive: tell them that eating smart will make them smarter/faster/taller/better at football or whatever and they will often fall over themselves to eat better than their pals.

Cooking the Life-Plan way doesn't involve enormous changes either; your family can still enjoy the same sort of meals, just with a twist. Grilled fish, rather than battered; wholemeal pasta rather than white; new potatoes rather than chips (if you really must have chips, make your own, thickly cut, brushed with olive oil and cooked in a medium oven).

THE LIFE PLAN

WEEK ONE

Your new life starts here. Remember, we're going to introduce the Life Plan a few steps at a time so you won't feel overwhelmed. At the beginning of this (and each) week, fill in your Progress Chart and also check your BMI. Don't be dispirited if they make depressing reading at first – you'll soon notice a huge difference. Don't make a song and dance about going on the programme; it's strange, but people will often try to tempt you off the straight and narrow if they know you're trying to reform your eating. Make your own silent commitment and just get on with it.

DIET CHALLENGE #1: REINTRODUCE FOODS

This week follows the end of your Detox. As you will recall, the Detox also acts as an Elimination Diet that allows you to discover if you have any hidden intolerances or allergies. This week, therefore, you will carefully and systematically be reintroducing different foods. Choose one food (let's take tomatoes as an example). You would need to eat tomatoes at two meals in a day – and in their purest form (so, raw tomato rather than pizza). Make a note in your food diary of the time you took the food and then be especially aware of any old or unusual symptoms – for example, heartburn, indigestion, itching, palpitations. If you get through the day without any adverse reactions, it is highly unlikely that food causes a problem for you. You can then continue testing a new food on the next day.

However, if you *do* get a reaction (e.g. to tomatoes), stop taking the food and wait another clear day before introducing anything else. In this case, it is very likely that the food that caused the reaction is one to which you are intolerant. Leave it out of your diet for the time being. **NOTE:** some people find that, once their bodies have been free of a problem food for some months, it can safely be reintroduced. And if raw tomato affects you adversely, try it cooked as it is less acidic.

DIET CHALLENGE # 2: GO ALKALINE

This week, and throughout the Life Plan, you will be aiming to keep your diet as alkaline as possible, bulking it up with the fruits and vegetables that are essential for good digestion and a healthy balance in the body. This will also continue (in a gentler way) the detox work you have done over the past three weeks, relieving stresses on the detox systems of your body. Refer to the charts on page 19 and 23 – in fact it's a good idea to copy those pages and take them with you to the shops.

BODY CHALLENGE #1: START YOGA OR PILATES

This week, I challenge you to find yourself a good yoga or Pilates teacher and get started with one of these wonderful exercise systems. Also, invest in a good beginner's DVD (your teacher will be able to recommend one for your abilities) and practise at home every day as well. The best time for your yoga or Pilates practice is in the morning, before breakfast. Maybe set your alarm clock an hour earlier, if you can face it! The Sun Salute on pages 52–5 is the perfect start to the day. Don't worry if your moves seem a bit stilted or if you can't reach very far – be very gentle with yourself and always work within your body's limits. If you cannot manage early mornings, you will need to find a time when you haven't eaten for at least two hours (it's essential to do these exercises on an empty stomach).

BODY CHALLENGE #2: TREAT YOURSELF TO A MASSAGE

You're going to be working hard and so a little pampering is called for. Pick any form of bodywork that appeals out of those described on pages 86–8. Pay attention to the touch; notice how your body responds. This week I'd suggest you choose something nurturing and soft such as aromatherapy, Trager, cranio-sacral therapy or MLD.

MIND CHALLENGE #1: MINDFULNESS

This week I want to introduce you very gently to the idea of meditation through the simple technique of mindfulness. I'd like you to set your watch, mobile phone or computer to give you a beep or reminder once an hour. Then just start being aware of what you are doing. If you are sitting at your desk, feel your buttocks on the chair, your feet on the floor. Notice if you are holding any tension anywhere in your body. Check your shoulders, legs, buttocks, neck, jaw – these are common culprits. Notice your breathing – is it deep or shallow. Could it go deeper? How do you feel in your body? How do you feel in your mind? What's worrying you? Is there anything you could do to make your body and mind happier right now? For just 5 minutes be aware of every thing you do – as you do it.

MIND CHALLENGE #2: WRITE YOUR DIARIES

Firstly, remember that you must keep a detailed food-and-mood diary throughout the Life Plan. Don't be tempted to skip this stage – it really is vital. Secondly, I'd like you start keeping a journal this week. Go out and buy yourself a lovely notebook or journal, one that really appeals to you. Maybe a good pen as well. Get in the habit of writing your journal every single day, ideally just before bedtime. Remember this is *your* journal and it's vital you are totally honest – keep it under lock and key if necessary.

Write down anything and everything that occurs to you – how you feel about the Life Plan, how you feel about your relationships, how you feel about your body, how you feel about your life.

BEAUTY CHALLENGE: DETOX YOUR DRESSING TABLE

Go through your bathroom cabinet and your dressing table and get rid of all your old cosmetics and beauty products. In the first place, throw out anything you've had for over a year – it just isn't hygienic any more.

Secondly, take a long hard look at the ingredients in your products – are you plastering chemicals on your skin? If you're brave, get rid of the lot and make your own (see Chapter 5). If you're not quite ready, cut it right down to a simple cleanser and light moisturiser.

YOUR DAY

This might seem like a lot to do. Let's see how a typical day would work. .

WAKING UP: During the Detox, you woke up to a cup of warm water and fresh lemon – it's a great way to start the day and I suggest you continue with it throughout the Life Plan.

If you can do your yoga practice now, that's wonderful. Maybe ease yourself into it, setting the alarm 5 or 10 minutes earlier each day.

BREAKFAST: Gluten-free muesli or porridge is a great start to the day, with almond, soya or rice milk. You can try reintroducing gluten – and it's worth testing each form of gluten (wheat, barley etc.). Cow's milk, even if you are not intolerant of it, is very mucus forming and so I don't advise it – but you could try sheep's milk as an alternative (testing it first of course). Eggs – scrambled eggs, omelettes or poached eggs on gluten-free bread – are another good option.

MID-MORNING: Don't let yourself go hungry. Rice cakes with humus make a great snack. So do sticks of carrot, cauliflower florets and mangetout. Don't be temped to gulp down vats of coffee: experiment with spice and herbal teas – they will help you keep calmer and more in control.

Are you remembering to practise mindfulness every hour? If you can't manage each hour, try four times a day and work up.

LUNCH: If you're at work, come prepared. Bring a nutritious packed lunch. Maybe you can heat up soup at work? As this Plan is much more flexible than a strict Detox, eating out is easier – but do take care (see the guidelines on pages 145–7).

If you possibly can, lunchtime is a great time of day for exercise: you could do some yoga in the office, or take a brisk walk or even a swim. Eat your lunch *after* you have exercised. Are you keeping your food and mood diary carefully?

Include *everything*, absolutely everything, you eat or drink.

TEA: Mid-afternoon is a common time for an energy slump, usually brought on by a heavy lunch packed with processed carbohydrates. However, even if your lunch was exemplary, you can still feel a dip – this is our natural siesta time. Wake yourself up with a handful of unsalted nuts and seeds (packed with essential fatty acids and energy-giving protein). If you're desperate for coffee, try a natural alternative, such as Wake-Up, which contains guaranine (a gentler stimulant than caffeine).

Take the opportunity to do some office yoga (see pages 60–1) to give yourself a natural wake-up call. Remember, drinking can be mindful, too – notice the warmth of the cup, the sensation of warm liquid in your mouth, the taste, the feeling of it sliding down your throat.
Sometimes I have a quick 15-minute power nap. I set my alarm, drift off quite deeply and wake up amazingly refreshed.

AFTER WORK: An ideal time for a yoga class – particularly if you're too busy in the morning. Remember, yoga is not competitive (or it shouldn't be) so pick a class in which you feel comfortable and where you like and trust the teacher.

One day this week (or more if you can), enjoy a gentle pampering session of bodywork. Enjoy the feeling of being in touch with your body.

SUPPER: Spend time cooking yourself the healthiest, most vibrant food you can, packing your meal full of those alkaline vegetables and pulses. A little lean meat, fish or eggs are fine but should be used more as flavouring than as the main focus of your meal. The recipes in the next chapter should fire you up. If you can, try to buy your food fresh each day – or several times a week. Tired food won't give you that vibrant energy you crave.

EVENING: Spend a little time during the week detoxing your beauty products and cosmetics. Don't be temped to hoard – just let go. Remember, letting go is really a wonderful way of making space for new, exciting things. Every evening, take the time to think over the day and write in your journal. This programme isn't just about your body; it's about your mind too. Try your hardest to write without censoring yourself – it isn't for publication!

BEDTIME: Wind yourself down gently if you want a good night's sleep. Don't be tempted to watch horror films or read thrillers just before bedtime. Sink yourself into a lovely warm bath, maybe adding a few drops of lavender, sandalwood or chamomile essential oils mixed in a tablespoon of milk.

LIFE-PLAN TOP TIPS

1. Always chew your food really well – at least 8–12 times. Eat slowly – and mindfully – encouraging good digestion.

2. Keep yourself well hydrated. Keep a bottle of clean, fresh, still, room-temperature water on your desk, or with you through the day. Don't drink cold water, especially not with meals as it slows your digestion. Aim for about 1–2 litres of water a day.

3. Keep blood sugar and energy levels even by eating smaller meals more times a day. *Vata*, in particular, benefits from this.

4. Use every opportunity for exercise – walk up the stairs or to the shops; squeeze in office yoga at odd moments through the day.

5. Get into the habit of using mindfulness – waiting for the train, in the shower, driving your car.

WEEK TWO

You should be in the swing of the Plan by now, and starting to feel some real benefits. No doubt, you'll be enjoying compliments, too, as your new healthy body starts to make itself highly visible. At the beginning of this week, remember to check your BMI and to fill in your Progress Chart.

Don't forget your food-and-mood diary, and your journal – each and every day. Get in the habit of popping them in your bag and taking them everywhere with you.

DIET CHALLENGE #1: START JUICING AND SPROUTING

This week, you continue with your alkalising diet, and you will probably still be reintroducing foods. Be patient – I know this is a long process, but it's vital you take it one step at a time and aren't tempted to cut corners. I'd also like you to start (if you aren't already) boosting your diet with freshly pressed juices. Review the information on pages 30–2 and start experimenting. Also, this week, I want you to use sprouts in your cooking – added to salads or stir-fries, or whizzed up in the juicer with your favourite vegetables. If you haven't tried sprouts before, please do so with an open mind. You may need to experiment – some will be more appealing than others. See page 25 for more information on these superfoods.

DIET CHALLENGE#2: EAT MINDFULLY

One of the very best times to practise mindfulness is when you're eating. Not only is it a wonderful way of focusing and stilling the mind, but it has the added benefit of encouraging you to eat more slowly, chew more thoroughly and aid your digestion. Become aware of each sense as you eat – how does your food look and smell? What is its texture? How does it sound as you eat it? How does it feel in your mouth before you chew, while you chew, as it slides down your throat? This week, you could also start each meal by saying a short prayer, or word, of thanks for the food – be aware of where it comes from, how it was harvested and by whom, how far it had to travel. Could you buy food that is more local, that has been grown more carefully, ethically, environmentally? Eat with a conscience if you can – you are what you eat.

DIET CHALLENGE #3: GET SPICY

If you're not already using herbs and spices in your cooking, now's the time to start. Spices and herbs make food zingy and take away the need for added salt. They also pack their own health kick – check out pages 24–5 for the properties of many herbs and spices. Try them in soups, stir-fries and stews, or fresh in salads. Add to vegetables for an extra burst of flavour or experiment with them by adding to your favourite juices.

BODY CHALLENGE #1: BREATHE DEEP

Continue this week with your yoga or Pilates practice. If you are going to a yoga class, ten to one you will naturally be introduced to breathing exercises. Spend this week specifically focusing on good breathing. Experiment with the exercises given on pages 57–8. Take it easy at first – they may sound easy but are pretty strong medicine. Don't strain; just as you have to build up your muscles in exercise, you need to build up strong lungs bit by bit.

BODY CHALLENGE #2: HYDROTHERAPY

Get wet this week. Take yourself along to a Turkish baths or steam room if you have one (go easy if you're a *Pitta*). If you have a spa nearby that does balneotherapy, hydrotherapy or thalassotherapy – indulge. Water is incredibly healing for the body and mind. Another wonderful water therapy is floatation; it's a superb mind de-stresser. Try my home-spa bath treats as well – in Chapter 5.

MIND CHALLENGE #1: FIRST STEPS IN MEDITATION

Now you're used to mindfulness, meditation is just one step beyond. This week I would like you to find 5 minutes a day for your meditation practice. Experiment with the various types of meditation on pages 75–7 and find the one that suits you best. Don't overdo it: 5 minutes is enough at this stage.

MIND CHALLENGE #2: EXPRESS YOURSELF

Start becoming aware of how you express yourself – both to yourself and to other people. Are you always putting yourself down, or saying 'Yes' when you would love to say a firm 'No!'? Just becoming aware is an important step. Use your journal to chart your negative thoughts and then to challenge them. Are you still parroting things you heard as a child? Are you holding on to self-beliefs that are no longer valid? Are unwanted emotions from your past that have no relevance to your present tarnishing your future?

BEAUTY CHALLENGE: MAKE YOUR OWN CLEANSER AND NOURISHER

Producing your own great beauty products is easy – truly. Make a list of what you need (the recipes are on pages 129–30) and buy your ingredients (you may need to order some ingredients – see Directory). Then simply put them together and give your skin a toxin-free treat.

YOUR DAY

You should find you have a good routine going by now – and you should be starting to feel good, too.

WAKING UP: Continue with your hot water and lemon. If you can, do some yoga – a run through of the Sun Salute is perfect and need not take too long. Each pose should be mindful. In the Ayurvedic tradition, it's common to meditate after yoga and before breakfast, and if you can squeeze in 5 minutes before work, you will set yourself up well for the day. If not, don't worry – you can do it later.

BREAKFAST: Whiz yourself a bumper smoothie for breakfast and give yourself the healthiest start to the day. Try some of the ideas on page 32 & 169 or invent your own. Remember, it's best not to mix fruit and vegetables – stick to one or other. If you like a creamy smoothie, you can add soya, almond or rice milk, or live sheep's yoghurt.

MID-MORNING: A snack mid-morning keeps energy levels high – stick to your crudités and dips or take a handful of nuts, seeds and dried fruits.

Mindfulness should be a way of life now – and keep up those yoga mini-exercises to keep stress under control and both body and mind feeling relaxed. Also, remember to keep an ear out for how you talk to yourself, and how you relate to other people: awareness is the first step to change.

LUNCH: Take yourself swimming or to the Turkish baths if you can. Exercise often makes you feel bizarrely less hungry, so keep your lunch light – a mix of protein and complex carbohydrates (vegetables, pulses, wholegrains, brown rice etc.). If lunch is a salad, remember to include some nutrient-rich sprouts. If you find it hard to digest your meals, try drinking a cup of ginger tea 5 minutes before you eat – it stimulates the digestive 'fire', known in Ayurveda as *agni*.

TEA: Chocolate cake may look tempting but resist! Cakes, cookies and biscuits will give you an energy spike followed by a serious energy slump. Stick to your nuts and seeds, or some rice cakes and hummus. Keep experimenting with new teas, there are some lovely spicy ones around: try those with ginger, cardamom, licorice, coriander and aniseed for a warming drink that also helps your digestion. Don't forget your 1–2 litres of water either – try to drink water in between meals so it doesn't dilute your digestive juices.

AFTER WORK: Hopefully you're enjoying your yoga or Pilates now. Don't be scared to talk over any problems or concerns with your teacher. Before you go out for the evening, or when you get home, do some breathing exercises – you will find you can energise yourself or calm yourself down, depending on the type you choose.

SUPPER: Don't be worried about entertaining while on the Life Plan – you'll find that you can still create gorgeous meals that, as an added bonus, will make your guests feel wonderful. Whether you are cooking for hoards or eating alone, don't forget to eat mindfully. If you fancy going to town with spices or herbs, pick a theme for your dinner party – a Southern Indian vegetarian feast, or fragrant Moroccan tagines or salads, piquant with fresh herbs and spices. Refer to the recipes at the back of the book for inspiration.

EVENING: If you didn't make time for meditation during the day, now is an excellent time to practise. Make sure you won't be disturbed – many people find it's good to dedicate a particular room or spot for meditation when you begin as it helps to focus your mind. But, truly, anywhere will do. Make up your very own cleanser and nourisher and give your skin some pampering. Get used to the simple routine described on pages 125–6.

BEDTIME: Try out the baths on pages 132–3 to put yourself in the mood for sleep. A cup of chamomile or vervain tea will put you in the mood for sleep. Make sure your room is airy. Some people, including me, find that watching mind-numbing sit-coms on TV puts them to sleep immediately. Occasionally I also use a sounds tape in the background. Gentle waves or the sounds of a babbling brook can be very relaxing.

Continue with this plan throughout the week. If you can do yoga every day, that's wonderful but, if not, three times a week is fine.

WEEK THREE

Well done! You're over halfway through and I suspect you're really noticing a big difference now. Don't forget, at the beginning of this week, to check your Progress Chart and also your BMI. You should be noticing real differences now – look back to where you started and I suspect you'll find you've come a long way. Don't be tempted to start cheating or lapsing – it can often happen at this stage in any programme. Keep up with your food-and-mood diary – to remind you why you're choosing healthy options. Don't forget your journal either. By this stage, you may well find a lot of old emotions coming to the fore. Write them all down. You may feel you need the help of a professional counsellor or psychotherapist – I'd encourage you to find one (see the Directory).

DIET CHALLENGE #1: BOOST YOUR GLYCONUTRIENT INTAKE

You should automatically be choosing healthy options now, opting for as much alkaline food as possible. Don't worry too much when you're eating out – you can't be too picky and, if your eating is spot-on the rest of the time, it will all balance out. Keep on juicing and sprouting – your body will thank you. This week, I want you to start adding in those wonderful glyconutrients that I talked about on pages 29–30. Put as many as possible of those superfoods on your shopping list this week and find ways of incorporating them into your diet on a daily basis.

DIET CHALLENGE #2: COOK MINDFULLY

You're already eating mindfully, but now I'd like you to try cooking mindfully, too. Remember that, in the Ayurvedic tradition, it's common for the cook to pray or chant while cooking, putting a sense of loving awareness into the food. Food cooked this way is considered to be full of *prana* (vital energy) and thus more nourishing on a cellular level. I think it's true that the one vital ingredient is love – there is nothing worse than eating somebody else's negative emotions. If that feels odd, then just use preparation and cooking time as a chance to practise mindfulness, being aware of how you're chopping, stirring, arranging.

BODY CHALLENGE #1: FIND A SPORT YOU LOVE

I want you to be as active as you possibly can. Exercise, alongside diet, is the bedrock of a healthy lean body. Keep up your yoga practice but, this week, I would like you also to find a sport or form of aerobic exercise that appeals to you. Look back at Chapter 2 and figure out what kind of exercise would suit your taste and your *dosha*. Check out the possibilities at your local gym or sports centre. Go for it.

BODY CHALLENGE #2: BODYWORK

This week, take your relationship with your body even deeper by investigating some of the more challenging forms of bodywork. This is the point where you will find bodywork as much a mental workout as a physical one, so don't be surprised if old memories or sudden insights pop up as you're on the couch. Choose a form of bodywork that is in line with your own, personal-pain threshold (see pages 87–7 for ideas – you can find practitioners via the organisations listed in the Directory).

MIND CHALLENGE #1: CLEAN UP YOUR RELATIONSHIPS

Think about your relationships. What works? What doesn't? Are you a doormat or a people pleaser? Maybe it's time to change all that. Review Chapter 3 and take time this week to do the exercises

I suggest. If you know you have serious problems in this area, I would suggest you get expert help from a counsellor – see Directory for organisations that can help.

BEAUTY CHALLENGE #1: HAVE FUN WITH FRUIT
This week, keep going with your new beauty regime, using your own home-made products. In addition, try out the fruit scrubs and deep-cleansing and exfoliating treatments in Chapter 5.

YOUR DAY

WAKING UP: Your cup of hot water and lemon should still be part of your routine. If you didn't manage to squeeze in pre-breakfast yoga last week, try it this week. There really is nothing like it to prepare you for the day. If you're really keen, you could even try an early-morning aerobic session: your body burns more calories in the morning so it's the most effective time of day to work out.

BREAKFAST: Make your breakfast a quite substantial meal. Remember the old adage: 'Breakfast like a king, lunch like a prince and dine like a pauper' – it really is true. Eggs and mushrooms contain vital glyconutrients, so try scrambled eggs and mushrooms on rye toast as a great start to the day, or go for brown-rice kedgeree (you can make a great vegetarian version with smoked tofu – see Chapter 8 for the recipe). Keep juicing, too – fresh fruits are high in glyconutrients: add some aloe-vera juice for a real burst.

MID-MORNING: Have you tried office yoga yet? If not, this is the time to start. Remember, many of the exercises can be performed right at your desk. Don't forget mindfulness, either: just because you're meditating every day, now, doesn't mean you should lose this vital and lovely practice.

LUNCH: Take a trip to your local gym or health club and see what's on offer. Could you do a lunchtime class? Be careful, however, not to skip lunch – it's an important meal in the day. Exercise first and then have a big bowl of salad (with some protein) or take a flask of warm, nourishing soup into work with you. It's always best to be prepared and take your own 'ready-meals' so that you're not tempted to grab a sandwich.

TEA: Are you still filling in your food-and-mood diary? Everything counts – down to the last raisin! However tempting that muffin might seem, turn away and have a warming comforting herbal tea with honey instead. Or eat a banana slowly – it will boost your energy levels in a balanced way. If you know you're a people pleaser, practise saying 'No!' at least once a day. You don't have to be bolshy – just firm.

AFTER WORK: Get some good bodywork this week – at least once. If you really want to shift your body and emotions, sign up for a course of Rolfing or Hellerwork – both of these systems can actually change the shape of your body as you straighten up and your fascia become unknotted. Expect emotional changes, too, as you release old hurts and traumas.

SUPPER: Your confidence should be growing, so look further afield for gorgeous recipes. By now, you will know what makes a healthy recipe – and how to adapt even ordinary recipes by choosing different methods of cooking and by slipping in a few new ingredients. Whether you're cooking for hoards or just for yourself, remember to buy and cook the best-possible food you can. You're worth it.

EVENING: As long as you're doing your regular yoga and exercising aerobically three times a week, you can spend your evenings as you wish.

But, stretch yourself – try new things. Don't just slump in front of the television (old associations die hard and, more than likely, you'll want to pour a glass of wine or open a packet of crisps). Get outside if the weather's good. Otherwise, go to the ballet, the theatre, the cinema or a comedy show. Meet up with friends. Life is for living.

BEDTIME: Your skin should be appreciating your new simple beauty routine by now. Remember, don't overdo scrubs and treatments – once a week is more than enough. Think back over the day – what went well, what didn't? Tell your journal all about it. If you find you're worrying about what needs to be done or what you have to do the next day, write down all your worries in your journal and then let them go – there's nothing you can do right now.

WEEK FOUR

You're nearly there. Look back in amazement at how you felt at the beginning of the Plan – are you feeling like a completely new person? I suspect so. How's your BMI? There should be good news there, too.

This week we continue with all the usual elements – alkaline diet, glyconutrients, meditation, exercise, yoga, boosting self-esteem – with just a tiny few extras. It's the final challenge.

DIET CHALLENGE #1: TWEAK YOUR DIET FOR YOUR DOSHA

This week is all about consolidation. Check you're not slipping and that you're still eating a predominantly alkaline diet, that you're juicing and sprouting, and that you're eating those wonderful glyconutrients at every opportunity. Look back at the list of superfoods on pages 27–9 – could you incorporate more into your diet? Be careful that you don't fall into the habit of using vegetables and salad as just an accompaniment to meat

and fish dishes – eat vegetarian a lot, and nibble on raw veggies in between meals as snacks.

In addition, this week I'd like you to think about adapting your diet to suit your predominant *dosha* (see the chart on page 34). This is really the beginning of a process I hope you'll continue in the weeks to come, testing out how avoiding certain foods makes you feel. Your intuition should be firing on all fronts, now, and your body will soon tell you if a food doesn't suit you – so trust the process.

DIET CHALLENGE #2: BE AN ETHICAL CONSUMER

You're already eating and cooking mindfully and, this week, I would like you to think about *shopping* mindfully. The best food is organic or biodynamic, and produced locally and seasonally. Food should be allowed to ripen naturally 'on the vine' or in the field, and not be air-freighted while still unripe (after all, why lose out on all those wonderful glyconutrients?). Champion small shops, box schemes, farmers' markets – anyone committed to producing good food. Some products can't be produced locally, of course; in those cases, pick Fair Trade produce.

Take care when choosing your food, too – smell it, feel it, ask where it comes from. This is your body's fuel – be picky.

BODY CHALLENGE #1: EXERCISE AS A WAY OF LIFE

Have you found your ideal exercise yet? If not, keep trying. Sometimes it takes a while to find something that really works for you. Try thinking outside the box – don't be limited by what's trendy, or what your friends are doing, or what sports are 'supposed' to be for men or women. Why not wrestling, if you're a woman (particularly a *Kapha* woman)? Why not ballet if you're a man (watch Billy Elliot if you've any doubts).

Also, this week, I want you to grab exercise wherever and whenever you can, not just in rigid time slots or classes. Could you cycle to work? Walk to the shops? Take the stairs, not the escalator or lift? Get your body working at every opportunity.

MIND CHALLENGE #1: VISUALISATION

Meditation and mindfulness should be ways of life now. If you are still uncomfortable with meditation, keep trying different forms. If you still baulk, you could try learning Autogenic Therapy, a very pragmatic Westernised form of meditation that is used by airline pilots and top management – see the Directory.

This week I'd like you to try visualisation, too. Follow the instructions on pages 78–9 and keep an open mind.

MIND CHALLENGE #2: DETOX YOUR ENVIRONMENT

Your body is about as clean and pure as it's possible to be after four weeks on the Plan (and your previous three weeks on the Detox). Now, you should be ready to clean up your home and office. Be brutal – think of this as making space for new opportunities, new challenges, new chances. Don't hang on to the old – let it go. Follow the ideas in Chapter 3 to get you started.

BEAUTY CHALLENGE: LEARN MASSAGE

Continue with your beauty regime. This week, take the time to learn head massage (see pages 134–5). Get your partner or a friend to learn with you so you can trade massages. It's well worth trading body massages, too – you'd be surprised how good you can get with a little practice.

YOUR DAY

WAKING UP: Use visualisation even before you get up, visualising yourself coping perfectly and effortlessly with the day ahead. Make time for your meditation and yoga practice if you possibly can. Hot water and lemon, still, please.

BREAKFAST: Check that your breakfast is as nutritious as it possibly can be. Are you juicing? Try adding wheatgrass to the mix for a potent pick-me-up. Track down medicinal mushrooms for their glyconutrient content and maybe add to an omelette or scrambled eggs. Remember to cook and eat mindfully.

MID-MORNING: Mindfulness, office yoga, visualisation – as important as the handful of nuts and seeds, or your mid-morning banana. Have you still got that jug of water on your desk? You could try a thermos of hot water, as well, if the weather is cold (or even if it's not) – it's an Ayurvedic way of dissolving *ama* – toxins – from the body.

LUNCH: The old pattern of long, heavy lunches should be a distant memory, now. If you don't feel like exercising, why not take yourself to a private room and meditate or do some visualisation to prepare yourself for the afternoon ahead? Have you tried adding pulses to your salads? Chickpeas, kidney beans, fava beans, borlotti beans or *chana dal* all work well. Adding nuts and seeds will also boost the protein balance of your meal.

TEA: Get up and walk around a bit during breaks. Remember that having regular breaks actually makes you more productive. Do some stretching or office yoga. Don't let your blood sugar dip – how about bringing in something like falafel for a snack?

AFTER WORK: Now your skin has settled into its routine, you could treat yourself to a facial. Don't, however, go somewhere that will pile back on chemical toxins. Dr Hauschka facials are excellent and use pure ingredients. Otherwise, find someone who does facial acupressure or shiatsu – wonderful techniques that act like a natural face-lift by relaxing tense muscles and smoothing frown lines.

Think about bringing exercise into your social life and family life too. Could you go to the gym or play tennis with your partner? Do an aerobics class with your friends? Go walking or swimming as a family?

And why not introduce your children to visualisation? It's a lovely tool and can help them feel relaxed. Remember, children get stressed too.

SUPPER: Are you confident about eating out? If you hit doubts, reread Chapter 1 and the guidelines for eating out given earlier in this chapter. Don't be afraid to experiment – so many of us eat the same foods every time we go to restaurants. Be bold. Also, don't beat yourself up if you do have the occasional slip. It's only human to make the odd mistake. It happened, let it go. If you're still not seeing that BMI as low as you'd like, try eating from a smaller plate. Don't cook too much food, and throw away any leftovers – in Ayurveda they are considered to be *tamasic* – food with inferior lethargic energy.

EVENING: Look back through your journal – what have you learned about yourself over this last month? Think about further steps you could take to boost your self-esteem or to improve your relationships. Set aside at least one evening a week for real communication with your partner – go out to dinner or cook a special meal at home and really talk about how you feel and what you want from life. This is especially important if you are both working hard, and even more so if you're juggling a family as well.

BEDTIME: By now, your sleep should have settled into a balanced pattern – although, if you have young children, this might still be a far-off dream. Do aim to get them into a regular sleep pattern though, so you have time for you. Otherwise, if, after the four-week plan, you still suffer from insomnia, I would suspect it's due to anxiety. Talk to your doctor and maybe consult a psychotherapist or hypnotherapist who can help with the underlying cause. Remember to keep your room well aired and cool.

HILLARY'S STORY

Nearly two years ago I was diagnosed with gout, which prompted me to embark on a mission to lead a healthier lifestyle. Shortly after my diagnosis I read an article on Joshi and as if by fate that day I bumped into a friend I hadn't seen for a while. She looked amazing – her secret? She had been going to see Joshi! My mind was made up and I booked my first appointment.

In addition to the gout I was suffering from stress and energy slumps throughout the day. Initially I was concerned that the Detox Programme would be hard to stick to as I travel a lot for work and often eat out. But actually it really wasn't that difficult and I felt so much better so quickly. I lost one and three quarter stone in eight weeks. My energy levels became consistent, there were no more peaks and troughs. One of the most dramatic things was the effect on my stress levels – I just felt much better able to cope and much better at stress management.

It has been two years since I went on the Detox Programme. I extended it on to the Maintenance and Life Plans and have basically now made it my way of life, aside from the occasional indulgence in chips! My troubles with the gout have all but vanished and I know that I will never go back to living the way I used to.

HILLARY SHAW WORKS IN THE MUSIC INDUSTRY AS AN ARTIST MANAGER. SHE IS BASED IN LONDON.

CHAPTER SEVEN
HOLISTIC WELLBEING

CONGRATULATIONS. HUGE CONGRATULATIONS. WELCOME TO AN ENTIRELY NEW YOU! I HOPE YOU'VE ENJOYED THE LIFE PLAN AND, IF YOU'VE FOLLOWED THE PROGRAMME THOROUGHLY, I KNOW YOU WILL BE FEELING ALL THE BENEFITS OF A SPRING-CLEANED BODY, MIND AND EMOTIONS. PROVIDING YOU HAVEN'T CHEATED, YOU WILL BE LOOKING SLIMMER AND SEXIER THAN EVER BEFORE – AND QUITE PROBABLY MANY, MANY YEARS YOUNGER. I HAVE PATIENTS WHO COMPLAIN THAT THEY ARE TOTALLY FED UP WITH PEOPLE ASKING WHETHER THEY'VE HAD BOTOX. I EXPECT YOU'VE BEEN HAVING A FAIR FEW COMPLIMENTS – ALONG THE LINES OF 'YOU LOOK WONDERFUL, HAVE YOU BEEN ON HOLIDAY?'; OR, 'TELL ME YOUR SECRET – OR THE NAME OF YOUR COSMETIC SURGEON'. AT WHICH POINT YOU CAN EITHER SUGGEST THEY BUY THIS BOOK, OR SIMPLY SMILE BRIGHTLY AND FEEL DEEPLY SMUG.

THE STEPS YOU HAVE TAKEN OVER THE LAST FOUR WEEKS ARE THE BASIS OF THE HEALTHIEST, HAPPIEST LIFE YOU CAN LIVE. I HAVE GIVEN YOU THE ULTIMATE TOOLKIT FOR A GREAT LIFE. AS YOU'VE SEEN, THERE'S NOTHING MYSTERIOUS OR PECULIAR ABOUT IT ALL – IT'S VERY SIMPLE. LET'S RECAP ONE LAST TIME.

→ Eat the very best possible diet you can. Your food is your body's fuel. Keep it alkaline and boost your diet with superfoods and glyconutrients. Tweak your diet according to your Ayurvedic Metabolic Type.

→ Exercise regularly and smartly. Choose forms of exercise you enjoy so you will stay committed.

→ Stretch your body with yoga or Pilates; expand your lungs with good breathing.

→ Give peace to your mind with meditation and visualisation. Learn to express your feelings and to communicate honestly and authentically.

→ Keep your entire life as toxin-free as possible – whether that means detoxing your bathroom cabinet, your soft furnishings or even your address book.

I want you to be aware that – unless you are a saint or truly blessed with ironclad willpower – there may well be times when you 'fall off the wagon'. I only say this so you're forewarned and won't become despondent if it happens. Remember, one minor setback will not undo all the good that you have already achieved.

As the song says, 'Pick yourself up, dust yourself off, and start all over again.' Look at obstacles as life's challenges that are there to be overcome. Remember that other people may well be jealous of your newfound energy, beauty, commitment and self-esteem. They may even try to coax you out of your healthy habits so that you don't shine so brightly. Don't give them the satisfaction. Sure, you could have a crème brulée every day – I'm not stopping you – but ask yourself how good it is for you. You have to decide once and for all whether it's worth eating certain foods if you're going to experience negative effects. I know, for my own part, that it isn't.

You need to lead your life with a sense of responsibility for your health and wellbeing. Your wellbeing is a duty to yourself. Learn to nurture yourself and, in being kinder to yourself, you will undoubtedly become healthier, happier and more fulfilled.

The Life Plan is just the start. I've given you the ground rules – the blueprint, if you like. Now, it's up to you. Keep up-to-date with what's new and exciting in health news. Until recently, nobody talked about glyconutrients, nobody really knew why blueberries or pomegranates were so wonderful for you. Keep informed, keep your body as healthy as it possibly can be. Never become complacent – whether it's your diet, your exercise, your work or your relationships. Ask yourself, how could I do this better? What would make my life work more wonderfully? How could I look better, feel better, *be* better?

Commit right here and now to living your life to the full. Who knows for sure what happens to us after we die? As the maxim goes, 'This [life] is it – not a dress rehearsal' – so get up there, put on your dancing shoes, and live your best life ever!

TOP TIPS FOR LIVING THE BEST LIFE YOU CAN

1. Take full responsibility for your health. Eat and exercise as well as you can, and have regular check-ups if you are at risk of chronic illness.

2. Remember you are an aquatic being – you need water. Drink two litres of room-temperature water a day and indulge in water treatments, hydrotherapy and swimming.

3. Mind your mind. Meditate and use mindfulness and visualisation to keep your mind in tip-top condition.

4. Be honest in your relationships. Learn to express yourself clearly and confidently. Wean yourself off toxic relationships.

5. Don't be scared to ask for help. Whether it's a counsellor, a gym instructor, a nutritional therapist or simply a friend, reach out and ask for the help you need.

6. Stretch yourself. Keep your attitude flexible. Yoga and Pilates automatically help this, but make conscious decisions to try new things, new ways of living, working and being.

7. Get out into nature, breathe the fresh air, stretch your limbs and your horizons.

8. Laugh, smile, giggle – have fun. Laughter actively releases endorphins, making you feel better and brighter. Get out with friends, focus on books/films/shows that make you laugh rather than cry or scream.

9. Hug your kids, snuggle up with your partner, have regular massages (if you can't afford them, trade with a friend). Be tactile – bodies love to be touched.

10. Realise just how lucky you are. Much of life's misery comes when we are envious or dissatisfied. Be grateful for what you have.

CHAPTER 8
RECIPES

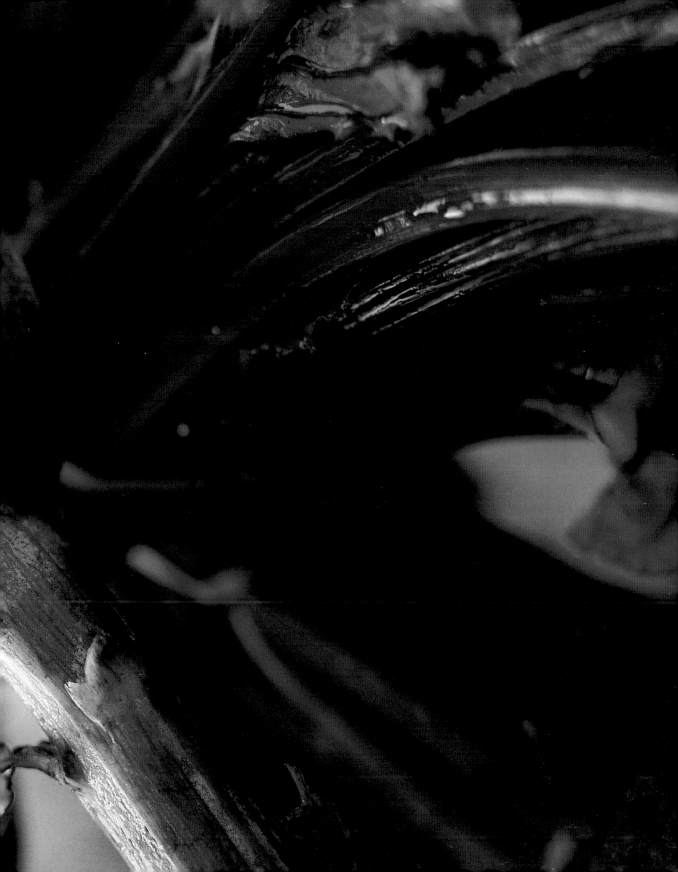

EATING SHOULD ALWAYS BE FUN AND ENJOYABLE – NEVER BORING AND A CHORE. SO YOU WON'T FIND DREARY DIET RECIPES HERE, BUT RATHER, DELICIOUS MEALS THAT WILL DELIGHT YOUR TASTE BUDS AS WELL AS GIVING YOU A HUGE HEALTH BOOST.

THEY REALLY ARE A MOVEABLE FEAST – I WOULD ENCOURAGE YOU TO ADAPT THEM AND EXPERIMENT WITH THEM – ADDING YOUR FAVOURITE TASTES OR SWAPPING INGREDIENTS FOR THOSE IN SEASON. PLAY AROUND WITH HERBS AND SPICES TOO – BUT REMEMBER, VERY SPICY FOOD IS TOO ACIDIC – SO GO FOR SUBTLE, NOT OUTRAGEOUS.

BE PREPARED TO BE OPEN-MINDED – I HAVE INCLUDED MANY DISHES FROM AROUND THE WORLD AND SOME OF THEM COULD BE UNFAMILIAR. GIVE THEM A GO – YOU MAY BE PLEASANTLY SURPRISED. A LARGE NUMBER OF THE DISHES ARE SIMPLE TO PREPARE AND COOK (I KNOW TIME IS OF THE ESSENCE). YET MANY ARE STILL SOPHISTICATED ENOUGH IN THEIR TASTES AND PRESENTATION TO PASS MUSTER AT THE SMARTEST DINNER PARTY.

BREAKFAST

You can buy gluten-free cereal from health shops and, served with soya milk, it's the standard Joshi breakfast. But sometimes a change can be welcome. Try some of these variations.

RICE PORRIDGE

SERVES 1

¼ LITRE/½ PINT WATER
2 TBSP GROUND BROWN RICE
1 TBSP DRIED FRUIT (MIX OF
SULTANAS/RAISINS/APRICOTS/PINEAPPLE)
15G/½ OZ GROUND ALMONDS
1 CARDOMOM POD (BROKEN OPEN TO PROVIDE
   ABOUT 3–4 SEEDS)
MAPLE SYRUP AND SOYA/ALMOND MILK TO TASTE

Put the water, ground rice, cardomom and dried fruit in a saucepan and bring to boiling point, stirring continuously. Continue cooking and stirring for about five minutes until the porridge is thick. Take off the heat and add the almonds. Serve with a little maple syrup and soya or almond milk, to your taste.

PAPAYA MANGO SMOOTHIE

SERVES 1

1 CUP DICED PAPAYA
1 CUP DICED MANGO OR MANGO PULP
CRUSHED ICE
1 TSP HONEY
½ TSP GINGER POWDER

Use a blender to combine the two fruits with the honey and crushed ice.
Pour into a glass, sprinkle ginger powder on the top and serve.

TOFU KEDGEREE

SERVES 1

3 TBSP BROWN RICE (COOKED)
½ PACK OF SMOKED TOFU, CUT INTO SMALL PIECES
1 EGG, HARD-BOILED AND ROUGHLY CHOPPED
1 MEDIUM WHITE ONION, CHOPPED
WHITE PEPPER/SEA SALT TO TASTE
A LITTLE TOASTED SESAME OIL OR GHEE

This tastes great cold too, so you could cook extra and have some for lunch.
Stir-fry the tofu and onion in the toasted sesame oil or ghee until lightly browned. Add the cooked rice and egg and mix together. Season to taste.

DOSAS

SERVES 4

115G/4 OZ URUD DHAL FLOUR (YOU CAN SUBSTITUTE
   CORNMEAL IF YOU CAN'T FIND URUD DHAL)
115G/4 OZ RICE FLOUR
500ML/8 FL OZ WATER
PINCH SEA SALT
½ TEASPOON OF OLIVE OIL OR GHEE

Put the flours and salt in a bowl and add the water, mixing well until you are left with a thin pancake mixture. Cover and leave overnight at room temperature. Heat a tiny bit of oil in a pan until it starts to smoke. Add two tablespoons of the mix and, with the back of a tablespoon, spread the batter out from the centre in a spiral. Once it starts to bubble, flip it over to do the other side (it can take a little practice to ensure they are cooked right through and don't go soggy in the middle). Serve with maple syrup or stewed or fresh fruit.

SPINACH MUSHROOM TORTILLA

SERVES 4

4 EGGS
300G/10 OZ SPINACH, RINSED, CHOPPED AND DRIED
300G/10 OZ SLICED MUSHROOMS (YOUR CHOICE BUT
AVOID BUTTON MUSHROOMS AND TRY TO INCLUDE
SOME MEDICINAL MUSHROOMS IN THE MIX)
1 LARGE ONION, CHOPPED
2 GARLIC CLOVES, THINLY SLICED
1 TSP FRESH THYME (OR ½ TSP DRIED)
1 TBSP FRESH DILL (OR 1 TSP DRIED)
GROUND BLACK PEPPER AND SEA SALT TO TASTE
2 TSP OLIVE OIL

Tortilla, frittata, omelette – call it what you will –
this makes a substantial and delicious breakfast,
packed with nutrients. It also makes a great
packed lunch, served cold.

Stir-fry the onions in just a teaspoon of oil
until golden-brown, then add the mushrooms,
spinach and herbs. Meanwhile beat the eggs
and seasonings in a large bowl. Take the
vegetable mixture off the heat and mix briskly
into the egg mixture.

Add the remaining oil to a frying pan or skillet and
when it's hot, add the egg and vegetable mixture.
Cook until the edges are firm and the bottom is
beginning to brown then either flip over or put in
the oven (if you have an oven-proof frying pan).

SOYA BREAKFAST SAVOURY

SERVES 1

1 TEA CUP SOYA GRANULES
2 TBSP SPLIT BLACK LENTILS
1 TSP CUMIN SEEDS
1 MEDIUM ONION, CHOPPED
½ CUP CHOPPED CABBAGE
½ CUP GRATED CARROTS
1 TSP GRATED GINGER
½ TSP ASAFOETIDA (MUSTARD)
1 GREEN CHILLI, FINELY CHOPPED
2 TBSP SUNFLOWER OIL
4 LEMON WEDGES (OPTIONAL GARNISH)
2 TBSP CHOPPED CORIANDER (OPTIONAL GARNISH)
SALT TO TASTE

Soak the soya granules in hot water for half
an hour. Drain and squeeze out the excess water,
put aside. Heat the oil in a non-stick pan and add
the cumin seeds. When they start to crackle, add
the lentils and fry gently until they turn light brown.
Add the asafoetida powder, ground ginger, green
chilli and onions and fry until the onions are
translucent. Then add the carrots and cabbage
and cook for 4–5 minutes. Add the soya granules
and mix well, and allow the mixture to cook for
another 3–4 minutes. Season with salt, mix well
and garnish with coriander and lemon wedges.

LUNCH

If you're out at work, lunch needs a little preparation. While it is possible to eat out on the Life Plan (and eat very well), it's not a great idea to do it every day, as the choices are inevitably more tempting than virtuous. It also calls for a more flexible attitude – lunch doesn't have to be a sandwich! You could take a flask of delicious nutritious soup, or pack a substantial salad.

CHICKPEA AND SPINACH SOUP

SERVES 6

2 TINS COOKED CHICKPEAS
BIG BUNCH OF GREENS, CHOPPED – YOUR CHOICE – SPINACH IS GREAT, BUT SO TOO ARE KALE, SPROUTING BROCCOLI, MUSTARD GREENS, DANDELION OR DARK GREEN CABBAGE.
1 TBSP SUNFLOWER OIL
1 TSP MUSTARD SEEDS
1 TSP TURMERIC
2 TSP SESAME SEEDS
3 TBSP LEMON JUICE
1 TBSP GROUND CORIANDER
SEA SALT TO TASTE
FRESH CORIANDER LEAVES (OPTIONAL)

Chickpeas and spinach go together beautifully. If you make this with less water, it stops being a soup and becomes a delicious curry instead – eat with brown rice, chapattis or dosas.
Stir-fry the mustard seeds in the oil until the seeds pop. Add the turmeric and mix. Combine with the chickpeas in a large pan and add the remaining ingredients and enough water to cover the greens. Stir and cook for about 15 minutes. Garnish with fresh coriander if you like.

BANG BANG CHICKEN

SERVES 4

450G/1LB CHICKEN, COOKED AND TORN INTO SHREDS
100G/4 OZ SPROUTED SEEDS – YOUR CHOICE
1 CUCUMBER, PEELED AND CUT INTO THIN STRIPS
4 CARROTS, PEELED AND CUT INTO THIN STRIPS
4 SPRING ONIONS (SCALLIONS) CUT INTO THIN STRIPS
1 TBSP SESAME SEEDS
½ LIME, SQUEEZED
DRESSING
150G/5 OZ SMOOTH PEANUT BUTTER
2 TBSP ROASTED SESAME OIL
1 TBSP OLIVE OIL
2 TBSP SWEET CHILLI SAUCE
½ LIME SQUEEZED

This makes a great packed lunch and is also a great lunch to serve to friends. Cut down on the portion size and it's also a useful starter for dinner. The peanut butter sauce *is* fattening (but delicious and OK as a treat) – you can cut down on the quantity of peanut butter if you're feeling virtuous. First make the dressing by warming the peanut butter in a *bain marie* until it melts. Take off the heat and add the other ingredients. Leave to cool. Toss the sesame seeds in a hot dry pan until pale gold and leave to cool. Combine all the salad ingredients. Just before eating add the lime juice, dressing and sesame seeds (you can take these to work in a small pot for a really fresh salad).

TORTILLA

SERVES 4

3 LARGE POTATOES, COOKED AND CUT INTO SMALL CUBES
2 LARGE ONIONS, SLICED AND STIR-FRIED UNTIL GOLDEN
4 EGGS
HERBS TO TASTE (THYME/DILL/BASIL/OREGANO
ARE ALL GOOD)
EXTRA VEGETABLES TO TASTE
(ASPARAGUS/BROCCOLI/SWISS
CHARD/PEPPERS/COURGETTES ARE ALL GREAT).
SIMPLY STIR-FRY UNTIL TENDER.
A LITTLE OLIVE OIL
SEA SALT AND BLACK PEPPER TO TASTE

A frittata or tortilla (as I've already said in the Breakfast section) makes a wonderful lunch on the go. It's substantial, packed with protein from the eggs, and will keep you going all afternoon. Furthermore you can adapt it so easily – pretty well any vegetables can go into it, and you can add fresh herbs in season. You could even add cooked pulses – chick peas work well. If you want to make this lower in calories, you can use 2 whole eggs and 4–6 egg whites. Experiment!

Mix the eggs in a large bowl with the seasoning. Stir in the cooked vegetables. Add a little olive oil to a frying pan and, when hot, add the egg and vegetable mixture and cook until the edges are firm and the bottom golden. Either flip over or transfer to the oven if you have an oven-proof pan.

SUSHI SALAD

SERVES 4

115G/4 OZ BROWN OR RED RICE
425ML/14 FL OZ WATER
1 CUCUMBER, PEELED AND DICED
2 CARROTS, PEELED AND DICED
1 RED PEPPER, SEEDED AND DICED
SMOKED SALMON OR TROUT (OPTIONAL)
MIXED LEAVES (ROCKET/YOUNG SPINACH/LETTUCE ETC)
1 TSP WASABI POWDER, DISSOLVED IN 1 TSP COLD WATER
(OPTIONAL)
DRESSING
75ML/2½ FL OZ RICE VINEGAR
2 TSP JAGGERY (AYURVEDIC SUGAR) OR HONEY
2 TSP FRESHLY GRATED GINGER ROOT
SEA SALT AND PEPPER TO TASTE
TOPPING
1 SHEET NORI SEAWEED (GRILLED FOR A FEW MINUTES
AND CRUMBLED)
1 TBSP SESAME SEEDS (DRY TOASTED UNTIL
GOLDEN-BROWN)

Sushi makes a great lunch – low in fat, high in nutrients and very satisfying. It's a great takeaway lunch but fiddly to make from scratch. However this salad gives the taste and can easily be made at home. If you're new to sushi, be warned that wasabi is very hot – so take it easy to begin with.

Cook the rice for about 40–45 minutes, until tender. Allow to cool. Meanwhile, bring a large pan of water to the boil and blanch the carrots and peppers for just a few minutes, so they're tender but still have bite. Allow to cool. Put a base of salad leaves at the bottom of a bowl. Mix the dressing ingredients together and add to the other ingredients. Toss well, and pile on top of the leaves. Just before serving add the topping.

INDONESIAN VEGETABLE SOUP

SERVES 4

1 LARGE ONION, CHOPPED
4 CARROTS, CUT INTO STICKS
1 SMALL CAULIFLOWER, CUT INTO SMALL FLORETS
2 HEADS BROCCOLI, CUT INTO FLORETS
ABOUT 10 MANGETOUT OR FRENCH BEANS, SLICED
1 INCH PIECE OF FRESH GINGER, GRATED
4 CLOVES GARLIC, SLICED
1 TSP FENUGREEK
1 TSP TURMERIC
½ TSP MUSTARD POWDER
½ TSP GROUND CUMIN
1 LITRE/2 PINTS VEGETABLE STOCK (HEATED)
50G/2 OZ COCONUT, GRATED
1 TBSP OLIVE OR COCONUT OIL
**25G/1 OZ TAMARIND SOAKED IN 150ML/¼ PINT HOT WATER
(SOAK FOR ABOUT HALF AN HOUR)**

Don't be put off by the large ingredient list – it's
a very simple soup to cook. Best of all it needs
to be made the day before so all the flavours
can meld together.

Stir-fry the onion, garlic, carrots and spices
(bar the tamarind) for about five minutes. Then
add the other vegetables and mix well. Strain the
tamarind water over the vegetable mix (discard
the tamarind) and simmer. Add the coconut and
the heated stock and simmer (covered) for about
15 minutes or until the vegetables are tender
but not soggy.

Put in the fridge overnight. You may need to add
a little extra stock or water the next day if the soup
is too thick for your taste.

FRESH SPRING GREEN SALAD

SERVES 2

**150G/5 OZ BROAD BEANS (IDEALLY FRESH BUT FROZEN
WILL DO), COOKED UNTIL TENDER**
BAG OF BABY SPINACH LEAVES
6–8 SHIITAKE OR CHESTNUT MUSHROOMS
HANDFUL OF FRESH PARSLEY OR CORIANDER
4 COOKED ARTICHOKE HEARTS (BOTTLED OR TINNED)
1 TBSP PINE NUTS
DRESSING
1 TBSP FRESH LEMON JUICE
2 TBSP WALNUT OIL
½ TSP MUSTARD POWDER
1 CLOVE GARLIC, FINELY CHOPPED

Whisk the dressing ingredients together. Pile
the rest of the ingredients into a bowl, add some
dressing and toss together (you probably won't
need all the dressing – the salad should be
lightly coated but not soaking).

CHICKEN AND SWEETCORN SOUP

SERVES 2

1 SHREDDED BOILED CHICKEN BREAST
2 CUPS ORGANIC CHICKEN STOCK
**2 TSP CORNFLOWER MIXED INTO A PASTE WITH A LITTLE
WATER**
1 EGG, BEATEN
1 SMALL TIN SWEETCORN
1 TSP SOY SAUCE
1 TSP SALT

Boil the chicken stock in a pan with the salt.
Add the shredded chicken to the boiling mixture,
then the cornflower paste, stirring all the time. Add
one teaspoon of the beaten egg at a time, stirring
gently. This will give the soup its thready look.
Serve with the soy sauce sprinkled over the top.
To make this dish vegetarian just substitute tofu
cubes for the chicken.

SPINACH DAL

SERVES 4

1 TBSP EACH OF CHANA DAL, MASOOR DAL, TUVAR DAL AND
MOONG DAL
50G/2 OZ FRESH SPINACH, WASHED AND TORN INTO PIECES
1 ONION, PEELED AND CHOPPED FINELY
2 GARLIC CLOVES, PEELED AND CHOPPED FINELY
1 TSP OLIVE OIL OR GHEE
½ TSP GROUND TURMERIC
1 TSP GROUND CORIANDER
1 TSP MILD CHILLI POWDER (OPTIONAL)
1 TSP GROUND GINGER

If you can get hold of the various different kinds of
dal used in this dish, it makes it more interesting –
but it's equally good with any combination or
even just with normal red lentils (simply adjust
the quantities).

Soak the dal for about 10 minutes in hot water,
drain. Using a large pan, stir-fry the onion and
garlic for a few minutes in the oil, then add the
spices and stir well. Add the dal and 600ml/1 pint
water, bring to the boil and cook until soft (about
30 minutes usually). You may need to add extra
water during the cooking process.

Serve on its own or with rice for a more substantial
dinner meal.

BLACK BEAN SOUP

SERVES 4

1 CUP DRIED BLACK BEANS
4 TSP EXTRA VIRGIN OLIVE OIL
1–2 SMALL JALAPENO CHILLIES, CHOPPED
1 TSP CORIANDER
1 LARGE CARROT, CHOPPED
1 CUP FINELY CHOPPED CELERY STALKS AND LEAVES
½ TSP ASAFOETIDA POWDER
1 TSP CUMIN POWDER
8 CUPS ORGANIC VEGETABLE STOCK
A DASH OF LIME JUICE
1–2 TEASPOONS SALT TO TASTE
½ TEASPOON PEPPER
FRESH CORIANDER TO GARNISH

Rinse the beans in water and allow to soak in a
lot of water (2 inches above the level of the beans)
for at least 4 hours or preferably overnight. Heat
the olive oil in a non-stick pan, when hot add the
chillies and sauté until translucent. Add the
asafoetida powder, celery, cumin and coriander,
stir and sauté for 4–5 minutes until the celery
appears translucent. Drain the beans and add
to the pan. Stir and add the vegetable stock and
carrot. Cover the saucepan and allow to cook on
a low heat for 1–1½ hours or until the beans are
softer. Remove the saucepan from the heat and
allow to cool. When cool put the cooked beans
into a blender and blend until smooth and creamy
in texture. When ready to eat, reheat the mixture
in a non-stick pan, add a dash of lime juice, salt
and pepper to taste and serve with a sprinkle
of fresh coriander leaves as a garnish.

ASPARAGUS AND SUNDRIED TOMATO PIZZA

SERVES 2

1 CUP FRESH BASIL LEAVES
1 BUNCH ASPARAGUS CUT INTO 1 INCH PIECES
½ CUP SUNDRIED TOMATOES
1 TBSP PINE NUTS
¼ TSP ASAFOETIDA POWDER
2 TBSP EXTRA-VIRGIN OLIVE OIL
SALT TO TASTE
2 TBSP GRATED PARMESAN OR PECORINO CHEESE
1 CUP GRATED MOZZARELLA CHEESE
1 CUP GRATED GOAT'S CHEESE
2 LARGE YEAST AND GLUTEN FREE SPELT PITTA BREADS

Preheat the oven to 350°F/180°C. Heat the olive oil in a non-stick pan on a moderate heat. When hot stir in the pine nuts and sauté until golden brown. Put the pine nuts in a blender, add two tablespoons of olive oil, the asafoetida powder, parmesan cheese and salt and blend until smooth. Steam the asparagus until tender. Spread the pine-nut sauce over the pitta breads, top with the asparagus, mozzarella and goat's cheese and sundried tomatoes. Bake in the preheated oven, until the cheese has melted and they are golden brown.

QUINOA TABBOULEH SALAD

SERVES 2

2 CUPS QUINOA
3½ CUPS WATER
2 TSP SALT
½ TSP ASAFOETIDA POWDER
¼ CUP FRESH LEMON JUICE
½ CUP OLIVE OIL
½ TSP COARSELY GROUND BLACK PEPPER
3 TBSP FRESH PARSLEY, FINELY CHOPPED
2 TBSP FRESH MINT LEAVES, CHOPPED
2 TBSP CUCUMBER, FINELY DICED
2 TBSP TOMATOES, FINELY DICED
LETTUCE LEAVES FOR SERVING

Rinse the quinoa in a large fine sieve under cold water until the water runs clear and then drain well. Place the water and 1 tsp salt in a heavy medium-sized saucepan and bring it to a boil over moderate heat. Add the quinoa, return to a boil, reduce the heat and simmer, covered, for 10–15 minutes or until the grains are translucent and fully cooked and the quinoa's spiral-shaped germ ring has separated. Remove the pan from the heat and set it aside, covered, for 10 minutes to allow the quinoa to firm up and cool. Combine it with the asafoetida powder, lemon juice, olive oil, the remaining salt, black pepper, parsley and mint in a large bowl. Add the cucumber and tomatoes and toss to combine all the ingredients. Chill and serve Quinoa Tabbouleh in lettuce leaves.

DINNER

SPICED CHICKEN WITH LENTILS

SERVES 2

2 CHICKEN BREASTS

MARINADE

3 TBSP SHEEP OR GOAT NATURAL YOGHURT

2 GARLIC CLOVES, CHOPPED

¼ TSP EACH OF GROUND CUMIN, GROUND CORIANDER AND TURMERIC

LENTILS

175G/6 OZ GREEN OR YELLOW LENTILS

1 LARGE ONION, CHOPPED

3 GARLIC CLOVES, CHOPPED FINELY

3 VINE-RIPENED TOMATOES, CHOPPED

1 ORANGE/YELLOW PEPPER, DESEEDED, GRILLED, SKINNED AND TORN INTO PIECES

½ TSP TURMERIC

SEEDS FROM 4 CARDAMOMS, CRUSHED

½ INCH FRESH GINGER ROOT, PEELED AND GRATED

500ML/16FL OZ CHICKEN OR VEGETABLE STOCK, WARMED

2 TSP OLIVE OIL

FEW SPRIGS OF FRESH CORIANDER (OPTIONAL)

This makes a great dinner party dish but equally works well as a cold salad (good for lunch too). Combine the marinade ingredients. Make several large slashes in the chicken breasts and work in the marinade. Set aside in the fridge for at least 2 hours (or overnight).

Stir-fry the onion and garlic in the olive oil until the onions are soft. Mix in the spices and cook for a further few minutes. Add the lentils and the stock and bring back to the boil. Now simmer for about 40 minutes, until the lentils are soft but not soggy. Remove from the heat and add the tomatoes and pepper. Keep warm.

Now grill the chicken for about ten minutes, or until well-cooked inside.

Place a puddle of the lentil mix on a plate and top with a piece of chicken. You can garnish with fresh coriander.

SEAWEED FISHY RICE

SERVES 2

200G/7 OZ SMOKED MACKEREL, TROUT OR SALMON FILLETS, ROUGHLY SHREDDED

200G/7 OZ SHORT GRAIN RICE, JAPANESE OR THAI FRAGRANT RICE

300ML/½ PINT WATER

2 TBSP FINELY CHOPPED SPRING ONIONS

LARGE HANDFUL FRESH SEAWEED

BUNCH OF ASPARAGUS

HEAD OF BROCCOLI

HANDFUL BROCCOLI SPROUTS

1 TBSP TOASTED SESAME SEEDS

DASH OF LEMON JUICE

1 TSP TAMARI

This may sound a bit odd but it's truly delicious. If you have never tried seaweed before, open your mind and give it a go – remember, it's packed with glyconutrients. Once again, this is a dish that works well either hot or cold.

Rinse the rice several times and then cook in the water until it is tender but still has a slight bite (usually about 20 minutes).

Steam the asparagus and broccoli (on top of the rice saves space). Alternatively (and deliciously) you can roast the vegetables with a tiny bit of olive oil.

Mix together the lemon juice, tamari and spring onions – season to taste. Toss everything together and sprinkle with the sesame seeds.

ASPARAGUS, BEETROOT AND POMEGRANATE SALAD

SERVES 4

300G/10 OZ COOKED BEETROOT

JAR COOKED ARTICHOKES

400G/14 OZ ASPARAGUS

BAG OF MIXED SALAD LEAVES (GO FOR PEPPERY PUNCHY
    FLAVOURS SUCH AS ROCKET, BABY SPINACH, WATERCRESS)

1 LARGE RIPE POMEGRANATE

1 LEMON, SQUEEZED

2 TBSP EXTRA-VIRGIN OLIVE OIL

2 CLOVES OF GARLIC, VERY FINELY SLICED

1 TSP HONEY

SMALL BUNCH OF CHIVES (OPTIONAL) AND/OR EDIBLE
    FLOWERS

This is a truly sophisticated salad, packed with
my favourite phytonutrients.

Roast or grill the asparagus until tender. Slice
the beetroot into very thin slices. Run your knife
around the skin of the pomegranate, twist hard
and break in half. Turn inside out and pull the
seeds away, catching any juice in a bowl. Slice
the artichokes finely. Mix the ingredients together
(lay the beetroot carefully on top or it will turn
everything bright purple). Whizz up a dressing with
the olive oil, lemon juice, pomegranate juice, garlic
and honey (you may like a little more honey – taste
and try). Drizzle over the salad and garnish with
chives if you like and any edible flowers
(nasturtium, borage, chive etc.).

CHICKEN SATAY

SERVES 4

1KG/2LB CHICKEN, CUT INTO SMALL CUBES

MARINADE

1 ONION, FINELY CHOPPED

2 GARLIC CLOVES, FINELY CHOPPED

1 TSP GROUND CORIANDER

1/2 TSP GROUND CUMIN

1/2 TSP MILD CHILLI POWDER

2.5CM/1 INCH PIECE OF GINGER, PEELED AND CHOPPED

2 TBSP TAMARI

1 TBSP LIME JUICE

1 TBSP TOASTED SESAME OIL

1 TSP MAPLE SYRUP OR HONEY

Mix the marinade ingredients in bowl. Put in the
chicken and make sure all the pieces are well
coated. Put in the fridge for at least two hours
(preferably overnight). Thread onto skewers
and grill for about ten minutes, turning often.
Serve with rice or salad and satay sauce (see
below).

SATAY SAUCE

You can buy ready-made satay sauce (bumbu sate)
but it will contain sugar and soy sauce. Try this –
it's easy to make and will keep in the fridge (in a
jar with a lid) for up to a week. You can also freeze
it. The basic ingredients are the same as those
for the marinade. To these, add 250g/8oz peanut
butter (choose one without added sugar or salt)
and whiz the whole lot in a blender or food
processor. Add olive oil to your favourite
consistency, then simmer until warm.

GADO-GADO

SERVES 4

125G/4 OZ GREEN BEANS/MANGE TOUT/SUGAR SNAP
    PEAS, CUT INTO DIAGONAL SLICES
125G/4 OZ CARROTS, PEELED AND THINLY SLICED
125G/4 OZ DARK GREEN CABBAGE, KALE OR SPRING
    GREENS, WASHED AND SHREDDED
125G/4 OZ CAULIFLOWER/BROCCOLI FLORETS
125G/4 OZ BEAN SPROUTS
1 POTATO, BOILED, PEELED AND SLICED
½ CUCUMBER, THINLY SLICED
2 HARD-BOILED EGGS, CUT INTO QUARTERS
BUNCH OF SALAD LEAVES (WATERCRESS/ROCKET/
    YOUNG SPINACH), WASHED AND TORN INTO PIECES
SATAY SAUCE (AS PAGE 177)

Another Indonesian dish, packed with
phytonutrients. It can be served with the sauce
warm, or cold for a packed lunch.
Steam the vegetables for about five minutes,
so they are soft but still have plenty of crunch.
Drain and set aside to cool.
Put the salad leaves in a bowl. Pile the vegetables,
beansprouts, potato, cucumber and eggs on top.
Warm the satay sauce and pour over the salad.

HERBY FISH WITH LIME

SERVES 4

4 FILLETS OF FIRM WHITE FISH
2 TBSP LIME JUICE, FRESHLY SQUEEZED
4 SHALLOTS, CHOPPED
4–6 SUN-RIPENED TOMATOES
4 GARLIC CLOVES, FINELY CHOPPED
BUNCH PARSLEY, CHOPPED
1 TSP FRESH ROSEMARY, CHOPPED
1 TSP FRESH THYME, CHOPPED
1 TSP PAPRIKA

This is really zingy with fresh herbs. If, however,
you can't get the herbs fresh, you can make do
with dried but cut the amount of herbs by one half.
Mix together all the ingredients (except the fish).
Place the fish fillets on a non-stick baking tray and
spread the herb/onion/tomato mixture over the
top. Cover tightly with foil and bake in the oven
for about half an hour, until the fish is well-cooked.
Serve with steamed vegetables/salad and
new potatoes.

CHICKEN KEBAB

SERVES 4

1.4KG/3LB CHICKEN, CUT INTO CUBES
3 CLOVES GARLIC, MASHED
JUICE FROM 2 LEMONS
1 TBSP OLIVE OIL
2 TSP FRESH THYME (OR ½ TSP DRIED)
8 SMALL SHALLOTS, PEELED BUT LEFT WHOLE
2 GREEN PEPPERS, CUT INTO SQUARES
8 SUN-RIPENED CHERRY TOMATOES
GROUND BLACK PEPPER

Mix together the oil, lemon juice, garlic, pepper and thyme. Add the chicken and make sure it's well coated. Leave for two hours minimum (ideally overnight). Thread the marinated chicken onto skewers, alternating with tomatoes, pepper and onions. Grill for about fifteen minutes, turning regularly.

QUICK QUICK CHICKEN

SERVES 1

180G SLICED CHICKEN BREAST (SLICED WITH A PAIR OF SCISSORS)
½ TBSP OF SUNFLOWER OIL
2 CLOVES GARLIC, CRUSHED
½ TSP OF RED CHILLI POWDER OR BLACK PEPPER
1 TSP SOY SAUCE
2 TSP OYSTER SAUCE
1 TSP SUGAR
6–8 BASIL LEAVES
SALT TO TASTE

Heat the oil in the pan and stir-fry the chicken for 2–3 minutes. Add all the other ingredients one at a time, stirring after each one is added to mix well. Serve garnished with basil leaves. To make this dish vegetarian just substitute thin slices of tofu for the chicken.

MOROCCAN SEA BASS WITH CHERMOULA

SERVES 2

2 SEA BASS (RED MULLET AND SEABREAM ALSO WORK WELL)
2 CLOVES GARLIC, PEELED
3 TBSP FRESH CORIANDER, FINELY CHOPPED
1 TSP FRESH PARSLEY, FINELY CHOPPED
1 TBSP OLIVE OIL
JUICE OF HALF A LEMON
1 TSP PAPRIKA
½ TSP GROUND CUMIN
½ TSP GROUND CORIANDER
½ TSP SEA SALT

Chermoula is a delicious herby spicy garlicky marinade that is a classic part of Moroccan cooking. You can use it on chicken or game too, and it also works well with lightly cooked vegetables, such as carrots, turnips or courgettes. Ideally you should use a pestle and mortar for grinding the spices, but you can use a food processor – just don't process them too far. Crush the garlic and sea salt together, then pound in the fresh herbs. Add the remaining ingredients (bar the fish) and mix well together.
Make several deep slashes across both sides of the fish. Spread the chermoula all over the fish, pressing it down into the gashes. Leave to marinade for at least 3 hours.
Grill the fish under a hot grill for about 10–15 minutes on each side.

TEMPEH-TOFU-TAMARI

SERVES 4

400G/14 OZ TEMPEH
350G/12 OZ TOFU
115G/4 OZ BEANSPOUTS
6 SPRING ONIONS, SLICED FINELY
2 STICKS CELERY, DE-STRUNG AND CHOPPED FINELY
½ INCH GINGER ROOT, PEELED AND CHOPPED FINELY
1 CLOVE GARLIC, CHOPPED FINELY
1 TBSP TAMARI
½ TSP WASABI (OPTIONAL, ACCORDING TO TASTE)
1 TSP RUNNY HONEY
6 TBSP WATER
A LITTLE OLIVE OIL FOR STIR-FRYING

Another useful dish than can be eaten hot or cold.
Serve with Japanese or wild rice, with a side order
of seaweed, asparagus or broccoli.
Cut the tofu and tempeh into thin pieces and grill
until they turn yellow. Turn over and repeat on the
other side.
Stir-fry the spring onion, celery, ginger and garlic
for a few minutes and then add the tamari, wasabi
and honey. Mix well together and add the water.
Bring to the boil and allow to simmer for about 2
minutes. The celery should make it naturally salty
so you shouldn't need to add any salt. Add the
tempeh, tofu and beansprouts. Stir and simmer
for just 2 more minutes.

FISH IN FOIL

1 SERVING

1 FISH STEAK
ONE SMALL LEMON
SIX CHERRY TOMATOES
¼ CUP MELTED BUTTER MIXED WITH 2 TBSP EXTRA-VIRGIN OLIVE OIL
1 CLOVE OF GARLIC, CRUSHED
1 TBSP DRY WHITE WINE
1 TSP PARSLEY, FINELY CHOPPED
1 CUP OF BOILED WILD RICE
A SQUARE PIECE OF ALUMINIUM FOIL

Preheat the oven to 350°F/180°C. Cut the lemon
into thin slices and arrange down the centre of the
aluminium foil (on the shiny side). Place the fish
steak on top, and cover with a few more lemon
slices. Arrange the cherry tomatoes along both
sides. Mix the butter, olive oil, white wine, garlic
and parsley and pour over the top. Fold the
aluminium foil sealing the contents securely
(this prevents the flavour escaping). Cook in the
preheated oven for approximately 20 minutes.
Serve in the foil with the wild rice.

FRIED INDONESIAN STYLE RICE

SERVES 2

2 CUPS BOILED RICE
1 LARGE BONELESS CHICKEN BREAST
1 TBSP SUNFLOWER OIL
1 SMALL TO MEDIUM SIZED ONION, SLICED
3 CLOVES GARLIC, CRUSHED
1 TSP CORIANDER POWDER
½ TBSP SOY SAUCE
SALT AND PEPPER TO TASTE
1 CUP PLAIN LIVE (SHEEP OR GOAT) YOGHURT
2 TBSP CORIANDER, CHOPPED
2 GREEN CHILLIES, FINELY CHOPPED

Heat the oil, add the onions and fry until they turn light brown. Add the cubed chicken and fry for 3–4 minutes. Add the crushed garlic and coriander powder and stir for one minute. Add the soy sauce and the cooked rice, with salt and pepper to taste and mix well. Serve with the yoghurt, garnished with the chopped coriander and green chillies, To make this dish vegetarian just substitute diced tofu for the chicken.

OKRA CURRY

SERVES 4

500 G OF CHOPPED OKRA INTO SMALL CUBES
2 TBSP SUNFLOWER OIL
¼ TSP CUMIN SEEDS
¼ TSP MUSTARD SEEDS
¼ TSP ASAFOETIDA POWDER
2 SMALL TOMATOES, CHOPPED
3 CLOVES OF GARLIC, CRUSHED
½ TSP TURMERIC POWDER
½ TSP CUMIN POWDER
½ TSP CORIANDER POWDER
½ TSP CHILLI POWDER
1 TSP SALT (TO TASTE)

Heat the oil in a non-stick pan, add cumin and mustard seeds. When they crackle add the asafoetida powder and stir for 5 seconds. Add the chopped okra and fry in the hot seasoning. Add tomatoes, garlic and all the remaining ingredients. Stir, cover and allow to cook for another 5 minutes. Serve with white or brown basmati rice.

SNACKS

FALAFEL
MAKES ABOUT 18 FALAFEL
450G/1LB COOKED CHICKPEAS
100ML/4 FL OZ WATER
2 TBSP SOYA FLOUR
4 EGGS (BEATEN)
2 TBSP FRESH PARSLEY (CHOPPED)
2 TSP TURMERIC
2 TSP CUMIN
2 TBSP BASIL (FRESH OR DRIED)
2 TBSP FRESH MARJORAM (OPTIONAL)
SALT AND PEPPER TO TASTE
A LITTLE OLIVE OIL

These make a great snack on their own, or you can pop them into pitta pockets (if you're not gluten-intolerant) or dosas (see breakfast recipes) or wheat-free chapattis (see below). They're delicious hot or cold.

Whizz the chickpeas in a food processor and add to the other dry ingredients. Stir together with the eggs until you get a firm mixture. Form into balls, about the size of golf balls, or flat patties. Place on an oiled baking sheet and drizzle a drop or two of oil over the top of each. Bake at about 160°C for around 20 minutes.

AUBERGINE DIP WITH RYE CRISPBREADS
SERVES 2
DIP
2 AUBERGINES
3 GARLIC CLOVES, CHOPPED FINELY
2 TBSP TAHINI
1 TBSP FRESH LEMON OR LIME JUICE
1 TBSP OLIVE OIL
¼ TSP GROUND CUMIN
CRISPBREADS
2 TBSP RYE FLOUR
1 TBSP BARLEY FLOUR
6 TBSP WATER
A LITTLE OLIVE OR SUNFLOWER OIL

A hugely versatile dip – scrumptious with crudités as well as these useful wheat-free crispbreads. It also makes a great accompaniment to kebabs or any grilled meat or fish.

First make the dip. Roast the aubergines until the skin is completely blistered – around 20–25 minutes. Scrape out the flesh and discard the skin. Put in a food processor with the rest of the ingredients and whizz to your preferred consistency (you can add a little water if it's too stiff a paste). Put in the fridge.

Now make the crispbreads. Heat the oven to 250°C/gas mark 9. Lightly grease a non-stick baking tray with the merest dab of oil. Mix together the flours and water and beat to a smooth batter. Using a tablespoon, pour spoonfuls of the batter onto the tray (they will spread out into circles). Bake on the top shelf of the oven for around 10 minutes (until they are crisp and golden). Allow to cool on a rack.

SUN-DRIED TOMATOES AND PINE NUTS

Makes 8

8 SUN-DRIED TOMATOES (DRAINED)
1 CLOVE GARLIC, CHOPPED FINELY
1 TBSP FRESH PARSLEY OR CORIANDER, CHOPPED
4 TBSP PINE NUTS, DRY-ROASTED OR GRILLED

Mix the pine nuts, garlic and parsley and pile a
dollop of the mixture over each of the sun-dried
tomatoes. Serve with olives as an appetiser
or snack. This is also good spread over the
crispbreads (above).

SALMON CARPACCIO WITH FRESH HERBS

SERVES 2

2 SALMON FILLETS, SLICED AS FINELY AS POSSIBLE
   (YOU CAN CAREFULLY HIT THE FISH WITH A ROLLING PIN
   TO MAKE THEM EVEN THINNER – PUT IT INSIDE AN OILED
   PLASTIC BAG BEFORE HITTING)
JUICE OF HALF A LEMON
1 TBSP OLIVE OIL
20 FRESH TARRAGON LEAVES
2 TBSP CHOPPED HERBS (YOUR CHOICE FROM A MIX
   OF THYME, PARSLEY, MARJORAM, CHIVES)

Sublime as an appetiser or light first course.
Mix the ingredients (bar the salmon) together –
season to taste.
Place the salmon on a plate and drizzle the
dressing over the top.

SPICED SWEETCORN

SERVES 2

1 TIN SWEETCORN (THE NO-ADDED SUGAR OR SALT VARIETY
   IF POSSIBLE)
1 TBSP FRESH CORIANDER, CHOPPED
1 ONION, FINELY CHOPPED
1 TSP MUSTARD SEEDS
1 TSP OLIVE OIL OR GHEE
1 TSP MILD CHILLI POWDER
1 TSP FRESH LEMON JUICE
A LITTLE SEA SALT

Stir-fry the mustard seeds in the oil. When they
start to pop, add the sweetcorn. Cook for about 2
minutes before adding the rest of the ingredients.
Cook for a further 5 minutes.

WHEAT-FREE CHAPATTIS

Makes 2

45G/1½ OZ RICE FLOUR
15G/½ OZ GRAM FLOUR
15G/½ OZ CORNFLOUR
5 TBSP WATER
PINCH SEA SALT
A LITTLE SUNFLOWER OIL OR GHEE

These are a boon if you miss a sandwich for lunch – simply fill with pretty well any filling you like (salads go well) and fold over like an envelope. Needless to say, they make a great alternative to rice with any curry.

Mix the flours, salt and water into a thin batter mix. Heat the oil or ghee in a non-stick frying pan. When it is hot, pour in half the mixture and allow to spread. Cook for about 2 minutes and then turn over. Cook on the other side for another 2 minutes.

PARSLEY AND YOGHURT SPREAD

2 SERVINGS

1 CUP LOW FAT ORGANIC GOAT, COW OR SHEEP'S YOGHURT.
1 TBSP FINELY CHOPPED PARSLEY
1 TBSP FINELY CHOPPED GREEN SPRING ONIONS OR CHIVES
2 CRUSHED GARLIC CLOVES
SALT TO TASTE

Pour the yoghurt into a muslin cloth, tie over the sink and allow to hang for 15–20 minutes. Put the yoghurt into a blender, add all the other ingredients and blend. Serve chilled. Garnish with some chopped parsley.

ORGANIC VEGETABLE SPREAD

2 SERVINGS

2 TBSP OF SOYA MILK
1 CUP LOW FAT GOAT CHEESE
2 TBSP CHOPPED CELERY
½ CUP CHOPPED CARROTS
½ CUP CHOPPED GREEN PEPPER
2 TBSP CHOPPED SPRING ONIONS OR CHIVES
1 SMALL FIRM TOMATO CHOPPED
¼ CUCUMBER CHOPPED
1 TBSP CHOPPED PARSLEY
SALT TO TASTE

Combine all the ingredients in a bowl, mix well. Chill for 2 hours. Store in a glass jar. Use as required on toasted spelt bread or as a garnish with your salad.

CHAPTER 9
DIRECTORY

* = international organisation or website giving international resources

THE JOSHI CLINIC
57 Wimpole Street,
London W1G 8YP
T: 020 7487 5456
www.joshiclinic.com

CHAPTER ONE

THE INSTITUTE FOR OPTIMUM NUTRITION (ION)
T: 020 8877 9993
www.ion.ac.uk

BRITISH ASSOCIATION OF NUTRITIONAL THERAPY (BANT)
T: 08706 061284
www.bant.org.uk

AUSTRALASIAN COLLEGE OF NUTRITIONAL AND ENVIRONMENTAL MEDICINE (ACNEM)
www.acnem.org

DIETICIANS OF CANADA
www.dieticians.ca

ALLERGY ELIMINATION (NAET METHOD)
NAET for Europe
T: 00 33 450 51 31 50
www.naeteurope.com

NAET (NORTH AMERICA AND WORLD-WIDE)
www.naet.com

JUICING/SPROUTING/WHEAT GRASS SUPPLIERS
Wholistic Research
T: 01438 833100
www.wholisticresearch.com

THE SPROUT PEOPLE*
www.sproutpeople.com

LIVING FOODS
T: 0845 330 4507
www.livingfoods.co.uk

ORGANIC FOOD
The Soil Association
T: 0117 314 5000
www.soilassociation.org

BIO-DYNAMIC FOOD
Biodynamic Agricultural Association
T: 01453 759501
www.anth.org.uk/biodynamic

DEMETER INTERNATIONAL *
www.demeter.net

THE NATIONAL ASSOCIATION OF FARMERS' MARKETS
T: 0845 230 2150
www.farmersmarkets.net

CHAPTER TWO

BRITISH WHEEL OF YOGA
T: 01529 306851
www.bwy.org.uk

YOGA NETWORK*
www.yoganetwork.org

THE PILATES FOUNDATION UK LIMITED
T: 07071 781859
www.pilatesfoundation.com

PILATES METHOD ALLIANCE*
www.pilatesmethodalliance.org

NATIONAL REGISTER OF PERSONAL TRAINERS (UK)
T: 0870 200 6010
www.nrpt.co.uk

CHAPTER THREE

BRITISH MEDITATION SOCIETY
T: 01460 62921
www.osteopath.plus.com/bms/

TRANSCENDENTAL MEDITATION
T: 08705 143733
www.t-m.org.uk

DHARMANET INTERNATIONAL*
www.dharmanet.org

CENTER FOR MINDFULNESS*
www.umassmed.edu/cfm

THE SAMARITANS
T: 08457 909090
www.samaritans.org.uk

BEFRIENDERS*
www.befrienders.org

DEPRESSION ALLIANCE
T: 020 7278 6747
www.depressionalliance.org

ANXIETY NETWORK*
www.anxietynetwork.com

RELATE
www.relate.org.uk

JOB STRESS NETWORK*
www.workhealth.org

INSTITUTE OF STRESS MANAGEMENT
www.isma.org.uk or www.isma-usa.org

WORLD HEALTH ORGANISATION (WHO)*
www.who.int

BRITISH ASSOCIATION FOR COUNSELLING AND PSYCHOTHERAPY
T: 0870 443 5252
www.bacp.co.uk (comprehensive links to support groups and helplines)

AUSTRALIAN COUNSELLING ASSOCIATION
www.theaca.net.au

CANADIAN COUNSELLING ASSOCIATION
www.ccacc.ca
www.psychotherapy.co.za (South Africa)

MENTAL HEALTH FOUNDATION
T: 020 7803 1100
www.mentalhealth.org.uk

**THE FLOATATION TANK
ASSOCIATION**
T: 020 7627 4962
www.floatationtankassociation.net

**MASSAGE THERAPY ASSOCIATION
SOUTH AFRICA**
www.mtasa.co.za

THE AROMATHERAPY CONSORTIUM
T: 0870 7743477
www.aromatherapy-regulation.org.uk

**CANADIAN FEDERATION OF
AROMATHERAPISTS**
www.cfacanada.com

**INTERNATIONAL FEDERATION OF
AROMATHERAPISTS (AUSTRALIA)**
www.ifa.org.au

**BIODYNAMIC PSYCHOTHERAPY
AND MASSAGE**
T: 07000 794725
www.lsbp.org.uk

THE BOWEN ASSOCIATION
T: 0700 269 8324
www.bowen-technique.co.uk
www.bowtech.com *

**THE SOMA INSTITUTE
(CHAVUTTI THIRUMAL)**
T: 07790 562781 www.chavutti.com

**BRITISH CHIROPRACTIC
ASSOCIATION**
T: 0118 950 5950
www.chiropractic-uk.co.uk

**THE WORLD CHIROPRACTIC
ALLIANCE***
www.worldchiropracticalliance.org

**THE CRANIO-SACRAL THERAPY
ASSOCIATION OF THE UK**
T: 07000 784735
www.craniosacral.co.uk

**THE SUTHERLAND SOCIETY
(CRANIAL OSTEOPATHY)**
www.cranial.org.uk

MLD UK
T: 01592 748008
www.mlduk.org.uk

VODDER SCHOOL (MLD)*
www.vodderschool.com

MCTIMONEY CHIROPRACTIC
T: 01865 880974
www.mctimoney.org.uk

GENERAL OSTEOPATHIC COUNCIL
T: 020 7357 6655
www.osteopathy.org.uk

**AUSTRALIAN OSTEOPATHIC
ASSOCIATION**
www.osteopathic.com.au

**ASSOCIATION OF
REFLEXOLOGISTS**
T: 0870 5673320
www.aor.org.uk

**INTERNATIONAL COUNCIL OF
REFLEXOLOGISTS***
www.icr-reflexology.org

THE ROLF INSTITUTE*
www.rolf.org

HELLERWORK INTERNATIONAL*
www.hellerwork.com

SHEN THERAPY*
www.shentherapy.info

**INTERNATIONAL ASSOCIATION FOR
KAIROS THERAPY***
T: 0131 478 4780
www.kairostherapy.co.uk

THE SHIATSU SOCIETY
T: 0845 1304560
www.shiatsu.org

**THE SHIATSU THERAPY
ASSOCIATION OF ONTARIO**
www.shiatsuassociation.com

**THE SHIATSU THERAPY
ASSOCIATION OF AUSTRALIA**
www.staa.org.au

TRAGER® ASSOCIATION*
www.trager.com

**WORLDWIDE AQUATIC BODYWORK
ASSOCIATION (WATSU ETC)***
www.waba.edu

ZERO BALANCING*
www.zerobalancing.com

**BIOMONITORING OF TOXIC
CHEMICALS.**
WWF and Co-Operative Bank's
Chemicals and Health Campaign –
www.wwf.org.uk/chemicals or
www.co-operativebank.co.uk/safer

CHAPTER FOUR

ALCOHOLICS ANONYMOUS (AA)
T: 0845 769 7555
www.alcoholics-anonymous.org.uk

AA (AUSTRALIA)
www.aa.org.au

AA (CANADA)
www.alcoholics-anonymous.org

AA (SOUTH AFRICA)
www.alcoholics.org.za

**ASH (ACTION ON SMOKING AND
HEALTH)**
www.ash.org.uk

**INSTITUTE FOR COMPLEMENTARY
MEDICINE (ICM)**
T: 020 7237 5165
www.i-c-m.org.uk

**BRITISH COMPLEMENTARY
MEDICAL ASSOCIATION (BCMA)**
T: 0845 345 5977
www.bcma.co.uk

**AUSTRALIAN COMPLEMENTARY
HEALTH ASSOCIATION**
www.diversity.org.au

**AUSTRALIAN NATURAL
THERAPISTS ASSOCIATION (ANTA)**
www.anta.com.au

**AUSTRALASIAN INTEGRATIVE
MEDICINE ASSOCIATION (AIMA)**
www.aima.net

**CANADIAN COMPLEMENTARY
MEDICAL ASSOCIATION (CCMA)**
www.ccmadoctors.ca

BRITISH ACUPUNCTURE COUNCIL
T: 020 8735 0400
www.acupuncture.org.uk

**AUSTRALIAN ACUPUNCTURE &
CHINESE MEDICINE ASSOCIATION**
www.acupuncture.org.au

**THE CHINESE MEDICINE AND
ACUPUNCTURE ASSOCIATION OF
CANADA**
www.cmaac.ca

**ALL AYURVEDA* (PORTAL SITE
WITH INTERNATIONAL LINKS)**
www.allayurveda.com

THE SOCIETY OF HOMEOPATHS
T: 01604 4506611
www.homeopathy-soh.com

**AUSTRALIAN ASSOCIATION OF
PROFESSIONAL HOMEOPATHS**
www.homeopathy.org.au

**NATIONAL UNITED PROFESSIONAL
ASSOCIATION OF TRAINED
HOMEOPATHS (CANADA)**
www.nupath.org

**HOMEOPATHIC ASSOCIATION OF
SOUTH AFRICA**
www.hsa.org.za

**GENERAL HYPNOTHERAPY
REGISTER***
T: 01590 683770
www.general-hypnotherapy-
register.com

THE HYPNOTHERAPY ASSOCIATION
T: 01257 262124
www.thehypnotherapyassociation.
co.uk

**NATIONAL INSTITUTE OF MEDICAL
HERBALISTS**
T: 01392 426022
www.nimh.org.uk

**NATIONAL HERBALISTS
ASSOCIATION OF AUSTRALIA**
www.nhaa.org.au

**ONTARIO HERBALISTS
ASSOCIATION**
www.herbalists.on.ca

**GENERAL COUNCIL AND REGISTER
OF NATUROPATHS**
T: 01458 840072
www.naturopathy.org.uk

**CANADIAN ASSOCIATION OF
NATUROPATHIC DOCTORS (CAND)**
www.naturopathicassoc.ca

**SOCIETY OF TEACHERS OF THE
ALEXANDER TECHNIQUE (STAT)**
T: 0845 230 7828
www.stat.org.uk

**THE AUSTRALIAN SOCIETY OF
TEACHERS OF THE ALEXANDER
TECHNIQUE (AUSTAT)**
www.alexandertechnique.org.au

**THE CANADIAN SOCIETY OF
TEACHERS OF THE ALEXANDER
TECHNIQUE (CANSTAT)**
www.canstat.ca

**THE SOUTH AFRICAN SOCIETY OF
TEACHERS OF THE ALEXANDER
TECHNIQUE (SASTAT)**
www.alexandertechnique.org.za

FELDENKRAIS GUILD UK
T: 07000 785506
www.feldenkrais.co.uk

**INTERNATIONAL FELDENKRAIS
FEDERATION***
www.feldenkrais-method.org

BUTEYKO METHOD*
www.buteyko.com

CHAPTER FIVE

The Spice Shop (stock essentials
such as gram flour, turmeric,
sandalwood and a wide variety of
essential oils – will ship overseas)
T: 020 7221 4448
www.thespiceshop.co.uk

DR HAUSCHKA*
www.drhauschka.com

REN*
T: 020 7724 2900
www.renskincare.com

WELEDA (UK)
T: 0115 9448 222
www.weleda.co.uk

WELEDA INTERNATIONAL*
www.weleda.com

SPIEZIA ORGANICS*
T: 0870 850 8851
www.spieziaorganics.com

MOOR MUD
www.torfspa.com *

DEAD SEA MUD
www.mineralseashop.com *

CHAPTER SIX

**BRITISH AUTOGENIC SOCIETY
(BAS)**
T: 020 7391 8908
www.autogenic-therapy.org.uk

INDEX

acid-forming foods 18–19, 101
acidosis 19
acne 102, 121, 124, 126, 127
acupressure 17, 88
acupuncture 82, 96
addictions 144
after-shave 121, 126
ageing process 29, 123–4
agni 22
alcohol 18, 22, 98, 108, 146, 147
    cancer 99
    diabetes 100
    heart disease 100
Alexander Technique 103
alkaline-forming foods 18–19, 105, 150, 164
allergies 75, 102, 106
food intolerances 17, 105, 106, 108, 110,
    111, 112, 113, 149
    hypoallergenic beauty products 121
    NAET testing 17, 108
almonds 123
aloe vera 30, 123
American food 148
amino acids 27, 30
anaemia 24, 111
anger 88, 89
angina 82
antioxidants 103, 123, 124
antiperspirants 121
anxiety 25, 29, 32, 35, 80, 81, 82
aphrodisiacs 32, 114
appetite, suppressing 25
aqua aerobics 41
aromatherapy 87, 131
    insomnia 82
    stress 74
arthritis 10, 18, 25, 29, 101
asbestos 89
ashwagandha 114
asparagus
    asparagus, beetroot and pomegranate
      salad 177
    asparagus and sundried tomato
      pizza 175
asthma 35, 48, 75, 102, 106, 117
    beauty products 117
athlete's foot 103
Attention Deficit Hyperactivity Disorder
    (ADHD) 28
aubergine 105
    aubergine dip with rye crispbreads 182
Autogenic Therapy 159
avocados 23, 123
    avocado mask for mature skin 128
Ayurveda 99
Ayurvedic five-nectar bath 132
Ayurvedic metabolic skin types (AMSTs)
    121–2

backache 48, 68, 103
bad breath 103
balding 104
balneotherapy 154
bananas 123
bang bang chicken 171
barbecued food 99
barley 28

basil 25
baths 133–5
beans 27
beauty products
    holistic 120, 126–38
    hypoallergenic 121
    toxic 94, 110, 121, 151
bed linen 94
beeswax body treat 135
berries 27
beta-carotene 26
bioflavonoids 111
bipolar disorder 28
biscuits 22
bites 104
black bean soup 174
bloating 24, 104, 113
    pre-menstrual 104
blood pressure 24, 25, 27, 40, 82, 102
    diabetes 100
blood, purifying 24
blood sugar 16, 28, 146
blueberries 27
body mass index (BMI) 104, 144–5
bodywork 86–7, 156
bones 28, 29, 48, 105, 131
Bowen technique 91
brain chemicals 15
bread 23, 147
breakfast recipes 168–70
breath freshener 25
breathing 22, 67–8, 153, 164
    alternate-nostril 68
    Ayurvedic 46
    breath of life (complete breath) 67–8
    Buteyko Method 102
    detox breath 68
    diaphragm 113
    for meditation 83
    Pilates 68
    pranayama 48, 49, 111, 113
    stress, relieving 82
broccoli 26, 27–8
bunions 104
burns 105
burnt food 99
Buteyko Method 102
butter 22

caffeine 15, 22, 28, 103, 113, 146
cakes 22
calcium 26, 27, 28, 33
calming 10, 32, 48
cancer 10, 24, 26, 27, 28, 29, 99
    beauty products 121, 122
candles 94
    candle meditation 77
    scented 131
cardamom 24
cardiovascular system 28
carnosine 124
carotenoids 27, 29
carpets 93
carrots 29, 120
celery 25
cellulite 105
chamomile 25

champagne hair treat 137
chapattis, wheat-free 184
charcoal tablets 104
cheese 22, 147
chest infections 25, 106
chewing, importance of 22, 104
chicken 20, 23
    bang bang chicken 171
    chicken kebab 179
    chicken satay 177
    chicken and sweetcorn soup 173
    quick quick chicken 179
    spiced chicken with lentils 176
chickpea flour *See* gram flour
children 149
chilli, red 24
chills 25
Chinese food 147
chiropractic 31, 107
    McTimoney 92
chocolate 18, 146
chocolate, hot 22
cholesterol 24, 27, 29
chromium 104
chronic illness, prevention 97, 99–101
cinnamon 24
circulation 24, 25, 48, 131
cleaning chemicals 90, 110
cleansers, skin 128–30, 154
cloves 24
coal tar 121
coconut oil and milk 122
coenzyme Q10 123
coffee 22
colds 24, 25, 40, 105, 112
colour therapy 74
complimentary medicine 99–100
concentration
    improving 32, 81, 135
    lack of 121
confidence, building 10, 86, 88–9
constipation 104, 106, 109
cookies 22
cooking 21, 156
copper 28
coriander 24
cortisol 87
cosmetics 94, 110, 121, 123, 151
    removal 128
coughs 24, 25, 106
counselling 88
cramps 24, 113
cranial osteopathy 87
cranio-sacral therapy 87
cravings 146
crisps 22, 147
croutons 21
cucumber 123
    cucumber cooling body lotion 133
cumin 24
curry, okra 181
cystitis 25

dairy produce 17, 22, 105, 106, 113, 115
dal, spinach 174
damp, eliminating 94
dandelion 25

decaffeinated drinks 22
deep detox mineral bath 135
dehumidifier 94
dehydration 110, 112
dementia 28
depression 25, 28, 29, 32, 35, 81, 82, 93
dermatitis 28, 110, 121
detox 16
    cosmetics and beauty products 94,
        110, 121, 151, 164
    deep detox mineral bath 135
    detox breath 76
    environmental 11, 93–4, 159, 164
    reintroducing foods 149–50
    relationships 86, 90, 156–7, 164, 165
diabetes 10, 24, 27, 28, 35, 82, 100
diaphragm breathing and massage 113
diarrhoea 24, 25, 107, 109
diary
    of emotions and feelings 89, 150, 154
    food 15–16, 150
diet 10, 11, 14–15, 164
    chemical additives and preservatives
        103, 113
    for children 149
    cooking 21, 156
    disease prevention 101, 103, 104, 105
    doshas 35–6, 158
    eating mindfully 22, 153
    eating socially 146
    fast and convenience foods 21, 22
    food diary 15–16, 150
    food intolerances 17, 81, 105, 106,
        108, 110, 111, 112, 113, 149
    glycemic load 103, 104
    habits, forming 16
    health snacks 32
    herbs 25
    leftover food 21, 94
    pH balance 17, 18–19, 105, 150, 164
    processed foods 102
    psychological factor 15
    restaurant food 146–8
    shopping 20, 23, 158
    spices 24
    stress-proofing 81
    superfoods 25–9, 123–4
    supplements 33
    weight loss 18, 28
    your relationship with food 15
digestion 25, 29, 35, 113
    bad breath 107
    sluggish 18
dinner recipes 176–80
diuretics 25
dosas 169
doshas 34–6, 41–3, 124–5, 158
dry cleaning 89

ear problems 112
eczema 35, 106, 117, 121, 134
eggs 120, 123
    egg-yolk deep conditioner 136
electric blankets 93
electrical appliances 93
electro-magnetic radiation 93
emotions
    bodywork 91–2
    dependent or destructive relationships
        86, 90, 156–7, 164, 165

expressing 84, 154, 164
    handling 83–4
energy 10, 32
environmental detox 11, 93–4, 159
Epsom salts 134
essential oils
    Ayurvedic metabolic skin types 132
    beauty care 128–9
    insomnia 87–8
    stress 87–9
ethical consumer, becoming 158
exercise 156, 158–9, 164, 165
    arthritis 105
    bloating and flatulence 108
    cellulite 109
    disease prevention 102, 103, 104
    facial 128
    fatigue 111
    finding time for 44
    generally 10, 11
    motivation 44
    and skin tone 123
    as stress-reliever 40, 68, 81
exfoliation 122, 127, 130–1, 133
eyes 28, 29, 112
    circles under 87
    exercises 67
    eye strain 93, 135
    palming 66–7
    soothing eye mask 131

face masks 126, 127, 130
faeces 24
falafel 32, 182
fascia 92
fast, one-day juice 32
fat 18, 131
fatigue 18, 111, 121, 123
fatty foods 146
fear 88, 89
Feldenkras Method 107
fennel 25
fevers 25
fires, open 93
first-aid kit 116
fish 23, 28
    fish in foil 180
    herby fish with lime 178
    Moroccan sea bass with chermoula 179
    salmon carpaccio with fresh herbs 183
    seaweed fishy rice 176
    sushi salad 172
fizzy drinks 22
flatulence 24, 25, 108, 113
flavonoids 28
flotation therapy 81, 154
flu 40, 105
fluid retention 108
fluorescent lighting 93
folate 28
food intolerances 17, 81, 105, 106, 108,
        110, 111, 112, 113, 149
food poisoning 24, 114
food storage 94
formaldehyde 121
four-week programme 138–61
frankincense 123
free radicals 123
French food 147
fresh air 93, 105, 165

fresh spring green salad 173
fried food 22, 103
fried Indonesian-style rice 181
fruit 27
    dried 32
    healthy snack 32
    juicing 30, 32
    preparation 21
fucose 31
fungal infections 107, 108

gado-gado 178
galactose 31
gall-bladder 35
garden chemicals 94
garlic 24
gastric upsets 24
genetic predisposition 101, 103
ginger 24
    tea 22
    warming ginger bath 134
glucosamine 29
glucose 31
gluten 22, 105, 106
glycemic load, dietary 103, 104
glyconutrients 29–31, 156, 164, 165
gram flour 123
    gram flour and turmeric facial mask 137
Greek food 148
grilling 21
guacamole 32
guilt 86, 88
gums 24, 28, 107, 111

habit
    destructive relationships 86, 156–7
    forming 16
hair 10
    analysis for toxic metals 105
    balding 104
    blonde 137
    champagne hair treat 136
    cleaning 135–6
    conditioners 126, 136
    dyes 121, 122
    frizzy 126
    Indian head massage 108, 134–5
    pH balance 137
    promoting growth 108, 126
    shampoos 121, 137
hangovers 108
headaches 25, 35, 80, 82, 93, 108,
        117, 134
    See also migraine
health screening 102, 103, 165
heart 27
heart disease 10, 28, 29, 99–100
heartburn 109
heating systems 93
hellerwork 88
help, asking for 165
henna 122
herbalism 95–6
herbs 25, 153
herby fish with lime 178
hiccoughs 25
homeopathy 82, 95
homocysteine 104
honey 123
hummus 32

hydrogenated fat 109
hydrotherapy 153–4, 165
hypnotherapy 95

iced drinks 147
immune system, boosting 10, 18, 29, 40, 78
Indian food 148
Indian head massage 104, 134–5
indigestion 24, 25, 103, 109
Indonesian vegetable soup 173
insomnia 24, 81–2, 108
interior decoration 93
iron 27, 33, 101
irritability 82
irritable bowel syndrome (IBS) 25, 35, 109
Italian food 147

Jahara Technique 92
Japanese food 148
jealousy 88
jet lag 109–10
joints 25, 29
    exercise 41, 48, 60
    See also arthritis
juicing 21, 30, 32, 153

Kairos Therapy 88
Kapha dosha 34–6, 42, 43, 124–5
kedgeree, tofu 169
kidney stones 24, 28
kidneys 24
kinesiology 17

laughter 81, 165
laxative foods 110
lecithin 123
lemon balm 25
lemons 18, 124, 151
libido 40, 87, 110
lipids 99
liver 24, 25, 28, 35
lunch recipes 171–5

McTimoney chiropractic 87
magnesium 27, 28, 29
manganese 27
mannose 31
manual lymphatic drainage (MLD) 87, 109
massage 122, 129–30, 150, 159
    Ayurvedic metabolic skin types 132
    biodynamic 87
    chavutti thirumal 31
    diaphragm 113
    facial 128–9
    Indian head massage 108, 135–7
    insomnia 88
    Jahara Technique 88
    Thai 88
    third eye, massaging 81
meat 18, 21, 22, 23, 113
meditation 73, 75–7, 100, 123, 154, 164, 165
    ambient sound meditation 77
    Autogenic Therapy 159
    breathing 76
    candle meditation 77
    counting meditation 76
    mantra meditation 76
    mindfulness 150

Transcendental Meditation 75
    walking meditation 77
    yoga nidra 48
memory, enhancing 25, 29
menopause 25, 28
mental state 10, 15
    effect on physical health 80
    focusing your mind 11, 24
    lack of sleep 87
water intake 24
metabolic types See doshas
metabolism 28
Mexican food 148
microwave ovens 94
Middle Eastern food 148
migraine 25, 35
milk 22, 23
mindfulness 21, 22, 150, 153, 156, 165
mint 25
miso 28
moisturisers 123, 128–9
morning sickness 114
Moroccan sea bass with chermoula 179
motivation 143
mould 94, 103
mouthwash 25
mucus production 115
muira puama 114
mushrooms 30
    spinach mushroom tortilla 170

N-acetylgalactosamine 31
N-acetylglucosamine 31
Nambudripad allergy elimination technique (NAET) 17, 108
naturopathy 96
nausea 24, 25, 93, 110, 121
neck pain 80
neck rolls 60
nectars 134
nervous exhaustion 25
nervous system 48
night sweats 25
nutmeg 24
nuts 28

oatcakes 32
oatmeal exfoliator, simple 133
oats 28, 124
okra curry 181
olive oil 21, 23, 120
olives 120
omega-3 fatty acids 28, 104, 105
organic vegetable spread 184
osteopathy 87, 107
    cranial 87
osteoporosis 18, 28, 29, 68

paints and varnishes 93
palming 60
panic attacks 93
pantothenic acid 29
papaya 124
    papaya exfoliator 128
    papaya mango smoothie 169
parasites 24, 29
parsley and yoghurt spread 184
peanuts 28
peas 27
pepper, black 24

peppers 105
period pains 24
pH balance 17, 18–19, 105, 150, 164
    hair 137
phytoestrogens 27, 28
Pilates 62–6, 108, 150, 164, 165
    breathing 68
    yoga-Pilates fusions 68
pineapple 124
    fruit peel 128
pistachios 28
Pitta dosha 34–6, 42, 43, 124–5
pizza, asparagus and sundried tomato 175
plants, indoor 94
plastic 24, 94
pollution, environmental 93–4, 106, 159
polyphenals 27
pomegranates 27, 120, 124
    asparagus, beetroot and pomegranate salad 177
postural imbalances 68
potassium 27, 28, 29
potatoes 18, 105
prana 21, 114
pranayama 50, 51, 109, 113
pre-menstrual bloating 104
processed foods 98
progress chart, keeping 143
psoriasis 121, 136
psychoneurimmunology (PNI) 78
psychotherapy 83, 96
    hypnotherapy 95
pulses 27
pumpkin 29

qi 114
quinoa 28
    quinoa tabbouleh salad 175

raisins 120
rapping, relaxing 82
refined (white) carbohydrates 22
reflexology 87
relationships
    dependent or destructive 85, 90, 156–7, 164, 165
    libido See libido
    physical interaction 131–2
relaxation response 48
repetitive strain injury (RSI) 68
resentment 88
responsibility, taking 165
restaurants, eating in 146–8
resveratrol 124
rheumatism 24, 25, 29
rice 23, 28
    fried Indonesian-style 181
    rice porridge 169
    seaweed fishy rice 176
    tofu kedgeree 169
rice cakes 32
rolfing 86, 88
rosemary 25

saffron 24
sage 25
salads 21, 146–7
    asparagus, beetroot and pomegranate 177
    fresh spring green 173

quinoa tabbouleh 175
sushi 172
salmon carpaccio with fresh herbs 183
salt
    dietary 102, 108, 146
    salt and pepper scrub 133
    skin care 124, 131
sandalwood 124
'sauna' salts bath 134–5
seafood 22
seasonal affective disorder (SAD) 93
seaweed fishy rice 176
seeds 28
    sprouted 26–7
selenium 28
self-esteem, building 86, 88–9
shampoos 121, 137
shellfish 23
SHEN therapy 88
shiatsu 86, 88
shopping 20, 23, 158
sialic acid 31
sinus problems 110–1, 135
skin 10, 18, 24, 29
    ageing process 123–4
    Ayurvedic metabolic skin types 121–2
    baths 131–3
    body care 129–33
    body masks 131
    cleansing 118, 125, 154
    creams 123, 127, 128–30, 154
    exfoliation 122, 127, 130–1, 133
    face masks 126, 127, 130
    healing spot vanisher 131
    holistic care 120, 126–38
    massage 131–3, 159
    skin care 118
    sun protection 102, 115, 123, 124
    sunburn 135
    superfood boosters 120
    toxic beauty products 117
    water, drinking 122, 123
skin brushing 109
skin conditions 35
sleep 10, 29, 32
    disease prevention 102
    and exercise 40
    insomnia 24, 87–8, 112
    jet lag 109–10
    REM sleep 87
    sleep hygiene 81
smoking 102
    cancer 103
    diabetes 104
    heart disease 104
smoothie, papaya mango 169
snacks, healthy 32
    recipes 182–4
soap 121
solanine 105
soups 21
    black bean 174
    chicken and sweetcorn 173
    chickpea and spinach 171
    Indonesian vegetable 173
soya 23, 28
    soya breakfast 170
spa body treats 131–5
spiced chicken with lentils 176
spiced sweetcorn 183
spices 24, 153

spinach 27–8
    chickpea and spinach soup 171
    spinach dal 174
    spinach mushroom tortilla 170
sport 41, 156
spots 126, 127
    healing spot vanisher 131
    See also acne
sprains 25, 111
sprouted seeds and grains 26–7, 153
squashes 29
stings 104
stir-fries 21
strains 107, 111
stress 10, 24, 25, 32, 73–4, 123
    acne 102
    constipation 106
    disease prevention 102, 104
    exercise as stress-reliever 40, 62, 73
    indigestion 113
    irritable bowel syndrome 113
    relieving 81–94
stress ball 81
stretching exercises 48–9
strokes 28
sugar 18, 22, 113, 115, 146
sugars 29–31
sulforaphane glucosinolate 26
sulphur 105
sun block 102
sunburn 111, 122, 126, 135
sunlight 102, 123, 124
sushi salad 172
sweet potatoes 29
sweetcorn
    chicken and sweetcorn soup 173
    spiced 183
sweeteners, artificial 22, 113
synthetic materials 93, 94

tanning 102
tastes chart 36
tea 22
    cat's claw 99
    ginger 22
    green 28, 99, 120
    herbal 23, 25
teeth 24, 28, 107
television 22, 93
tempeh 23, 28
    tempeh-tofu-tamari 180
tension 35, 80, 123, 135
Thai food 147–8
thalossotherapy 127, 154
third eye, massaging 81
throat
    infections 24
    sore 25, 111
thyme 25
tofu 23, 28
    kedgeree 169
    tempeh-tofu-tamari 180
tomatoes 17, 18, 105
    asparagus and sundried tomato
        pizza 175
    sun-dried tomatoes and pine nuts 183
tortilla 172
    spinach mushroom 170
traditional Chinese medicine (TCM) 96
trager 88
travel sickness 25, 114

trimethylglycine 104
tuna 23, 28
turkey 23, 120
Turkish baths 153–4
Turkish food 148
turmeric 24, 124
    gram flour and turmeric facial mask 127

ujjayi 104
ulcers 35
urethritis 25
urinary disorders 24, 25

Vata dosha 34–6, 41–3, 124–5
vegetable spread, organic 184
vegetables
    as healthy snack 32
    juicing 21, 30, 32
    preparation 21
visualisation 78–9, 104, 159, 164, 165
    beauty ritual 128
    confidence visualisation 79
    safe-place visualisation 78
vitamin A 33
vitamin B complex 26, 27, 29, 104, 114
vitamin C 27, 28, 29
vitamin D 105
vitamin E 27, 28, 29, 33
vitamin K 26, 28

warts 112
water 15, 24, 108, 146, 165
    at mealtimes 22
    bottled 24
    cellulite 109
    constipation 110
    purification 24, 90
    skin care 122, 123
    sparkling 22, 108
    stress, relieving 82
WaterDance 88
watsu 88
weight
    body mass index (BMI) 104, 144–5
    diabetes 104
    and disease prevention 102, 103, 104
    weight loss 18, 28, 40, 48
wheat 17, 22, 108, 113
wheatgrass 26–7

xylose 31

yawning 74
yoga 50–61, 108, 111, 150, 151, 164, 165
    Child Posture 59, 61
    The Mountain 56
    office yoga 60–1
    pranayama 50, 51, 109, 113
    Prayer Posture 57
    Sun Salute 52–5, 104
    The Tree 58
    types 51
    weight loss 50
    yoga-Pilates fusions 62
yoghurt 23, 29, 124
    parsley and yoghurt spread 184

zero balancing 86, 88
zinc 28, 113, 114